Perry D. Hoffman, PhD
Penny Steiner-Grossman, EdD,
Editors

Borderline Personality Disorder: Meeting the Challenges to Successful Treatment

Borderline Personality Disorder: Meeting the Challenges to Successful Treatment has been co-published simultaneously as *Social Work in Mental Health*, Volume 6, Numbers 1/2 2008.

Pre-publication REVIEWS, COMMENTARIES, EVALUATIONS . . .

"This book's goals to bring knowledge about borderline personality disorder to social workers and encourage social workers to assume a more central place in their care are complementary and timely. . . . These highly significant public health goals are served admirably by this book's collection of chapters by our foremost clinical experts."

John G. Gunderson, MD
Professor, Psychiatry
Harvard Medical School
Director
Borderline Treatment
and Research Center
McLean Hospital

Borderline Personality Disorder: Meeting the Challenges to Successful Treatment

Borderline Personality Disorder: Meeting the Challenges to Successful Treatment has been co-published simultaneously as *Social Work in Mental Health*, Volume 6, Numbers 1/2 2008.

Monographic Separates from the *Social Work in Mental Health*

For additional information on these and other Haworth Press titles, including descriptions, tables of contents, reviews, and prices, use the QuickSearch catalog at http://www.HaworthPress.com.

Borderline Personality Disorder: Meeting the Challenges to Successful Treatment, edited by Perry D. Hoffman, PhD, and Penny Steiner-Grossman, EdD, MPH (Vol. 6, Nos. 1/2, 2008) *A unique resource offering social work clinicians access to the knowledge neede for effective treatment of Borderline Personality Disorder.*

Community Collaborative Partnerships: The Foundation for HIV Prevention Research Efforts, edited by Mary M. McKay, PhD, and Roberta L. Paikoff, PhD (Vol. 5, Nos. 1/2 and 3/4, 2007). *Exploration of ways to develop, design, and evaluate strong community partnerships to support youth health prevention efforts in the United States and around the world.*

Clinical and Research Uses of an Adolescent Mental Health Intake Questionnaire: What Kids Need to Talk About, edited by Ken Peake, DSW, Irwin Epstein, PhD, and Daniel Mederios, MD (Vol. 3, Nos. 1/2, 2004, and Vol. 3, No. 3, 2005). *"Clinical and Research Uses of an Adolescent Mental Health Intake Questionnaire: What Kids Need to Talk About" explores the research on adolsecent behavior culled from the answers to a clinician-designed intake questionnaire given to adolescent clients asking how they view their own risks, what they worry about, and what theywish to talk about. Respected authorities discuss the enlightening findings and present ways to reshape services, taking into account customer preference, risk and worry, and youth development (YD) perspectives while presenting practical clinical strategies to engage at-risk adolescents in mental health treatment.*

Social Work Approaches in Health and Mental Health from Around the Globe, edited by Anna Metteri, MSocSc, Teppo Kröger, PhD, Anneli Pohjola, PhD, and Pirkko-Liisa Rauhala, PhD (Vol. 2, No. 2/3, 2004). *"BROAD-BASED AND UNIQUE . . . . A much-needed publication for training and practice." (Charlene Laurence Carbonatto, DPhil, Senior Lecturer, Department of Social Work, University of Prestoria, South Africa)*

Psychiatric Medication Issues for Social Workers, Counselors, and Psychiatrists, edited by Kia J. Bentley, PhD, LCSW (Vol. 1, No. 4, 2003). *"OUTSTANDING . . . . All social workers, counselors, and psychologists working in the mental health field would benefit from reading this outstanding book." (Deborah P. Valentine, PhD, MSSW, Professor and Director, School of Social Work, Colorado State University)*

Borderline Personality Disorder: Meeting the Challenges to Successful Treatment

Perry D. Hoffman, PhD
Penny Steiner-Grossman, EdD, MPH
Editors

Gary Rosenberg, PhD
Andrew Weissman, PhD
Series Editors

Borderline Personality Disorder: Meeting the Challenges to Successful Treatment has been co-published simultaneously as *Social Work in Mental Health*, Volume 6, Numbers 1/2 2008.

The Haworth Press
www.HaworthPress.com

Published by

The Haworth Press, 10 Alice Street, Binghamton, NY 13904-1580 USA.

Borderline Personality Disorder: Meeting the Challenges to Successful Treatment has been co-published simultaneously as *Journal of Social Work in Mental Health* Volume 6, Numbers 1/2 2008.

Library of Congress Cataloging-in-Publication Data

Borderline personality disorder: meeting the challenges to successful treatment/ Perry D. Hoffman, and Penny Steiner-Grossman, editors.
 p. cm.
 "Co-published simultaneously as social work in mental health, vol. 6, no. 1/2 2008."
 Includes bibliographical references and index.
 ISBN 978-0-7890-3233-1 (hard cover : alk. paper)
 ISBN: 978-0-7890-3234-8 (soft cover : alk. paper)
 1. Borderline personality disorter–Treatment I. Hoffman, Perry D., 1944- II. Steiner-Grossman, Penny.
 [DNLM: 1. Borderline Personality Disorder–therapy. W1 S0135Q v. 6 no. 1-2. 2008/ WM 190 B666 2008
 RC569.5.B67B6892 2008
 616.85′85206–dc22   2007035365

The HAWORTH PRESS

Abstracting, Indexing & Outward Linking

PRINT *and* ELECTRONIC BOOKS & JOURNALS

This section provides you with a list of major indexing & abstracting services and other tools for bibliographic access. That is to say, each service began covering this periodical during the year noted in the right column. Most Websites which are listed below have indicated that they will either post, disseminate, compile, archive, cite or alert their own Website users with research-based content from this work. (This list is as current as the copyright date of this publication.)

Abstracting, Website/Indexing Coverage . . . . Year When Coverage Began

- *Academic Search Premier (EBSCO)*
  <http://search.ebscohost.com> **2006**
- *Academic Source Premier (EBSCO)*
  <http://search.ebscohost.com> **2007**
- *AgeLine Database (AARP) <http://research.aarp.org/ageline>* **2006**
- *Alternative Press Index (Print, online & CD-ROM from NISC)*
  <http://www.altpress.org> **2005**
- *Alzheimer's Disease Education & Referral Center (ADEAR AD LIB Database) <http://www.nia.nih.gov/alzheimers/Resources/ Search Health Literature/>* **2006**
- *British Library Inside (The British Library)*
  <http://www.bl.uk/services/current/inside.html> **2007**
- *Cambridge Scientific Abstracts (ProQuest CSA)*
  <http://www.csa.com> **2006**
- *Child Welfare Information Gateway (formerly National Adoption Information Clearinghouse Documents Database, and formerly National Adoption Information Clearinghouse on Child Abuse & Neglect Information Documents Database) <http://www.childwelfare.gov>.* **2006**
- *CINAHL (Cumulative Index to Nursing & Allied Health Literature) (EBSCO) <http://www.cinahl.com>* **2003**

(continued)

(continued)

(continued)

Bibliographic Access

- *Cabell's Directory of Publishing Opportunities in Psychology <http://www.cabells.com>*

- *MedBio World <http://www.medbioworld.com>*

- *MediaFinder <http://www.mediafinder.com>*

- *Ulrich's Periodicals Directory: The Global Source for Periodicals Information Since 1932 <http://www. bowkerlink.com>*

Special Bibliographic Notes related to special journal issues (separates) and indexing/abstracting:

- indexing/abstracting services in this list will also cover material in any "separate" that is co-published simultaneously with Haworth's special thematic journal issue or DocuSerial. Indexing/abstracting usually covers material at the article/chapter level.
- monographic co-editions are intended for either non-subscribers or libraries which intend to purchase a second copy for their circulating collections.
- monographic co-editions are reported to all jobbers/wholesalers/approval plans. The source journal is listed as the "series" to assist the prevention of duplicate purchasing in the same manner utilized for books-in-series.
- to facilitate user/access services all indexing/abstracting services are encouraged to utilize the co-indexing entry note indicated at the bottom of the first page of each article/chapter/contribution.
- this is intended to assist a library user of any reference tool (whether print, electronic, online, or CD-ROM) to locate the monographic version if the library has purchased this version but not a subscription to the source journal.
- individual articles/chapters in any Haworth publication are also available through the Haworth Document Delivery Service (HDDS).

AS PART OF OUR CONTINUING COMMITMENT TO BETTER SERVE OUR LIBRARY PATRONS, WE ARE PROUD TO BE WORKING WITH THE FOLLOWING ELECTRONIC SERVICES:

AGGREGATOR SERVICES

- EBSCOhost • Ingenta • J-Gate • Minerva
- OCLC FirstSearch • Oxmill • SwetsWise

LINK RESOLVER SERVICES

- 1Cate (Openly Informatics) • ChemPort (American Chemical Society)
- CrossRef • Gold Rush (Coalliance) • LinkOut (PubMed)
- LINKplus (Atypon) • LinkSolver (Ovid) • LinkSource with A-to-Z (EBSCO)
- Resource Linker (Ulrich's) • SerialsSolutions (ProQuest) • SFX (Ex Libris)
- Sirsi Resolver (SirsiDynix) • Tour (TDnet) • Vlink (Extensity)
- WebBridge (Innovative Interfaces)

 Phone: 800–429–6784 • Fax: 800–895–0582 • Web: www.HaworthPress.com

ABOUT THE EDITORS

Perry D. Hoffman, PhD, is President of the National Education Alliance for Borderline Personality Disorder (NEA-BPD) and a member of the voluntary faculty at The Mount Sinai School of Medicine. She received her doctorate in clinical social work from New York University. Dr. Hoffman is co-creator of Family Connections, the 12-week psycho-education course for families that is available in many parts of the US and in several other countries. Principal Investigator on two grants from the National Institute of Mental Health (NIMH), Dr. Hoffman is also co-principal investigator on several NMIH grants focusing on families who have a relative with BPD. She is co-editor, with John G. Gunderson, MD, of the book *Understanding and Treating Borderline Personality Disorder. A Guide for Professionals and Families*, published in 2005 by the American Psychiatric Press, Inc. Dr. Hoffman has directed several Dialectical Behavior therapy programs and is in private practice in the New York area.

Penny Steiner-Grossman, EdD, MPH, is Assistant Dean for Educational Resources and an Associate Professor in the Department of Family and Social Medicine at the Albert Einstein College of Medicine, Bronx, NY. She completed her MPH degree at Columbia University School of Public Health in 1981and her doctorate in education at Teachers College-Columbia University in 1993. In addition to her administrative and teaching responsibilities, Dr. Steiner-Grossman has written extensively about the experience of illness, with the aim of using clear language to help patients and their providers understand such chronic medical conditions as inflammatory bowel disease, lupus, genetic diseases, and, more recently, psychiatric disorders. She was a collaborator, with John G. Gunderson and Perry D. Hoffman, in the preparation of the book *Understanding and Treating Borderline Personality Disorder: A Guide for Professionals and Families.*

Borderline Personality Disorder: Meeting the Challenges to Successful Treatment

CONTENTS

About the Contributors

Ann H. Appelbaum, MD, completed a residency in psychiatry at the Menninger Clinic in 1956, and was graduated as a psychoanalyst at the Topeka Institute for Psychoanalysis. She directed the diagnostic service of the clinic and taught at the Topeka Institute until 1980, when she joined the staff of the New York Hospital, Westchester Division, as chief of a unit for borderline patients, and joined the research project on the treatment of borderline patients headed by Dr. Otto Kernberg. Currently, Dr. Appelbaum chairs a study group on psychotherapy of borderline patients and is a member of the faculty of the Center for Psychoanalytic Training and Research at Columbia University.

Anthony W. Bateman, MD, is Consultant Psychiatrist in Psychotherapy at several hospitals in the UK, Visiting Professor at University College London, and Visiting Consultant at the Menninger Clinic and the Menninger Department of Psychiatry and Behavioral Sciences at the Baylor College of Medicine. In collaboration with Dr. Peter Fonagy, he has developed mentalization-based treatment for personality disorder and is conducting clinical research trials on its effectiveness. He is an expert member of National Institute for Clinical Excellence (NICE) development group for treatment guidelines for Borderline Personality Disorder in the UK. He has authored numerous research articles and book chapters on personality disorder and the use of psychotherapy in psychiatric practice. His several books include *Psychotherapy for Borderline Personality Disorder: Mentalization-Based Treatment* and *Mentalization-Based Treatment for Borderline Personality Disorder: A Practical Guide*, both co-authored with Peter Fonagy.

Donald W. Black, MD, is currently Professor of Psychiatry at the University of Iowa Roy J. and Lucille A. Carver College of Medicine. He is a graduate of Stanford University and the University of Utah College of Medicine. He completed his training in psychiatry and a fellowship in psychiatric epidemiology at the University of Iowa. Dr. Black's research has been supported by NIMH, NIDA, private foundations, and the pharmaceutical industry. He has received the University of Iowa Collegiate Teaching Award for excellence in teaching and is listed in *Best Doctors in America*. He also serves as a consultant to the Iowa Department of Corrections. His book *Bad Boys, Bad Men–Confronting Antisocial Personality Disorder,* was published by Oxford University Press in 1999.

Nancee Blum, MSW, is a clinical faculty member in the Department of Psychiatry at the University of Iowa, and Adjunct Instructor in Medicine, Nursing, and Social Work, and a Diplomate of the American Psychotherapy Association. She co-authored the *Structured Interview for DSM-IV Personality* (with Bruce Pfohl and Mark Zimmerman), and *STEPPS Group Treatment Program for Borderline Personality Disorder* (with Norm Bartels, Don St. John, and Bruce Pfohl), and authored or co-authored numerous journal articles and book chapters. She is on the scientific advisory board of the Treatment and Research Advancements Association for Personality Disorder (TARA). Ms. Blum presents numerous workshops nationally and internationally.

Ellie Buteau, PhD, has conducted research with the National Education Alliance for Borderline Personality Disorder (NEA-BPD) since its inception in 2001. She has co-authored several research articles examining the knowledge, need for support and interpersonal relationship dynamics among families suffering from BPD. Through her work with NEA-BPD and Dawkins Productions, Inc., Dr. Buteau has developed the research designs for multiple NIMH-funded grants aimed at creating and improving services for family members.

Kevin Dawkins, MS, executive producer of Dawkins Productions, has developed educational media programs addressing borderline personality disorder, depression, substance abuse, cancer, asthma and cystic fibrosis. Before founding Dawkins Productions in 1987, Mr. Dawkins worked as a television producer for NBC, CBS News, Metromedia Television, and WCVB-TV, Boston. Dawkins Productions has produced health education programs for the Public Broadcasting System, Lifetime Medical Television, Hospital Satellite Network, Guilford Publications, the US Department of Health and Human Services, National League for Nursing, Eastern Paralyzed Veterans Association, and other clients.

Jill C. Delaney, MS, is on the Clinical Voluntary Faculty, Department of Psychiatry at the Weill Medical College of Cornell University. She is a member of the Personality Disorders Institute of Weill-Cornell, where she teaches and supervises Transference-Focused Psychotherapy. She maintains a private psychotherapy and psychoanalysis practice in New York City and Connecticut specializing in treating personality disorders.

Peter Fonagy, PhD, is Freud Memorial Professor of Psychoanalysis and Director of the Sub-Department of Clinical Health Psychology at University College London. He is also Chief Executive of the Anna Freud Centre,

London, and Consultant to the Child and Family Program at the Menninger Department of Psychiatry at Baylor College of Medicine. He is a clinical psychologist and a training and supervising analyst in the British Psycho-Analytical Society in child and adult analysis. His clinical interests center around borderline psychopathology, violence and early attachment relationships, and his work attempts to integrate empirical research with psychoanalytic theory. He also co-chairs the Research Committee of the International Psychoanalytic Association and is a fellow of the British Academy. He has published over 300 chapters and articles and has authored or edited several books.

Freda B. Friedman, PhD, LCSW, RN CS, has a private practice in Chicago and Northfield, Illinois. She has held clinical and administrative leadership positions in inpatient, partial hospitalization, and intensive outpatient settings specializing in the treatment of BPD, both in New York and Chicago. She frequently leads workshops and seminars, and serves as a consultant to professional and consumer groups on working with multi-problem, difficult-to-treat clients, and on Dialectical Behavior Therapy. She is co-author of *Surviving a Borderline Patient* and the author of "When Parents Age: Unique Stressor of Adult Children," in Catherall, D. (ed.) *Handbook of Stress, Trauma and the Family*.

Alan E. Fruzzetti, PhD, is Associate Professor of Psychology and Director of the Dialectical Behavior Therapy and Research Program at the University of Nevada in Reno. He received his BA from Brown University and MS and PhD from the University of Washington in Seattle. His research focuses on the interplay between psychopathology and couple and family interactions, and the development of effective individual and family treatments for these problems. Dr. Fruzzetti is Research Director and a member of the board of directors of the National Education Alliance for Borderline Personality Disorder, and is the co-creator of the NEA-BPD Family Connections program. He maintains a clinical practice with individuals and families, and has provided extensive training in the United States, Europe, and Australia in DBT with individuals, couples, and families. He has authored or co-authored dozens of scholarly articles and book chapters on these and related topics, and a recent book on DBT for high-conflict couples and families.

Nira Golombeck, PhD, is Research Scientist at the New York State Psychiatric Institute (NYSPI), Department of Neuroscience, in New York City. At NYSPI, she is Project Coordinator of a research study attempting to develop a systematic classification of suicidal ideation and behavior in an emergency room setting. She is also a primary assessor on a prospective study to determine state and trait predictors of suicide attempts. She is a past student representative of the American Psychological Association's Society of Clinical Psychology Section on Clinical Emergencies and Crises. Dr. Golombeck received her BA from New York University and her doctorate in clinical psychology from St. John's University.

Marianne Goodman, MD, is Assistant Professor of Psychiatry at The Mount Sinai School of Medicine in New York, where she is involved in teaching, research and clinical care. She conducts research on Dialectical Behavior Therapy in borderline personality disorder and is interested in adolescent precursors to the development of personality dysfunction. She is currently the recipient of an Advanced Career Development Award from the Veterans Administration. She completed her medical training and residency in psychiatry at the University of California-San Francisco (UCSF).

John Gunderson, MD, is Professor of Psychiatry at Harvard Medical School. At McLean Hospital, he is Director of the Center for Treatment and Research on Borderline Personality Disorder. His seminal studies on the diagnosis, families, psychodynamics, treatment and pathogenesis helped transform the borderline diagnosis from a psychoanalytic construct into an empirically validated and internationally recognized disorder. He chaired the DSM-IV work group on personality disorders, and currently is the principal investigator on major NIMH-funded studies on the longitudinal course of personality disorders and on the genetics and family phenotypes of BPD.

Richard G. Hersh, MD, is Assistant Clinical Professor of Psychiatry at the Columbia University College of Physicians and Surgeons and the Associate Director of the Intensive Outpatient Program at Columbia University Medical Center. He graduated from Stanford University and the George Washington University School of Medicine and completed his residency in psychiatry at Northwestern University. He previously served as an Instructor in Psychiatry at the Harvard Medical School and as an attending psychiatrist at McLean and Massachusetts General Hospitals. He is currently a candidate at the Columbia Center for Psychoanalytic Training and Research.

Cedar R. Koons, MSW, is the co-founder and team leader of Santa Fe DBT Consultation, an outpatient private practice group that provides comprehensive DBT and other evidence-based treatment in Santa Fe, New Mexico. In the 1990s, Ms. Koons introduced DBT at the Veterans Administration Medical Center in Durham, North Carolina, where she was principal investigator on a randomized, controlled study of DBT for women veterans with borderline personality disorder. She has also conducted a pilot study of an adaptation of DBT for the vocational rehabilitation of persons with severe personality disorder. Ms. Koons is a trainer and consultant for Behavioral Tech, a training and research agency that disseminates DBT and other evidence-based treatments.

Alec L. Miller, PsyD, is Associate Professor of Psychiatry and Behavioral Sciences and Chief, Child and Adolescent Psychology at Montefiore Medical Center/Albert Einstein College of Medicine, in the Bronx, New York. In addition, he is a Fellow of the American Psychological Association (APA), Past-President of the APA's Society of Clinical Psychology Section on Clinical Emergencies and Crises, Associate Editor of Cognitive and Behavioral Practice, and serves as a consultant on the FDA's Suicide Classification Project, and to other organizations. Dr. Miller received his BA from the University of Michigan and his doctorate in clinical psychology from the Ferkauf Graduate School of Psychology of Yeshiva University.

Deborah Neft, PhD, completed her clinical psychology internship at the Montefiore Medical Center/Albert Einstein College of Medicine. As an intern she worked in the Adolescent Depression Suicide Program, which provided intensive training in Dialectal Behavior Therapy for multi-problem youth who often presented with symptoms of severe depression, suicidality, self-injurious behavior and other symptoms of borderline personality disorder. Dr. Neft received her BA from Brown University and her doctorate in clinical psychology from Rutgers University.

Antonia New, MD, is Associate Professor of Psychiatry at The Mount Sinai School of Medicine. Her research focuses on emotion dysregulation, and she uses brain imaging techniques, genetic studies, and laboratory assessment of behavior to explore mechanisms of treatment and to develop novel treatments for emotion dysregulation. Dr. New is the principal investigator of grants from the NIH and from the Veterans Affairs Research Division, and she received a Career Development Award from the Veterans Administration. She completed her residency in psychiatry at New York Hospital/ Payne Whitney Clinic and a postdoctoral research fellowship at Mount Sinai. She received her medical degree from Cornell University School of Medicine.

Joel Paris, MD, was born in New York City but has lived most of his life in Canada. He obtained his medical degree from McGill University in 1964, where he also trained in psychiatry. Dr. Paris is Professor in Psychiatry at McGill and a Research Associate at the SMBD-Jewish General Hospital. He also served as Chair of Psychiatry at McGill from 1996 to 2007. Dr. Paris is a Past President of the Association for Research in Personality Disorders. His main research interest has been in personality disorders, focusing on the causes and outcome of borderline personality. He has published 125 peer-reviewed papers and nine books. Dr. Paris also has been an active practitioner and educator and has won awards for his teaching.

Dixianne Penney, DrPH, is a co-founder and Executive Vice President of the National Education Alliance for Borderline Personality Disorder (NEA-BPD). She is co-director of an NIMH conference grant focusing on BPD. She is a co-leader in NEA-BPD's Family Connections program, a 12-week education/skills course for relatives of persons with BPD. Dr. Penney was Administrative Director of the Center for the Study of Issues in Public Mental Health, Nathan Kline Institute, Assistant Regional Director, Adult Services, NYC Regional Office, NYS Office of Mental Health, and President, Board of Visitors, Rockland Children's Psychiatric Center. She is a frequent speaker on BPD, nationally and internationally, particularly as it affects families.

S. Charles Schultz, MD, completed his undergraduate training in History at the University of Southern California, and obtained both his medical degree and residency training at the UCLA School of Medicine. He then became a clinical associate at the National Institute of Mental Health, where he worked in the Neuropsychopharmacology Section at the Clinical Center. Since 1999, Dr. Schultz has been Professor and Head of the Department of Psychiatry at the University of Minnesota, continuing his research in psychopharmacology and brain imaging of BPD. He is principal investigator of the MIND Institute's applied research program. He is also active in community work with People, Inc., Suicide Awareness Voices of Education (SAVE), the Mental Health Association of Minnesota (MAHM), and the National Alliance on Mental Illness (NAMI).

Michael P. Rafferty, MD, completed his medical and psychiatric training at the University of Minnesota Medical School. While in residency, he joined the Dialectical Behavior Therapy consultation group and later received intensive training in DBT through Behavioral Tech, LLC. He completed a Harold Lawn endowed research fellowship focused on borderline personality disorder, and in addition to assisting with ongoing studies of BPD, he maintained a medication clinic aimed at alleviating symptoms of BPD. He currently resides in North Texas and works in a rural community-supported mental health center, which includes work on an Assertive Community Treatment team.

Ellen J. Safier, MSW, is a social worker and family therapist in private practice in Houston, Texas. She is on the adjuct faculty in psychiatry at Baylor College of Medicine and a consultant in family therapy to the Menninger Clinic. She was Director of Social Work Training and Senior

Family Therapy Faculty at the Menninger Clinic in Topeka, Kansas. Ms. Safier received her undergraduate degree in psychology and her masters in social work from the University of North Carolina in Chapel Hill.

Chad Shenk, MA, is currently completing his clinical psychology internship at the University of Rochester Medical Center in Rochester, New York. He received his BA from the Pennsylvania State University and his MA from the University of Nevada in Reno where he is currently completing his PhD. His research interests involve identifying variables that affect an individual's ability to regulate emotional arousal and how difficulties regulating emotional arousal lead to various forms of psychopathology in children and adolescents. He has published several articles related to this area of interest.

Maureen Smith, LICSW, is Director of Family Services for the Outpatient Personality Disorders Clinic and the Center for the Treatment of Borderline Personality Disorder at McLean Hospital in Belmont, Massachusetts. After receiving her MSW from Smith College School for Social Work, she practiced in a number of medical settings before coming to McLean 19 years ago. Since then she has worked in various levels of care, helping families cope with the psychiatric illness of a loved one. Ms Smith serves on the Board of the New England Personality Disorder Association, and assists in organizing monthly family workshops and local conferences on BPD.

Joseph Triebwasser, MD, graduated from Harvard College and the Harvard Medical School. He completed his psychiatry residency at McLean Hospital, where he subsequently helped direct an Affective Disorders Program inpatient unit. He currently works in the Mood and Personality Disorders Program at The Mount Sinai School of Medicine and the Bronx Veterans Administration Medical Center.

Kiera Van Gelder, MFA, is a writer, artist and educator. She is the founder and director of Middle Path, Inc. a borderline personality disorder consumer advocacy and education organization based in Waltham, MA. She is also on the board of directors of the New England Personality Disorder Association and is the Massachusetts Consumer Council Representative for the National Alliance on Mental Illness (NAMI). Ms. Van Gelder is an international speaker and presenter on borderline personality disorder and the recovery process.

Frank E. Yeomans, MD, PhD, is Clinical Associate Professor of Psychiatry at the Weill Medical College of Cornell University, Director of Training at the Personality Disorders Institute of Weill-Cornell, Lecturer in Psychiatry at the Columbia University Center for Psychoanalytic Training and Research, and Director of the Personality Studies Institute. Dr.

Yeomans' primary interests are the development, investigation, teaching, and practice of psychotherapy for personality disorders. He has helped establish training programs for psychodynamic therapy of personality disorders internationally. He has authored and co-authored numerous articles and books, including *A Primer on Transference-Focused Psychotherapy for the Borderline Patient*, and *Psychotherapy for Borderline Personality*, co-authored with Drs. John Clarkin and Otto Kernberg.

Foreword

Borderline personality disorder research is a young area of study, the disorder having been added to DSM only in 1980, and is minute in both absolute size and relative to the research on longer recognized disorders and the public health implications of this serious mental illness. So an overarching priority is for more research. Investigators will review the extant research in planning new studies. However, these findings also should be considered for their potential to lift the burden of suffering that the disorder inflicts while research seeks even better understanding and more effective interventions and, ultimately, prevention and a cure.

Happily, the extant research has been amazingly productive, yielding findings that require discarding much of the clinical lore about BPD and replacing it with research findings and practices that have the potential for immediate positive impact. These findings include:

- The identification of genetics as a major factor in the etiology of BPD;
- Family members benefiting from training in dialectical behavior therapy (DBT), improving their interactions with and helping their BPD-inflicted relative;
- Imaging studies demonstrating the involvement of the brain, not just the mind, in BPD;
- A diminishing of BPD symptoms over time, accompanied by remission from the disorder, rather than the persistence of symptoms as the expressions of a supposedly "enduring" personality psychopathology;
- Evidence for the efficacy of an array of specialty psychosocial treatments: dialectical behavior therapy (DBT), mentalization, transfer-

[Haworth co-indexing entry note]: "Foreword." Breiling, James P. Co-published simultaneously in *Social Work in Mental Health* (The Haworth Press) Vol. 6, No. 1/2, 2008, pp. xxxv-xxxvi; and: *Borderline Personality Disorder: Meeting the Challenges to Successful Treatment* (ed: Perry D. Hoffman, and Penny Steiner-Grossman) The Haworth Press, 2008, pp. xxv-xxvi. Single or multiple copies of this article are available for a fee from The Haworth Document Delivery Service [1-800-HAWORTH, 9:00 a.m. - 5:00 p.m. (EST). E-mail address: docdelivery@haworthpress.com].

Available online at http://swmh.haworthpress.com
© 2008 by The Haworth Press. All rights reserved.
doi:10.1300/J200v06n01

ence-focused therapy, schema therapy, and group psychoeducation and skills training adjunctive to individual therapy;
- High rates of continuity of patients with their therapists; and
- A growing evidence base for the informed use of pharmacotherapy.

Yes, BPD patients continue to be challenging, but for most of them the diagnosis now means hope for remission from the disorder. The clinician who provides one of the specialty treatments for which there is research support has a good likelihood of providing meaningful help. Indeed, a new and better world is possible in the here and now for most BPD patients, and there is new satisfaction for the clinician, as well.

To be sure, challenges remain. A minority of BPD patients does not show significant abatement of symptoms. For the majority, however, remission means a better life, but it does not mean cure. For many, there are residual impairments; social and vocational functioning are often problems, and physical health issues may emerge. There is still important research to be done, but the train has moved far down the track toward a good life.

Research findings are important, but for these findings to make a difference, clinicians - psychiatrists, psychologists, psychiatric nurses, and social workers - must learn of the existence of these research-based treatment methods for BPD, and then incorporate them into clinical practice. To build this new knowledge base, recent and emerging findings need to be translated from research papers (often neither readily accessible nor understandable) for effective dissemination to and utilization by clinicians and others. Fortunately for those with BPD and their families, some efforts are underway, although more are needed. Of special note are the conferences about BPD research sponsored by the National Educational Alliance for Borderline Personality Disorder (NEABPD). Videos of presentations at recent meetings are available at the NEA-BPD web site (http://www. borderlinepersonalitydisorder.com).

The work of Marsha Linehan provides a prime example of how research effectively disseminated and used in everyday clinical practice can lift the burden of suffering for BPD patients around the country. Dr. Linehan sought to prevent the high risk of suicides by BPD patients and thereby give them the opportunity to achieve a life worth living. To do this, she developed an innovative psychosocial treatment, dialectical behavior therapy (DBT), which she then subjected to rigorous evaluation. When she found evidence of DBT's efficacy in National Institute of Health (NIH) funded treatment research evaluations, she presented her findings at scientific meetings and in research papers in scientific journals. Rather than rely on these venues for what is often slow dissemination and partial utilization in clinical practice, she wrote books and organized workshops for clinicians. Because of the magnitude of the need, she enlisted collaborators for NIH-funded research on the effective use of computer technology to teach DBT skills and trained and certified therapists (48 were listed in December 2007) to train other therapists in the use of DBT. For a listing, see the directory of DBT trained therapists at http://www.behavioraltech.com.

Significantly, graduate level programs are now considering evidence-based treatment models in preparing new clinicians, and many are offering training about DBT so that their new clinicians can offer empirically supported treatment at the beginning of their clinical work. And since DBT skills also have proved useful to family members with a BPD sufferer, there now are programs for family members, e.g., Family Connections, in which the dissemination and effective utilization of DBT skills is a major focus.

Despite the effective dissemination and utilization of DBT skills in conferences at which consumers and family members communicate with each other, there still is a significant gap between the need for and the availability of DBT therapists. An analogous yawning gap exists between other new research findings about BPD and what is believed and acted upon in clinical practice. Linehan's example of disseminating and promoting the utilization of research findings needs widespread replication. Every adoption of new knowledge and skills will mean that more clinicians are empowered to give effective help to individuals and their families affected by borderline personality disorder.

James P. Breiling, PhD
Program Chief
Psychopathology, Behavioral Dysregulation,
and Measurement Development Research
National Institute of Mental Health

Introduction

We would like to welcome you to this volume on borderline personality disorder. BPD is a psychiatric disorder that has been, and remains, controversial and challenging. The symptomatology of BPD occurs in the context of relationships, and the resultant behaviors can greatly affect both those who live with the disorder–sufferers, family members, and friends–and the mental health professionals who treat them. The complex symptom constellation of BPD itself leads to behaviors that promote a cycle of symptom exacerbation, often making it difficult or impossible for the individual to sustain relationships. This interpersonal core of the disorder has obvious ramifications not only for personal relationships, but for therapeutic ones as well. Such conflicts can predispose premature terminations in relationships that, in turn, promote the most prevalent BPD symptom, fear of abandonment.

Unfortunately, BPD lags far behind other disorders such as schizophrenia in terms of research and treatment interventions; the lag time often cited is more than two decades. Ongoing debates persist about diagnosis, etiology, neurobiology, genetics, medication, and treatment. These realities, coupled with the fact that social workers most often are on the "front lines" and yet may lack the most recent information and research on the disorder, were the impetus for the preparation of this collection.

This volume is intended to offer social work clinicians easier access to the knowledge needed for effective treatment by providing, in one volume, the most current research, information and treatment considerations. Of equal importance is our wish to make treatment providers aware of the perspective of sufferers themselves, and to offer them the opportunity to understand the experiences of family members who are often devastated by their relatives' struggles with BPD.

[Haworth co-indexing entry note]: "Introduction." Hoffman, Perry D., and Penny Steiner-Grossman. Co-published simultaneously in *Social Work in Mental Health* (The Haworth Press) Vol. 6, No. 1/2, 2008, pp. 1-3; and: *Borderline Personality Disorder: Meeting the Challenges to Successful Treatment* (ed: Perry D. Hoffman, and Penny Steiner-Grossman) The Haworth Press, 2008, pp. 1-3. Single or multiple copies of this article are available for a fee from The Haworth Document Delivery Service [1-800-HAWORTH, 9:00 a.m. - 5:00 p.m. (EST). E-mail address: docdelivery@haworthpress.com].

Available online at http://swmh.haworthpress.com
doi:10.1300/J200v06n01_01

Although there has been an increasing interest in the disorder in terms of research funding, treatment advancement, and an acknowledgement of family perspectives over the past 10 years, the fact remains that BPD is a highly stigmatized disorder. The evidence for this is seen among several groups: mental health professionals who often turn BPD patients away as difficult or untreatable; insurance companies who often do not recognize treatment of the disorder as reimbursable; and families who experience the "excess stigma and burden" of caring for their loved ones. Tragically, these families may still be seen as causative agents and may remain as such until the biological underpinnings of BPD are understood more completely, as they were eventually with schizophrenia and autism.

It may be years before all the aspects of the BPD symptomatology are teased apart and effective treatments become widely available. But even today, BPD is viewed increasingly as a diagnosis with a relatively good prognosis (Zanarini et al., 2006). The symptomatology of the disorder is documented to decline over time, and many people have been able to leave the world of mental illness to lead lives that are satisfying and fulfilling. Since this accomplishment requires the benefit of good treatment, this volume represents an important step toward that end.

The authors contributing to this volume were invited because they are leading experts in the field of BPD. Their interest and investment in writing their particular chapters for this collection for social workers speaks to their level of commitment to the field of service delivery. While the chapters were formatted to offer the information in a practical fashion, the high quality of the writings recommend this volume as essential reading for all mental health professionals working toward the betterment of those affected by BPD.

This volume joins other initiatives of the National Education Alliance for Borderline Personality Disorder (NEA-BPD) to promote understanding of the disorder. Beginning in 2002, the National Institute of Mental Heath funded annual conferences for 2003-2007 on BPD, and the proceedings of conferences have been published by the American Psychiatric Association (2005) in *Understanding and Treating Borderline Personality Disorder: A Guide for Professionals and Families*, edited by John G. Gunderson, M.D., and Perry D. Hoffman, Ph.D. Materials from these conferences are now available through the Web site, www.borderlinepersonalitydisorder.com, again thanks to the dedication and commitment of the conference presenters.

We hope you will find the variety of topics in this volume stimulating and provocative and that you will be encouraged to continue to work closely with this community of patients and their families. While the challenges to successful treatment are great, the rewards can be even greater.

Perry D. Hoffman, PhD
Penny Steiner-Grossman, EdD, MPH

REFERENCE

Zanarini MC, Frankenburg FR, Hennen J, Reich DB, Silk KR. Prediction of the 10-year course of borderline personality disorder. Am J Psychiatry. 2006 May;163 (5):827-32.

Borderline Personality Disorder: An Overview

John Gunderson

SUMMARY. Our knowledge about borderline personality disorder (BPD) has taken some unexpected turns: BPD is less stable, it is more genetic, and it is more treatable than we would ever have imagined even 15 years ago. These developments have profound implications for understanding and treatment of individuals with BPD. doi:10.1300/J200v06n01_02 *[Article copies available for a fee from The Haworth Document Delivery Service: 1-800-HAWORTH. E-mail address: <docdelivery@haworthpress.com> Website: <http://www.HaworthPress.com> © 2008 by The Haworth Press. All rights reserved.]*

KEYWORDS. Borderline personality disorder, remission, heritability, psychotherapy

REMISSION OF BORDERLINE SYMPTOMS

The fact that borderline psychopathology is not stable has emerged dramatically from two major NIMH-funded perspective research projects: the McLean Study of Adult Development (MSAD) (Zanarini et al., 2003) and the Collaborative Longitudinal Personality Disorder Study (CLPS) (Gunderson et al., 2000). Both studies have shown that about

[Haworth co-indexing entry note]: "Borderline Personality Disorder: An Overview." Gunderson, John. Co-published simultaneously in *Social Work in Mental Health* (The Haworth Press) Vol. 6, No. 1/2, 2008, pp. 5-12; and: *Borderline Personality Disorder: Meeting the Challenges to Successful Treatment* (ed: Perry D. Hoffman, and Penny Steiner-Grossman) The Haworth Press, 2008, pp. 5-12. Single or multiple copies of this article are available for a fee from The Haworth Document Delivery Service [1-800-HAWORTH, 9:00 a.m. - 5:00 p.m. (EST). E-mail address: docdelivery@haworthpress.com].

Available online at http://swmh.haworthpress.com
© 2008 by The Haworth Press. All rights reserved.
doi:10.1300/J200v06n01_02

50% of BPD patients remit by two years and that, once remitted, it is un-usual for them to relapse. There are many reasons why borderline patients remit, but in a detailed examination of 16 who remitted within six months, the most common reason was situational change (Gunderson et al., 2003). Individuals with BPD who leave highly stressful environments and/or attain highly supportive new environments become dramatically less symptomatic; anger, impulsivity, dissociative experiences, and emp-tiness all can disappear quickly. This does not make these individuals healthy in a functional way, an issue to be discussed below, but it does mean that major sectors of borderline psychopathology are remarkably reactive to situational stress.

This sensitivity to situational stress is consistent with longstanding clinical observations wherein borderline patients who seem desperately suicidal or otherwise wildly out of control can quickly become calm and cooperative upon being placed within hospitals. It is also evident within therapies where, when borderline patients feel understood and attached, they can be wonderfully insightful and collaborative. Fonagy (Fonagy et al., 1995) has suggested that this sensitivity to situational stress is specifically an issue of interpersonal attachment. The inability to sus-tain thinking when attachments are threatened is, he believes, the core psychological handicap of individuals with BPD. This theory has been supported by demonstrations that the systems that govern and reflect at-tachment can become "hyper-activated," and that this state interferes with an individual's capacity to think clearly or realistically about oneself or others (Bartels & Zeki, 2004).

The observations about the borderline patients' instability, i.e., their surprising capacity for remissions, have implications for social work-ers. The first implication is that assessment of available social supports is a central aspect of treatment planning for borderline patients. Estab-lishing treatment goals often should begin by addressing this issue. For example, interventions that diminish alienation from one's family may have profound effects. Exchanging an abusive partner for someone more supportive can dramatically diminish desperation. Offering the support of a nanny may allow the person with BPD who is otherwise overwhelmed by becoming a new mother to resume self-esteem sus-taining functions in another sphere. Within therapies, the development of a needed attachment to a therapist (i.e., accepting a borderline patient's dependence) can provide a critical buffer against impulsivity and affective storms.

A GENETIC BASIS FOR BPD

The fact that BPD has significant genetic determinants (Torgersen et al., 2000) has not been integrated into the work of most clinicians. This delayed integration of a genetic perspective is connected to the almost exclusive emphasis on psychosocial sources as an explanation for this disorder. The primary reason that the borderline diagnosis ever emerged as distinctive was the result of the singular responses they evoked in caretakers–both appeals for rescue and hostilities when feeling deceived. Borderline patients have always distinguished themselves by the splits within themselves that can leave them mercilessly beaten by shame or just as mercilessly enraged by their perceived betrayals. Their significant others will invariably be torn between tender protectiveness and unexpected betrayals. These interpersonal dynamics all seem so immediate and so personal that it has remained difficult to recognize how the resulting turmoil might have significant genetic roots.

Still, when viewed with scientific dispassion from outside the interpersonal turmoil, it actually becomes hard to imagine that borderline psychopathology could develop *without* significant heritability. Normal personality traits have significant heritability (Tellegen et al., 1988; Jang et al., 1996), as do all the other forms of major mental illness, including even post-traumatic stress disorder (PTSD) (Stein et al., 2002). Moreover, the facts that siblings of those with BPD can emerge as well adjusted, and that most children survive the same forms of childhood trauma without developing this disorder have been neglected reasons to suspect the role of genes. What is inherited, however, still remains a mystery; it is probably not the illness *per se*. More likely, what is inherited is some combination of the predisposing temperaments ("phenotypes") believed to underlie borderline psychopathology. These temperaments have been conceptualized as poor behavioral/impulse control and poor emotional/affective control (Siever & Davis, 1991; Skodol et al., 2002). However, the hypersensitivity within relationships noted earlier may also prove to be a predisposing temperament (Gunderson, unpublished ms.).

The implications of BPD's genetic base for clinical practice are only beginning to be considered. Perhaps the clearest implication is that a medical "disease" model applies as surely to BPD as it has to schizophrenia, major depression, bipolar disorder, obsessive compulsive disorder, or other "brain disorders." For BPD, however, the application of a medical model occurs within a clinical context in which the borderline patients' putative phenotypes (i.e., their impulsive behaviors, emotionality, and interpersonal volatility) have been shown to respond to psychosocial interventions. The observed effectiveness of psychosocial intervention to treat the behaviors and affects that are believed to have a significant genetic base makes it unlikely that these interventions will be forfeited in hopes that treatment can focus on medications–a focus that in the past has evolved for the other major psychiatric disorders once evidence for their heritability was established.

A more direct clinical consequence of recognizing the genetic contribution to BPD has been the emergence of national parent/family organizations–the National Education Alliance for Borderline Personality Disorder (NEA-BPD), the New England Personality Disorder Association (NEPDA), and the Treatment and Research Advancements Association for Personality Disorder (TARA)–where families are seen as necessary allies rather than malevolent causes. Clinicians are beginning to appreciate the value of psychoeducation. Patients and their families are beginning to be informed about this diagnosis. The reluctance to do so by clinicians should now be consigned to the category of a "counter-transference problem"–a reluctance deriving from our own misapprehensions and pejorative attitudes towards this disorder. In truth, BPD's prognosis, its origins, and its treatability should make disclosure of the diagnosis and education about it welcome to these patients and their families.

TREATMENT ADVANCES IN BPD

The third major development in our knowledge about borderline personality disorder involves its treatment. Psychoanalysts were responsible for bringing borderline patients to our attention. No fewer than 52 books on psychoanalytic psychotherapy for BPD were written between 1975 and 1994 (Gunderson, 2001). In retrospect, the most remarkable feature of this literature is that while they fostered an attitude of treatability, these books usually documented the failures of psychoanalytic methods. In a recent overview, Fonagy and Bateman (2006) suggest that the poor prognosis traditionally associated with BPD was in part a byproduct of the prior generation of clinicians' mistreatment of them. The thesis that prior mistreatments fostered negative attitudes towards borderline patients gains support from the history of their treatment in modalities other than psychoanalysis. Behavioral therapy and psychopharmacology have had similar histories. When practiced by clinicians who believed that borderline patients would gratefully conform to their prescriptions for health, these treatments would fail. Marsha Linehan has often remarked that be-havior therapy did not work until she discovered, via Zen, the need to first provide ample acceptance or validation for the borderline patients' ex-periences. The same discovery made by the psychoanalyst, Gerald Adler (1986), helped a second generation of analysts to recognize that validation and other supportive interventions are an essential aspect of alliance building that is in itself therapeutic. The early literature about psychopharmacology emphasizes the problems with non-compliance, overdosing, missed sessions, and splits with the psychotherapists. Here too, when treatment accommodations were made that recognized the need to first establish an alliance, these problems largely disappeared.

Current developments of treatment for BPD have several major themes: the need for disorder-specificity; the importance of motivated and well-informed therapists; and the value of short-term focused inter-ventions. The past 15 years have seen the emergence of three long-term empirically validated treatments (EVTs) specifically designed for borderline patients. Dialectical Behavior Therapy (DBT) (Linehan, Heard & Armstrong, 1993) was the first, Mentalization-Based Therapy (MBT) (Bateman & Fonagy, 2004) followed and, most recently, a vari-ant of the traditional psychoanalytic approach called Transference-Fo-cused Therapy (TFP) has entered the competition (Clarkin et al., 2007). Each therapeutic approach attempts to treat the whole BPD person, but each sees the core issue differently. DBT focuses on emotional and be-havioral control, MBT focuses on cognitive disabilities and learning new ways of thinking, while TFP focuses on distortions in perceptions of oneself and others. The most significant lessons to be learned from these three therapies may derive from recognizing how the approaches overlap: all convey hope and expect that patients can and will change; all emphasize the recognition of feelings and identifying the situa-tions that prompt them; all require that the patient be involved with the therapist and form an alliance around specified treatment goals; and all require therapists who like working with borderline patients, are committed to the particular therapy, and have had special training. In all three models, therapists are proactive within sessions and provide con-sistent rules for crisis coverage between sessions.

Also emerging in current treatment developments are investigations of shorter-term interventions. In contrast to the three empirically vali-dated longer-term BPD-specific treatments described above, short-term focused interventions are treatments designed to target discrete aspects of borderline psychopathology. The explanation for such treatments is derived in part from the modern managed care and EVT environment, which has forced clinical interventions into briefer durations of treatment and more measurable outcomes. This development also is consistent with the new knowledge about instability, which, as described above, lends itself to crisis management and situational rather than psychological solutions.

The primary focus of short-term interventions has been deliberate self-harm (DSH). British investigators developed Manual-Assisted Cognitive Treatment (MACT), a six-session individual therapy requiring only two days of training (Evan et al., 1998; 20; Tyrer et al., 2004). MACT showed initial promise but subsequently was disappointing when a sub-sample with BPD was examined. A second DSH targeted short-term therapy involves 14 sessions of group therapy in which BPD patients are encouraged to accept (rather than control or avoid) their feelings (Gunderson & Gratz, 2005). Other research has demonstrated that short-term stays in partial hospital settings significantly improve anxiety, depression, and parasuicidality (Gratz, LaCrosse, & Gunderson). These studies offer hope that future treatment of borderline patients may evolve into a sequence of goals with a corresponding sequence of modalities appropriate for each goal. The more discrete the goals and the duration of the treatment, the less significant prior training in either cognitive-behavioral or psychodynamic technique would be required.

One implication of this development is that social workers soon will have the option of learning a wide variety of distinct treatment protocols. Certainly, the exclusive "trade-guild" requirements for conducting psychoanalyses, and to a lesser extent DBT, can be expected to give way before the pressures for shorter-term focused interventions. Adapting this approach will go a long way toward demystifying treatments and giving these impatient and distrustful patients the hope for shorter-term relief or for change, without requiring what are otherwise often unfeasible time commitments or levels of interpersonal attachment.

CHALLENGES THAT REMAIN

An overall clinical implication that derives from the evidence about instability, genetics, and treatment involves the significance of social rehabilitation. Just as the positive symptoms of schizophrenia (delusion and disorganization) can respond relatively quickly to medication, but the negative symptoms (lack of friends and employment) persist, the same is true for BPD. Symptoms such as dysphoric feelings and self-injurious behaviors can respond more rapidly to treatment than do the social handicaps of distrust and lack of vocational skills (Skodol et al., 2005). These persistent social disabilities remain the major obstacle to attaining a full and satisfying life for borderline patients. Because longer-term psychosocial treatments of borderline patients have been successful, the field may be in a position to develop a social rehabilitative care system. Social workers should expect to be central in advocating, developing, and implementing such a system.

Readers of this text will be surprised at the diversity and energy of current efforts to improve treatment. A cadre of clinically wise and outcome-sensitive professionals has begun to create a new aura of hope for borderline patients. Developments in our understanding suggest that social workers should become ever more central to the provision of their care.

REFERENCES

Adler, G. (1986). *Borderline psychopathology and its treatment.* New York: Jason Aronson.

Bartels, A. & Zeki, S. (2004). The neural correlates of maternal and romantic love. *Neuro-Image,* 21, 55-1166.

Bateman, A. & Fonagy, P., (2004). *Psychotherapy for borderline personality disorder: Mentalization-based treatment.* Oxford, U.K.: Oxford University Press.

Clarkin, J.F., Levy, K.N., Lenzenweger, M.F., & Kernberg, O.F. (2007). Evaluating three treatments for borderline personality disorder: A multiwave study. *American Journal of Psychiatry.* 164 (6), 922-928.

Evans, K., Tyrer, P., Catalan, J., Schmidt, U., Davidson, K., et al. (1998). MACT: A randomized controlled trial of a brief intervention for bibliotherapy in the treatment of recurrent deliberate self-harm. *Psychiatric Medicine,* 29, 19-25.

Fonagy, P. & Bateman, A. (2006). Progress in the treatment of borderline personality disorder. *British Journal of Psychiatry,* 188, 1-3.

Fonagy, P., Leigh, T., Kennedy, R., Mattoon, G., Steele, H., Target, M., Steele, M., & Higgit, A. (1995). Attachment, borderline states and the representation of emotions and cognitions in self and other, in *Emotion, Cognition, and Representation.* Rochester symposium on Developmental Psychopathology Vol. 6. Cicchetti D, Toth SL, et al. (eds.). Rochester, NY: University of Rochester Press, pp. 371-414.

Gratz, K.L., LaCrosse, D.M., & Gunderson, J.G. (2006). Measuring changes in BPD following short-term treatment. *Journal of Psychiatric Practice,* 12(3), 153-159.

Gunderson, J.G., Bender, D., Sanislow, C., Yen, S., Bame Rettew, J., Dolan-Sewell, R., Dyck, I., Morey, L., McGlashan, T.H., Shea, M.T., & Skodol, A.E. (2003). Plausibility and possible determinants of sudden "remissions" in borderline patients. *Psychiatry,* 66, 111-119.

Gunderson, J.G., Gratz, K.L., Neuhaus, E.C., Smith, G.W. (2005). Levels of Care. In A.E. Skodol, D.S. Bender, J. Oldham (Eds.), *Textbook of Personality Disorders* (pp. 239-256). Arlington, VA: American Psychiatric Publishing, Inc.

Gunderson, J.G., Shea, M.T., Skodol, E.A., McGlashan, T.H., Morey, L.C., Stout, R.I., Zanarini, M.C., Grilo, C.M., Oldham, J.M., & Keller, M.B. (2000). The collaborative longitudinal personality disorders study I: Development, aims, design, and sample characteristics. *Journal of Personal Disorders*, 14(4), 300-315.

Gunderson, J.G. (2001). *Borderline personality disorder: A clinical guide.* Washington, DC: American Psychiatric Press, Inc.

Gunderson, J.G. The Borderline's disturbed relationships as a phenotype: evidence, possible endophenotypes and implications. Unpublished manuscript.

Jang, K.L., McCrae, R.R., Angleitner, A., Reimann, R., & Livesley, W.J. (1998). Heritability of facet-level traits in a cross-cultural twin sample: Support for a hierarchical model of personality. *Journal of Personality and Social Psychology*, 74, 1556-1565.

Linehan, M.M., Heard, H.L, & Armstrong, H.E. (1993). Naturalistic follow-up of a behavioral treatment for chronically parasuicidal borderline patients. *Archives of General Psychiatry*, 50(12), 971-974.

Siever, L.J. & Davis, K.L. (1991). A psychobiologic perspective on the personality disorders. *American Journal of Psychiatry*, 148, 1647-1658.

Skodol, A.E., Pagano, M.E., Bender, D.S., Shea, M.T., Gunderson, J.G., Yen, S., Stout, R.L., Morey, L.C., Sanislow, C.A., Grilo, C.M., Zanarini, M.C., & McGlashan, T.H. (2005). Stability of functional impairment in patients with schizotypal, borderline, avoidant, or obsessive-compulsive personality disorder over two years. *Psychological Medicine*, 35, 443-451.

Skodol, A.E., Siever, L., Livesley, W.J., Gunderson, J.G., Pfohl B., & Widiger, T.A. (2002). The borderline diagnosis II: biology, genetics, and clinical course. *Biological Psychiatry*, 51, 951-963.

Stein, M.B., Jang, K.L., Taylor, S., Vernon, P.A, & Livesley, W.J. (2002). Genetic and environmental influences on trauma exposure and posttraumatic stress disorder symptoms: A twin study. *American Journal of Psychiatry*, 159, 1675-1681.

Tellegen, A., Lykken, D.T., Bouchard,T.J., & Wilcox, K.J. (1988). Personality similarity in twins reared apart and together. *Journal of Personality and Social Psychology*, 4, 1031-1039.

Torgersen, S., Lygren, S., Øien, P.A., Skre, I., Onstad, S., Edvardsen, J., Tambs, K., Kringlen, E. (2000). A twin study of personality disorders. *Comprehensive Psychiatry*, 41(6), 416-425.

Tyrer, P., Tom, B., Byford, S., Schmidt, U., Jones, V., et al. (2004). Differential effects of MACT in the treatment of recurrent deliberate self-harm and personality disturbance: The POPMACT study. *Journal of Personality Disorders*, 18,102-116.

Zanarini, M.C., Frankenburg, F.R., Hennen, J., & Silk, K.R. (2003). The longitudinal course of borderline psychopathology: 6-year prospective follow-up of the phenomenology of borderline personality disorder. *American Journal of Psychiatry*, 160, 274-283.

doi:10.1300/J200v06n01_02

Confronting Myths and Stereotypes About Borderline Personality Disorder

Richard Hersh

SUMMARY. The clinician treating a patient with borderline personality disorder (BPD) is often faced with complicated challenges, from making and communicating an accurate diagnosis, to implementing an appropriate, informed plan for treatment. Myths and stereotypes about BPD, and the individuals who may carry the diagnosis, likely complicate effective recognition and treatment of the disorder. BPD has been a controversial diagnosis among clinicians since its inception, and it is poorly understood among the general public. Pressures to avoid an explicit exploration of the diagnosis stemming from myths and stereotypes about the disorder can come from a number of sources, including other clinicians, family members and patients themselves. The results of minimizing or ignoring the contribution of borderline pathology may be detrimental. Clinical decisions based on outmoded thinking about diagnosis, prognosis, treatment efficacy, and availability of resources may deny patients optimal care. Integrating current findings into consideration of a BPD diagnosis and design of appropriate treatment, free of misconceptions about the condition, may help limit the untoward effects associated with failure to appreciate elements of borderline personality.
doi:10.1300/J200v06n01_03 *[Article copies available for a fee from The Haworth Document Delivery Service: 1-800-HAWORTH. E-mail address: <docdelivery@haworthpress.com> Website: <http://www.HaworthPress.com> © 2008 by The Haworth Press. All rights reserved.]*

[Haworth co-indexing entry note]: "Confronting Myths and Stereotypes About Borderline Personality Disorder." Hersh, Richard. Co-published simultaneously in *Social Work in Mental Health* (The Haworth Press) Vol. 6, No. 1/2, 2008, pp. 13-32; and: *Borderline Personality Disorder: Meeting the Challenges to Successful Treatment* (ed: Perry D. Hoffman, and Penny Steiner-Grossman) The Haworth Press, 2008, pp. 13-32. Single or multiple copies of this article are available for a fee from The Haworth Document Delivery Service [1-800-HAWORTH, 9:00 a.m. - 5:00 p.m. (EST). E-mail address: docdelivery@haworthpress.com].

Available online at http://swmh.haworthpress.com
© 2008 by The Haworth Press. All rights reserved.
doi:10.1300/J200v06n01_03

KEYWORDS. Borderline personality disorder, comorbidity, diagnosis, stereotypes

INTRODUCTION

Despite recent advances in the understanding and treatment of the borderline personality disorder, a number of powerful, lasting myths and stereotypes persist, both about BPD and about the individuals who may receive the diagnosis. These myths and stereotypes are widespread, insidious, and likely to impede the optimal identification and treatment of the disorder. Clinicians charged with caring for patients with BPD may face challenges on a number of fronts in the course of treating an individual with the disorder. A careful examination of prejudices and unintentional sequelae of certain kinds of outmoded thinking may be of use in improving the care and prognosis of patients with this syndrome.

One review by Nehls (1998) on the subject of BPD and stigma outlined the different pejorative terms used by clinicians over the years including: "not sick," "manipulative," "hateful," and "angry, noncompliant," among others. This review linked stigmatizing terms used about persons with BPD to "a lack of empathy toward persons with borderline personality disorder and the potential for misdirected treatment."

There may be myths and stereotypes about any number of psychiatric disorders, but it is fair to say that personality disorders in general, and BPD in particular, may be unusually vexing and confusing for mental health professionals. BPD can and does present in a wide variety of ways, sometimes even in the same patient. Paris (2005) has described BPD as "protean" or ever changing, and its place in psychiatry has been compared to the historical description of syphilis in medicine as "the great imitator." Indeed, patients with BPD often use the vocabulary of other disorders to communicate their experience of symptoms; emptiness or boredom can be described as "depression," impulsivity as "mania," fear of abandonment as "anxiety." To further complicate this, research has shown high rates of comorbid psychopathology in borderline patients (anxiety disorders, mood disorders, post-traumatic stress disorder, eating disorders and substance abuse), making accurate diagnosis a challenge (Oldham et al., 1995; Zanarini et al., 1998; Zimmerman & Mattia, 1990).

For many clinicians, particularly trainees, elements of borderline pathology can evoke tremendous distress, anxiety and hate. While BPD can be associated with suicidality, impulsivity and rage, the same can be said about other psychiatric diagnoses. These other presentations, particularly Axis I conditions, do not usually elicit comparable negative responses to both the patients *and* to the diagnosis. It is possible to treat patients with many Axis I disorders using a straightforward "medical model" approach. Work with patients with BPD presents unique challenges, and clinical thinking can be shaped by complex countertransferential responses including gratification, rescue- fantasies, revulsion and fear.

The following experiences of a young social worker in a clinical setting will serve to illustrate and then to explain a number of unfortunate myths and stereotypes about BPD:

> Janet's first job after completing social work school is on an inpatient general psychiatry unit in a highly regarded academic medical center in a large northeastern city. She is assigned to work with a team including one attending psychiatrist, two resident psychiatrists, one staff psychologist, and an occupational therapist. The unit treats adults with a variety of diagnoses, usually for short stays of days to weeks. The population of the unit was initially described to Janet as being primarily affective disorders, psychotic disorders and substance abuse disorders, but during rounds on her first day, Janet is struck by the significant number of cases presented to the team with identifiable borderline pathology.

MYTH: BPD IS A RARELY SEEN CONDITION

BPD is a common clinical presentation in almost all contemporary mental health treatment settings. Surveys in the community have noted rates of BPD in the population of approximately 1-2 %, which makes its prevalence similar to those of other major psychiatric illnesses such as schizophrenia (Torgersen, Kringlen & Cramer, 2001; Swartz et al., 1990). Prevalence rates of BPD in various treatment settings are considered to be significantly higher than rates noted above in community samples (Zimmerman, Rothschild & Chelminski, 2005). One review estimated that 10 % of general psychiatric outpatients and 20% of psychiatric inpatients met criteria for BPD (Widiger & Weissman, 1991). Studies have also shown that BPD patients are unusually high utilizers of all kinds of mental health services, including a wide variety of psychotherapies, treatment programs and hospital-based services (Zanarini et al., 2001). Patients with BPD are known to consume as many or more mental health services than patients with other personality disorders or patients with major depression (Bender et al., 2001).

It would be unusual for clinicians in general mental health settings *not* to see patients with BPD. So how is it possible to understand clinicians in various settings who maintain that they rarely or never see patients with BPD?

1. Clinicians may see patients with BPD in their work but fail to explore aspects of the patients' histories or presentations that would suggest a BPD diagnosis. One study showed that patients seen in research settings were more likely than those seen in clinical settings to receive a BPD diagnosis (Westen, 1997); another showed that patients seen in general clinical settings are more likely to be diagnosed with personality disorders, including BPD, if structured interviews are administered in addition to the standard clinical examinations (Zimmerman & Mattia, 1999).

2. Clinicians may conflate two elements of the evaluation process, the chief complaint and the diagnosis, in an effort to be supportive and validating of patients' self-assessments. The chief complaint should reflect the factors contributing to a patient's presentation to a clinician for assistance, but it may often include diagnoses patients make themselves or carry over from previous assessments. While self-diagnoses or previously made diagnoses may be of significance, they should not substitute for fresh, rigorous, unbiased formulations. It is possible for clinicians to miss BPD if they rely exclusively on patients' self-reports, given the lack of understanding and acceptance of the diagnosis among many individuals who might meet criteria for the disorder.

3. Clinicians may recognize BPD, but for philosophical reasons stress alternative explanations for certain symptom constellations. For example, clinicians focusing on pharmacotherapeutic interventions for mood disorders may stress the elements of BPD easily confused with elements of bipolar disorder or atypical depression, rather than identify the more narrowly defined boredom, emptiness or affective instability of BPD. Some clinicians might say that since the two symptom pictures may look similar, it is *always* to a patient's advantage to assume first that the symptoms are part of a mood disorder, instead of entertaining diagnoses of both mood and personality disorders from the start.

4. Some clinicians may reject the idea of descriptive psychiatry alto-
gether. These individuals may not find it of help to think in terms
of diagnostic categories, may not use the DSM-IV-TR, and may
utilize alternative systems for understanding pathology. Such clinicians would most certainly not integrate recognition of BPD
symptoms into their conceptualization of diagnosis or treatment.

During her first supervision session with the attending psychologist
at her new job, Janet describes a number of the cases on her service and
remarks that she has gone back to review some of her notes from school
and training because of the prominence of borderline pathology she has
observed. She tells her supervisor that she plans to ask one patient in
particular (and this patient's parents) more questions about her back-
ground and history in an effort to clarify a possible BPD diagnosis. Her
supervisor responds that this plan makes sense given the patient's history of recurrent hospitalizations, persistent threats of suicide, and lack
of response to treatment for recurrent depression. Janet adds that if the
data she collects support a BPD diagnosis, she will share her conjecture
in team meeting. To Janet's surprise her supervisor responds, "You
know a lot of clinicians think BPD has no validity and think of it as 'a
waste-basket diagnosis.'"

MYTH:
BPD IS A DIAGNOSIS UNIQUE
FOR ITS LACK OF VALIDITY

In his recent review, "The Diagnosis of Borderline Personality Disorder: Problematic but Better than the Alternatives," Paris (2005) con-
fronts the widespread criticism of the BPD construct and the questions
about the validity of the diagnosis. He addresses four areas of concern:
that the name itself is misleading; that the disorder is uniquely lacking in
validity; that the comorbidity associated with the disorder is unusual,
excessive and invalidating; and that the disorder is better conceptualized as a variant of affective disturbance. A theme in Paris' review is the
particularly vehement negative response to shortcomings in the BPD diagnosis and the extent to which similar shortcomings might be found in
any number of other psychiatric (and medical) diagnoses.

For many, the word "borderline" remains confusing, implying an inadequately defined set of symptoms not fitting into any well-described
category of illness. As the term "borderline" is an artifact of earlier investigations into clinical presentations on the border between psychotic

and neurotic states, it may not neatly communicate the essential elements of the condition. The same complaint could be made about the term "schizophrenia," of course, but clinical experience suggests generally less dissatisfaction among patients, families and clinicians about this and other imprecise diagnostic terms.

BPD may be dismissed as "invalid" or "a waste-basket diagnosis" by some, suggesting it is unique in its limitations as a psychiatric disorder. As Paris points out, however, the failure of BPD to meet all the rigorous criteria of validity (clear-cut clinical description; laboratory studies; delimination from other disorders; follow-up studies documenting characteristic outcome; and family prevalence studies) makes it no different than other widely accepted diagnoses.

Zanarini et al. (1998) have proposed that the Axis I comorbidity seen in BPD follows a specific pattern, which may have utility as a marker in aiding clinicians in their multiaxial assessment of patients. They do not view Axis I comordity as weakening the validity of the BPD diagnosis; rather, they maintain that a pattern of "complex comorbidity," described as meeting criteria for disorders of affect and impulse, is a useful predictor of likely BPD psychopathology.

Recent controversy has raised questions about the links among pharmaceutical company support, academic research, and the establishment of certain diagnostic entities. This controversy brings to light the complex process by which diagnoses attain wide acceptance. It may be important in reviewing the debate about BPD as a "valid" diagnosis to keep in mind that no pharmacotherapeutic agent has thus far been approved by the Food and Drug Administration for the treatment of BPD. There clearly has been no concerted effort by drug manufactures or public health agencies to promote the BPD diagnosis with extensive professional education programs or public outreach.

> *Janet's patients on her new job include a middle-aged woman, Anne, with a history of multiple suicide gestures and attempts who is admitted after taking an overdose of acetaminophen (Tylenol) following an argument with her mother. Janet has an opportunity to review Anne's history with her therapist of six years; the therapist outlines for Janet Anne's long history of self-injury, mercurial moods, and unstable relationships. Anne's therapist describes Anne's presentations as "consistent with borderline personality disorder." When Janet reviews the case with the resident on her team, he responds: "I guess Anne must be giving her therapist a*

*hard time; I'm sure she says she has borderline personality be-
cause she has been difficult."*

MYTH:
*BPD IS A DIAGNOSIS CLINICIANS GIVE
TO PATIENTS WHO MAKE THEM ANGRY
OR PATIENTS THEY DO NOT LIKE*

BPD was first described in 1938 (Stern, 1938), but the disorder was
not fully accepted into psychiatric nomenclature until its inclusion in
DSM-III in the 1980s (American Psychiatric Association, 1980). Since
then a number of authors have suggested that the diagnosis is widely
misused by clinicians to brand those patients who frustrate them or
whom they find unlikable. One paper by Reiser and Levenson (1984)
outlined a number of "abuses" of the BPD diagnosis, suggesting, among
others, "expression of countertransference hate" as a common reason
why the BPD diagnosis might be made. The authors of this paper also
maintained that use of the term borderline would lead to a breakdown of
empathy between therapist and patient. Another study by Lewis and
Appleby (1988) invited psychiatrists to review case vignettes, then
asked them to complete questionnaires assessing their attitudes towards
the cases. The study concluded that patients given a previous diagnosis
of personality disorder were seen as more difficult and less deserving of
care compared to control subjects who were not. This study concluded
that the personality disorder diagnosis was an "enduring pejorative
judgment" rather than a clinical diagnosis and recommended that the
concept of personality disorder be abandoned.

In her best-selling autobiographical work, *Girl, Interrupted*, published in 1994, Susanna Kaysen recounts a conversation with her psychiatrist during her extended hospitalization at McLean Hospital:
"What *does borderline personality mean*, anyhow? It appears to be a
way station between neurosis and psychosis: a fractured but not disas-
sembled psyche. Thus to quote my . . . psychiatrist: 'It's what they call
people whose lifestyles bother them.' He can say that because he's a
doctor. If I said it, nobody would believe me."

Many treaters seem to accept the conclusion that making a BPD diagnosis must result from a negative experience of a particular patient. By
DSM-IV-TR criteria, BPD can theoretically present in a multitude of
different manifestations; some, it is true, are marked by anger or affective instability, but other presentations might be notable for docility or

vulnerability. Zanarini and Silk (2001) distinguish between different types of BPD presentations in their review, "The Difficult-to-Treat Patient with Borderline Personality Disorder." They present borderline pathology as occupying a continuum, with some patients having "mild cases of BPD" or demonstrating borderline traits only. Still others, they note, are only intermittently self-destructive with extended periods of stability. The "difficult-to-treat" borderline patients they describe often have persistently chaotic lives with marked disabilities and limited functioning; this group of patients, who use the most mental health services, in their words "lead to the most distress among clinicians."

Because BPD can present in myriad ways, and because individuals with BPD can have waxing and waning symptom pictures, many clinicians may reserve a borderline diagnosis only for those most chronic or symptomatic patients. This unfortunate tendency may limit accurate communication about patients between treaters, may limit clinicians' ability to guide and educate patients and families, and may preclude referral to specific services for all but the most disabled patients with BPD.

> *Janet is assigned to work with Bill, a graduate student with a history of multiple difficulties in school and in his personal life. Bill's frequent angry outbursts began in his early 20s, with markedly conflictual relations with his family, often leading to periods of estrangement. Bill often uses drugs or alcohol in binge patterns when he feels he is not getting the attention he needs from his parents When Bill receives a letter from his girlfriend who is overseas telling him of her wish to break up, he called his parents and told them he planned to take an overdose of his antidepressant and mood stabilizer medications. Bill's parents called the police, who went to Bill's apartment and took Bill to the hospital against his will. Over the years Bill has been given a number of diagnoses from different therapists and psychopharmacologists: depression, atypical depression, rapid-cycling bipolar disorder and attention-deficit hyperactivity disorder, among others. During a meeting on the unit, Janet asks Bill's psychopharmacologist about the possibility of some kind of personality disorder symptoms in Bill's current presentation. He responds, "I guess he could, but I wouldn't feel comfortable suggesting that now; I'd rather give him the benefit of the doubt."*

MYTH:
DELAYING THE DIAGNOSIS OF BPD UNTIL TREATMENT FOR ANY PLAUSIBLE AXIS 1 DISORDER HAS FAILED GIVES PATIENTS THE "BENEFIT OF THE DOUBT"

Clinicians treating patients with BPD alone, or BPD comorbid with other conditions, often feel compelled to give these patients "the benefit of the doubt" by minimizing or ignoring the contribution of borderline pathology to their clinical presentations. Clinicians may have a number of reasons for doing so, including the conventional wisdom that a BPD diagnosis cannot and should not be made if a patient exhibits concurrent Axis I symptoms.

Trainee clinicians are often advised to wait until any Axis I disorder has fully remitted before entertaining an Axis II diagnosis, and this advice is often reflected by the practice of putting "deferred" under Axis II in a routine manner. Apprehension about "branding" patients as having BPD when an Axis I diagnosis is under consideration can make clinical sense, informed by research on the state-dependent nature of some personality symptoms or dimensions, or it can reflect either anachronistic thinking about the disorder or countertransferential resistance.

Although DSM-IV-TR clearly allows for distinguishing personality disorder pathology as "primary" or "reason for visit," there may be a widespread feeling that doing so reveals an absence of diagnostic rigor or therapeutic resolve (American Psychiatric Association, 2000). The supposition may be that a personality disorder diagnosis is what should be made only after all Axis I treatment possibilities have been thoroughly exhausted.

Triebwasser and Siever (2007) have noted that there may be reasons to be skeptical about concluding that it is wholly impossible to arrive at a reasonable Axis II diagnosis in clinical settings when Axis I pathology is in evidence. They note that few of the studies concluding that what seem like personality disorder traits are likely complications of Axis I conditions are designed to be similar to standard extended evaluation processes most likely to be done by skilled clinicians. They point out that studies based on self-report questionnaires, or on interviews with subjects only, cannot approximate a comprehensive process of serial interviews with patients and collateral interviews with spouses or family members.

BPD can account for disturbances in spheres of affect, impulsivity and cognition; most of the Axis I alternatives proposed in clinical situations that engender an Axis I vs. BPD debate do not offer a comparable economy of diagnosis. The delay in entertaining a borderline diagnosis is not just an academic matter; it can have genuine and deleterious effects on patient care.

1. Failure to appreciate borderline pathology can contribute to misapprehension about risk of suicide. Clinicians may understand recurrent suicide threats or gestures as part of borderline pathology and avoid unnecessary, regressing hospitalizations. Clinicians unwilling or unable to acknowledge borderline pathology (with or without comorbid Axis I conditions) may feel compelled to hospitalize patients repeatedly, incurring great expense and causing marked disruption in their patients' lives. On the other hand, risks of suicide might be *underestimated* in patients with borderline pathology seen as having Axis I conditions only; for example: patients with affective disorder symptoms and unexplored borderline pathology may be given inappropriately large amounts of medications like tricyclic antidepressants or mood stabilizers that are toxic in overdose.

2. Patients with BPD with or without comorbid Axis I disorders often end up on complex, sometimes inconsistent, medication regimens. It is common to see BPD patients on a regimen consisting of some combination of antidepressant, antipsychotic, sedative-hypnotic, anxiolytic and psychostimulant medications. Because patients with BPD are likely to have symptoms in a variety of dimensions, including affective disturbance, impulsivity, and transient psychosis, it follows that clinicians might feel compelled to prescribe unwieldy medication combinations. Patients and family members are understandably confused and concerned when patients first fail to respond to standard treatment recommendations for the Axis I conditions they are told they have, and are then treated with complex, unconventional medication combinations, often with prominent side effects and drug-drug interactions.

3. Patients and family members become discouraged with good reason when patients fail to respond to treatments widely believed to be effective for Axis I disorders. Keeping patients and family members in the dark about the contribution of BPD symptoms may contribute to the inevitable non-compliance that follows such limited responses. When the possibility of a BPD is finally raised, patients and families, weary of months or years of costly, ineffective treatments, some with profound side effects, often ask: "How come it took them so long to tell us?"

Janet interviews a new patient to the unit; Marcia is a 21year-old senior at a highly regarded women's college who was admitted by way of the emergency room after the college Dean's office insisted that she be evaluated. Marcia's roommate brought to the resident advisor's attention that Marcia had been cutting herself repeatedly on her inner thighs and now has medically concerning wounds bilaterally. Marcia is admitted to the unit, but soon thereafter asks Janet to contact her treating psychologist to facilitate a rapid discharge. Janet is able to make contact with the psychologist who describes Marcia's past year of symptoms including: self-injury, specifically superficial cutting on her arms and thighs; bulimia nervosa symptoms; and frequent drug use. Janet asks the therapist if she had ever entertained a BPD diagnosis for Marcia. She responds, "Well, yes, I think she's borderline but I haven't brought it up with her. I don't think it would serve any point and it might make things worse."

MYTH:
PATIENTS WITH BPD SHOULD NEVER BE TOLD THEIR DIAGNOSIS; IT WOULD CAUSE THEM UNDUE DISTRESS

The practice of withholding information to patients about their diagnosis, once widespread in many branches of medicine, changed significantly in the second half of the 20th century (Hassan & Hassan, 1998). For decades it was standard to withhold certain diagnoses, especially cancer, from most patients. At the time, the general thinking was that patients could not tolerate such dire news and that communicating such information might precipitate an exacerbation of the illness or even sudden death. More recently, a focus on assisting patients with informed consent and decision-making has changed this practice considerably; almost all patients in this country are now made aware of their medical diagnoses (Paranscandola, Hawkins & Danis, 2002). Research on the disclosure of cancer diagnoses has underscored a number of factors contributing to this trend, including: an improvement in therapy for some cancers; a focus on comfort and palliative care for patients; and a rise in consumer empowerment and a rethinking of the physician-patient relationship (Goldberg, 1984; Green & Gantt, 1987).

In a similar vein, disclosure of a schizophrenia diagnosis to patients has changed considerably in recent years (Atkinson, 1989). Arguments for withholding a reliably made schizophrenia diagnosis from patients have included: uncertainly regarding the validity of the diagnosis; a perception that patients might not be able to understand the meaning of the diagnosis; and a fear that the diagnosis might demoralize or stigmatize a patient or family. Some clinicians polled on this subject maintained that a frank discussion about diagnosis might be in a patient's best interest (MacDonald-Scott, Machizawa & Satoh, 1992). These clinicians cited the possibility that withholding the diagnosis of schizophrenia might *contribute* to stigmatization, implying that the diagnosis is "too terrible to tell the patient and too awful to discuss." Other potential benefits cited include: the possibility of greater treatment compliance; the utility of psychoeducation about the nature of schizophrenia in reducing feelings of blame, anger and helplessness in families; and the opportunity for informed patients and families to participate fully in treatment planning and forecast of future treatment needs.

There is scant research on the subject of the risks and benefits of disclosing a diagnosis of BPD to a patient. Collective experience suggests that many patients diagnosed with BPD are not told their diagnosis for a variety of reasons. As noted, some clinicians might not accept the validity of the BPD diagnosis; others may feel that a patient's condition might worsen if he or she were told of the diagnosis; still others may fear a rageful, explosive response to such information. One pilot study designed to look at the possibility of risks or benefits of disclosure of the BPD diagnosis found no untoward effects of communication of this information; in fact, the results suggested the possible benefits of such a disclosure coordinated with pertinent psychoeducation (Zanarini & Frankenburg, 2004).

> *Janet and her team are treating Martha, a 25-year woman employed as a legal secretary, with a three-year history of self-mutilation, bulimia and notable mood shifts often lasting only hours. This patient's psychiatrist referred her for an inpatient hospitalization after she cut herself with a razor when her boyfriend of six months told her that he wanted to break off their relationship. While she is in the hospital, Martha's outpatient psychiatrist, in consultation with the inpatient team, arranges a meeting to review with Martha their thoughts about her diagnosis and treatment plan. Janet is able to join the meeting and is struck that Martha seems to be open to considering a diagnosis of BPD when her doctor reviews with her the criteria in the DSM-IV-TR. Martha cries briefly when the diagnosis is suggested, but she is able to ask*

thoughtful questions about prognosis and treatment options and even expresses some relief. Later she tells Janet: "I thought for a while that I had some kind of depression that just never got better with medication. Now I understand I have a disorder with a name and some specific treatments."

MYTH:
COMMUNICATING A DIAGNOSIS OF BPD WILL HINDER, NOT HELP, A PATIENT'S TREATMENT

Clinicians may want to disclose a diagnosis of BPD to a patient for a number of reasons, with the intent of aiding them in their recovery. Despite almost universal concern about engendering anger or suicidality by talking openly about the BPD diagnosis with such patients, there are a number of good reasons to think that such an intervention will be to the patient's benefit.

In recent years, a premium has been placed on encouraging patient autonomy. Informed-consent procedures are now routine in all areas of medicine, including psychiatry, with an emphasis on educating patients so that they can make the best, informed, final decisions about their treatment. The balance between a clinician's desire to do what is best for the patient and a patient's need for independent decision-making has been influenced by social trends emphasizing truth-telling and patients' self-determination.

Effective psychoeducation about BPD for patients and families is not possible without disclosure of the diagnosis. Patients and families members may well express relief when a name and a set of symptoms and specific treatment options are communicated; as noted, many patients can go for months or years believing they are grappling with an unusually treatment-resistant form of an illness such as depression or bipolar disorder–illnesses they believe to be treatable for everyone but themselves. Bolton and Gunderson (1996) wrote about the relief patients may feel when they are educated about BPD and understand "that there are others who struggle with it and that there are effective, albeit time-consuming, treatments available."

Recent data from two important prospective studies (Zanarini et al., 2003; Gunderson et al., 2003) have added to a growing shift in thinking about the course of BPD, suggesting that a significant number of patients diagnosed with the disorder may demonstrate remission over time. A growing literature on psychological interventions and pharmacotherapy in BPD has added to a more optimistic thinking about long-term prognosis, leading to increased opportunities for psychoeducation of patients and families.

Psychoeducation about BPD can guide patients and families toward effective treatments and away from poorly informed and potentially dangerous interventions. Patients and families can access services through Websites of organizations like the National Alliance for the Mentally Ill (NAMI), the National Education Alliance for Borderline Personality Disorder (NEA-BPD), and the Treatment and Research Advancements Association for Personality Disorder (TARA). Family members may benefit from books written for the lay public like *I Hate You, Don't Leave Me* (Kreisman & Strauss, 1989), *Borderline Personality Disorder Demystified* (Friedel et al., 2004), and *Stop Walking on Eggshells* (Mason & Kreger, 1988).

Patients and families versed in the details of BPD and its treatment options can work with clinicians to craft care-plans with appropriate expectations. Patients can be educated about the limited goals of pharmacotherapy of BPD, with an expectation that medications can be of use for specific symptom relief (e.g., cognitive-perceptual disturbance, impulsivity), but will not likely result in remission of the disorder. Patients can be educated about the reality that any modality of psychotherapy will require time, effort and perseverance, with likely periods of frustration and blame directed at treaters and at self. Disclosure of a BPD diagnosis also allows patients and their families to access treatments specific for the disorder. Participation in treatments like Dialectical Behavioral Therapy (DBT) as outlined by Linehan (1993), or the Systems Training for Emotional Predictability and Problem Solving (STEPPS) as outlined by Blum et al. (2002), require awareness of the BPD diagnosis.

Communicating a diagnosis of BPD may be a boon to clinicians as well (Lequesne & Hersh, 2004). Clinicians faced with a group of treatment-seeking patients, often presenting in crisis, will be better able to avoid iatrogenic complications such as cumbersome, dangerous polypharmacy regimens and unnecessary, regressing hospitalizations, if patients, family members and other treaters are clear about the centrality of borderline pathology in any specific case.

In practical terms, many patients with BPD will eventually suspect or come to learn their diagnoses, either by talking with other patients, doing research about their symptoms, or reading a chart or insurance form. With the widely increased availability of medical information, in part from the Internet, it is now common for patients to come to clinicians armed with informed questions about diagnoses. Clinicians may run the risk of finding themselves explaining why they withheld a borderline diagnosis: what was so bad about the diagnosis, patients may wonder, that he or she could not be told in a straightforward manner?

After Janet opens her private practice, she is referred a new patient, Maria, who carries diagnoses of recurrent major depression, alcohol abuse and BPD. During Janet's initial evaluation period she takes a detailed history and obtains collateral information, confirming, in her view, the diagnoses already made. She gets permission from Maria to contact her previous therapist, whom she saw for two years. That therapist had decided to end treatment with Maria during Maria's most recent hospitalization; at that time Maria had become despondent over learning of her boyfriend's infidelity, combined alcohol and sleeping medication, and while intoxicated, called 911 threatening suicide. When Janet speaks with Maria's former therapist he explains to Janet that while he felt he had a decent treatment alliance with Maria and believed he could be of help to her, he chose to end treatment out of concern about his liability: "I just didn't think it was possible to protect myself against possible lawsuits."

MYTH:
TREATING PATIENTS WITH BPD LEADS TO INEVITABLE, INSOLUBLE LIABILITY PROBLEMS

The *Practice Guideline for the Treatment of Patients with Borderline Personality Disorder*, published by the American Psychiatric Association in 2001, stresses the particular importance of attending to risk management issues in this population. The *Guideline* is frank in its assessment of the challenges inherent in treating patients with BPD; in fact, the guideline for treating patients with BPD was the first of the APA Guideline series to include a special section on this subject.

Borderline patients *do* present complicated risk management challenges, reflecting key elements of the disorder including acute and chronic suicidality, intermittent anger and impulsivity, and frequent, crisis-driven demands for symptom relief. The Guideline's recommendations underscore the literature on the subject, emphasizing the importance of attention to boundary violations; thoughtful management of

suicidal thoughts, gestures and attempts; and the need for frequent consultation in problematic situations.

Treating patients with BPD does require additional awareness, and
sometimes additional effort, for clinicians who are clear about the diagnosis and understandably concerned about their liability. More concerning would be clinicians who are not fully aware of a patient's borderline
traits or disorder, and therefore more vulnerable to finding themselves
in at-risk situations. Such clinicians may find themselves making ex-
ceptions to their usual practice, influenced by unexplored countertransferential reactions, which can include urges to rescue or to abandon
a patient. Mental health professionals resolved never to treat patients
with borderline pathology may not always be successful in doing so. It
may be more likely that grave risk management situations–patient abandonment, financial or sexual boundary violations–will grow out of ignoring or minimizing borderline pathology. Treating patients with BPD
safely may require extra focus, extra documentation and extra consultation, but these precautions should allow treaters to care for these patients without undue distress.

> *Janet meets with the parents of a 19 year-old woman on her ser-*
> *vice as part of planning for the patient's discharge from the*
> *hospital. Suzanne had been hospitalized a year earlier after a*
> *suicide attempt by overdose of zolpidem (Ambien). Suzanne was*
> *hospitalized this time after taking eight 0.5 mg tablets of*
> *clonazepam (Klonopin) and drinking two beers in an effort to*
> *"get some sleep" after getting into an argument with another*
> *woman in her DBT group. Suzanne maintains that she was not*
> *attempting to harm herself as she had the previous year. Su-*
> *zanne's inpatient treatment team has decided to discharge her*
> *from the hospital to her parents' home for the weekend, before*
> *Suzanne can return to her own apartment. Suzanne's parents*
> *are both professionals; her father is an attorney and her mother*
> *is a health insurance company executive. When Janet reviews*
> *with them Suzanne's discharge plan, including her return to*
> *DBT and to her psychiatrist, Suzanne's mother winces when*
> *Janet asks about their understanding of Suzanne's diagnoses of*
> *alcohol abuse and borderline personality disorder. "We went*
> *over the diagnosis with Dr. Fielding when we met with him and*
> *with Suzanne last year, and we all agreed that the diagnosis*

seemed accurate, but why can't they change that name?" Su-
zanne's father adds, "I hear from a friend who's in the psychi-
atric field that they want to do away with the borderline
diagnosis anyway."

MYTH:
STIGMA ASSOCIATED WITH BPD WOULD BE REMOVED
IF THE NAME WERE CHANGED,
THE DIAGNOSIS MOVED TO A DIFFERENT CATEGORY
OR A NEW WAY OF ASSESSING PERSONALITY DISORDER
SYMPTOMS EMPLOYED

In response to the stigma associated with the diagnosis of BPD, pro-
posals to change the terms used to describe the pathology have been put
forward. Some have suggested renaming BPD using a more easily
grasped term or one that more clearly communicated key elements of
the condition. At different times, moving BPD to Axis I has been proposed, including suggestions that BPD be recast as a form of bipolar
disorder, atypical depression, or post-traumatic stress disorder. Others
suggest that it would be more useful to identify personality disorder
symptoms based on dimensions and not on categories. Still others call
for the elimination of the diagnosis entirely.

In the current debate on moving from a categorical to a dimensional
model for describing personality disorders, proponents of the change
have stressed clinicians' discomfort with current categories. As always,
discomfort about BPD seems to dominate discussion about clinicians'
discontent with the terms now used. Would a dimensional model be of
assistance to clinicians in identifying and treating what we now think of
as borderline pathology? Would it add clarity to clinical thinking, help
with educating patients and families, and assist with increasing public
awareness? Or would a shift to dimensions signify a retreat in facing
head-on the current crisis of this understudied, under-funded disorder?
These important issues have yet to be explored adequately in the debate
about moving from a categorical to a dimensional conceptualization of
personality disorders.

Renaming, reclassifying or moving BPD to a dimensional model
may be of utility in research and, perhaps, even in certain aspects of
clinical care, but it is not likely to remove the stigma associated with
borderline pathology. It may be testimony to the challenges inherent in

caring for such patients that periodically the borderline *diagnosis* is attacked, often from all sides. The current state of understanding about BPD–high morbidity and mortality, limited treatments, modest improvements over time–understandably contributes to frustration and a periodic wish to re-examine essential elements of the disorder and its description.

Stigma, myths and stereotypes are born of patients' considerable and often burdensome experiences of inner turmoil and pain. Clinicians do the best they can with a disorder marked by contradictions, unpredictability and risk. To quote Birnbaum (2004) in his introduction to a "Clinical Controversy" entitled "Borderline, Bipolar, or Both?":

> Abandoning the construct of BPD may help mitigate therapeutic nihilism and reduce stigma. These are worthy considerations. It does not seem to me, however, that the driving force behind our development of a diagnostic schema should be derived from the cultural sphere. HIV carries a tremendous burden of stigma . . . *but it is what it is* (italics added), and we did not soften our scientific language in order to arrive at a politically acceptable conception of the disease. We should, nevertheless, of course, be tireless in our efforts to educate those who are nihilistic or prejudiced, or who misappropriate psychiatric terminology.

REFERENCES

American Psychiatric Association. (1980). *Diagnostic and statistical manual of mental disorders* (3rd ed.). Washington, D.C.

American Psychiatric Association (2000). *Diagnostic and statistical manual of mental disorders* (4th ed., text revision). Washington, D.C.

American Psychiatric Association. (2001). Practice guideline for the treatment of patients with borderline personality disorder. *American Journal of Psychiatry*, 158, 1-152.

Atkinson, J. (1989). To tell or not to tell the diagnosis of schizophrenia. *Journal of Medical Ethics*, 15, 21-4.

Bender, D., Dolan, R,. Skodol, A., et al. (2001). Treatment utilization by patients with personality disorders. *American Journal of Psychiatry*, 158, 295-302.

Birnbaum, R. (2004). Borderline, bipolar or both? *Harvard Review of Psychiatry*, 12, 146-149.

Blum, N., Pfohl, B., St. John, D., et al. (2002). STEPPS: A cognitive-behavioral systems-based group treatment for outpatients with borderline personality disorder–a preliminary report. *Comprehensive Psychiatry*, 43, 4, 301-310.

Bolton, S. & Gunderson, J. (1996). Distinguishing borderline personality disorder from bipolar disorder. *American Journal of Psychiatry*, 153, 1202-7.

Friedel, R,. Hoffman, P., Penney, D., & Woodward, P. (2004). *Borderline personality disorder demystified: An essential guide for understanding and living with BPD.* New York: Avalon Publishing Group.

Goldberg, R. (1984). Disclosure of information to adult cancer patients: Issues and update. *Journal of Clinical Oncology,* 2, 948-55.

Green, R. & Gantt, A. (1987). Telling patients and their families the psychiatric diagnosis: A survey of psychiatrists. *Hospital and Community Psychiatry,* 38, 666-8.

Gunderson, J., Bender, D., Sanislow, S., et al. (2003). Plausibility and possible determinants of sudden "remissions" in borderline patients. *Psychiatry,* 66 (2), 111-119.

Hassan, A. M., & Hassan, A. (1998). Do we always need to tell patients the truth? *Lancet,* 352, 1153.

Kaysen, S. (1994). *Girl, interrupted.* New York: Vintage Books.

Kreisman, J, & Straus, H. (1989). *I hate you, don't leave me: Understanding the borderline personality.* New York: Avon Books.

Lequesne, E. & Hersh, R. (2004). Disclosure of a diagnosis of borderline personality disorder. *Journal of Psychiatric Practice,* 10, 3, 170-176.

Lewis, G., & Appleby, L. (1988). Personality disorder: the patients psychiatrists dislike. *British Journal of Psychiatry,* 153, 44-49.

Linehan, M. (1993). *Dialectical behavioral therapy of borderline personality disorder.* New York: Guilford Press.

Mason, P. & Kreger, R. (1988). *Stop walking on eggshells: Taking your life back when someone you care about has borderline personality disorder.* Oakland, CA: New Harbringer Publications.

McDonald-Scott, P., Machizawa, S., & Satoh, H. (1992). Diagnostic disclosure: A tale in two cultures. *Psychological Medicine,* 22, 147-57.

Nehls, N. (1998). Borderline personality disorder: Gender stereotypes, stigma, and limited system of care. *Issues in Mental Health Nursing,* 19, 97-112.

Oldham, J,. Skodol, A., Kellman, H., et al. (1995). Comorbidity of axis I and axis II disorders. *American Journal of Psychiatry,* 152, 571-78.

Paranscandola, M., Hawkins, J., & Danis, M. (2002). Patient autonomy and the challenge of clinical uncertainty. *Kennedy Institute of Ethics Journal,* 12, 245-64.

Paris, J. (2005). The diagnosis of borderline personality disorder: problematic but better than the alternatives. *Annals of Clinical Psychiatry,* 17, 1, 41-46.

Reiser, D., & Levenson, H. (1984). Abuses of the borderline diagnosis: a clinical problem with teaching opportunities. *American Journal of Psychiatry,* 141, 12, 1528-1532.

Stern, A. (1938). Psychoanalytic investigation of and therapy in the borderline group of neuroses. *Psychoanalytic Quarterly,* 7, 467-89.

Swartz, M., Blazer, D., George, L., et al. (1990). Estimating the prevalence of borderline personality disorder in the community. *Journal of Personality Disorders,* 4, 257-72.

Torgersen, S., Kringlen, E., & Cramer, V. (2001). The prevalence of personality disorders in a community sample. *Archives of General Psychiatry,* 58: 590-96.

Triebwasser, J., & Siever, L. J. (2007). Pharmacotherapy of personality disorders. *Journal of Mental Health,* 16 (1), 5-50.

Westen, D. (1997). Divergences between clinical and research methods for assessing personality disorders: Implications for research and the evolution of axis II. *American Journal of Psychiatry,* 154, 895-903.

Widiger, T. & Weissman, M. (1991). Epidemiology of borderline personality disorder. *Hospital and Community Psychiatry*, 42, 1015-1021.

Zanarini, M., Frankenburg, F., Dubo, E., et al. (1998). Axis I comobidity of borderline personality disorder. *American Journal of Psychiatry*, 155, 12, 1733-1739.

Zanarini, M. & Silk, K. (2001). The difficult-to-treat patient with borderline personality disorder. In M. Dewan, R. Pies (Eds.) The difficult-to-treat psychiatric patient. (pp. 197-208). Washington, D.C.: American Psychiatric Publishing, Inc.

Zanarini, M., Frankenburg, F., Khera, G., & Bleichmar, J. (2001). Treatment histories of borderline inpatients. *Comprehensive Psychiatry*, 42, 2, 144-150.

Zanarini, M., Frankenburg, F., Hennen, J., & Silk, K. (2003). The longitudinal course of borderline psychopathology: 6-year prospective follow-up of the phenomenology of borderline personality disorder. *American Journal of Psychiatry*, 160, 274-83.

Zanarini, M. & Frankenburg, F. (2004). A randomized trial of psychoeducation for patients with BPD. No. 100E, Report Sessions of American Psychiatric Association Meeting.

Zimmerman, M. & Mattia, J. (1990). Axis I diagnostic comorbidity and borderline personality disorder. *Comprehensive Psychiatry*, 40, 245-52.

Zimmerman, M, & Mattia J. (1999). Differences between clinical and research practices in diagnosing borderline personality disorder. *American Journal of Psychiatry*, 156, 1570-1574.

Zimmerman M, Rothschild L, Chelminski I. (2005). The prevalence of DSM-IV personality disorders in psychiatric outpatients. *Am J Psychiatry*, 162, 10, 1911-1918.

doi:10.1300/J200v06n01_03

Biological Underpinnings of Borderline Personality Disorder

Marianne Goodman
Joseph Triebwasser
Antonia New

SUMMARY. Biological understanding of a personality disorder is best achieved by examining the disorder's component dimensions, which for borderline personality disorder include impulsive aggression and affective instability. Current biological research into BPD aims to identify the neurotransmitters and brain regions implicated in each of these key domains. Because of advancing technologies and analytic strategies, structural and functional neuroimaging are at the forefront of such efforts. Structural neuroimaging, primarily in the form of magnetic resonance imaging (MRI) scans, gives information about the anatomy of the brain, while functional neuroimaging, primarily functional MRI (fMRI) and positron emission tomography (PET) scans, gives information about brain activity and neurotransmitter systems at the molecular level. BPD neuroimaging studies to date have implied the involvement of several neurotransmitter systems, principally serotonin, along with dysfunction of select brain regions, including the prefrontal cortex and amygdala, suggesting a "dual-brain pathology": "hyperarousal-dyscontrol syndrome." However, the exact mechanisms of all these putative etiologies remain unknown. doi:10.1300/J200v06n01_04 *[Article copies available for a fee from The Haworth Document Delivery Service: 1-800-HAWORTH. E-mail*

[Haworth co-indexing entry note]: "Biological Underpinnings of Borderline Personality Disorder." Goodman, Marianne, Joseph Triebwasser, and Antonia New. Co-published simultaneously in *Social Work in Mental Health* (The Haworth Press) Vol. 6, No. 1/2, 2008, pp. 33-47; and: *Borderline Personality Disorder: Meeting the Challenges to Successful Treatment* (ed: Perry D. Hoffman, and Penny Steiner-Grossman) The Haworth Press, 2008, pp. 33-47. Single or multiple copies of this article are available for a fee from The Haworth Document Delivery Service [1-800-HAWORTH, 9:00 a.m. - 5:00 p.m. (EST). E-mail address: docdelivery@haworthpress.com].

Available online at http://swmh.haworthpress.com

doi:10.1300/J200v06n01_04

KEYWORDS. Personality disorder, borderline personality disorder, impulsive aggression, affective instability

THE DIMENSIONAL APPROACH
TO PERSONALITY DISORDERS

In a landmark paper, Siever and Davis (1991) proposed a dimensional approach to the study of personality disorders. The core vulnerabilities that they argued contribute to characterological dysfunction included affective instability/sensitivity, impulsivity, aggression and cognitive/perceptual disturbances. With some modifications, and allowing for differences of opinions among various researchers, Siever and Davis's formulation of the dimensions of personality has continued to inform our understanding of both temperament and the Axis II diagnoses that represent the most severe forms of personality pathology.

Recent research that has brought into question the stability and boundaries of the borderline diagnosis has lent support to the application of this dimensional approach to borderline personality disorder. Longitudinal studies of BPD in a non-clinical sample show only moderate stability (.28-.62) over a two-year period (Trull et al.,1998). Cross-sectional studies of personality disordered populations show a high degree of co-morbidity among these disorders, particularly between BPD and paranoid (14.5%), schizotypal (14.3%), histrionic (13.5%) narcissistic (16.0%) and passive aggressive (13.4%) personality disorders. This co-morbidity among and within clusters also undercuts the distinctness of the three personality disorder clusters posited by DSM-IV (Watson et al., 1998).

Factor analyses of the phenomenology of BPD further suggest that a dimensional approach may be more appropriate than the categorical model that underlies the DSM, with impulsive aggression, affective instability, and identity disturbance the core dimensions of the disorder (Blais et al., 1997). A factor analysis of DSM-III-R criteria for BPD has suggested that impulsivity and affective instability, along with a relatedness factor, comprise the three homogenous factors underlying the condition (Sanislow et al., 2000); a subsequent, larger multi-center longitudinal study (Sanislow et al., 2002) has provided further evidence for this formulation.

Neuroendocrine findings, too, have tended to lend credence to the validity of the dimensional rather than categorical model of BPD, as have heritability data: monozygotic-dizygotic twin studies suggest that while personality disorder diagnoses themselves are not heritable, the traits of impulsive aggression or assertive aggressiveness are (Alnaes et al., 1989; Coccaro et al., 1993; Torgersen et al., 1994).

Our current understanding of the neuroanatomic circuitry and neuromodulators involved in the key dimensions of BPD is described in Figure 1. The dimensions of impulsivity, aggression and affective instability have been studied most extensively and will therefore be the focus of the remainder of this review.

IMPULSIVE AGGRESSION IN BPD

Phenomenology

Individuals with BPD often require psychiatric attention because of their difficulty with behavioral control and manifest a spectrum of impulsive aggressive acts, such as violence and assault, spousal abuse, property damage, self-mutilation and suicide attempts (Hamberger et al., 1986; Mikolajczak et al., 1978), resulting in difficulty in maintaining jobs (Skodol et al., 2005) and disrupted family relationships. As pharmacological and other treatments for mood disorders and psychotic disorders have improved, an increasing proportion of psychiatric hospitalizations are precipitated by an actual or threatened act of aggression directed towards self or others in patients with a primary personality diagnosis (Hansson et al., 1989; Breslow et al., 1993; Molinari et al., 1994).

Neuroendocrine Studies

Abnormalities in central serotonergic activity have consistently been found to be associated with measures of impulsive aggression in patients with personality disorders, including BPD (Coccaro et al., 1989; O'Keane et al., 1992; Siever & Trestman, 1993). Studies of cerebrospinal fluid have shown that a decrease in 5-hydroxyindolacetic acid, a metabolite of serotonin (5-HT), is associated with impulsive aggression in patients with BPD, as well as in depressed patients, volunteers, and violent alcoholic offenders (Linnoila et al., 1989; Linnoila et al., 1994; Virkkunen et al., 1994). Peripheral measures of 5-HT activity, includ-

FIGURE 1

Brain Systems in Borderline Personality Disorder

Dimension	Neuroanatomic Circuitry	Neuromodulator
Impulsivity/Aggression	Orbital frontal cortex / Anterior cingulate cortex / Amygdala	Serotonin
Affective Instability	Amygdala / Enterorhinal Cortex	Acethycholine, norepinephrine
Cognitive Disorganization	Prefrontal cortex / Striatum	Dopamine

ing platelet 5-HT levels and paroxetine binding, measures believed to reflect central nervous system serotonin activity, are similarly decreased in impulsive aggression (Verkes et al., 1998; Mann et al., 1992).

Neuroendocrine challenge studies have played a key role in linking 5-HT hypofunction to the pathophysiology of impulsive aggression. Such studies measure receptor-mediated neurohormonal responses to an agent that normally triggers the secretion of 5-HT, thereby providing data on system responsivity. The earliest challenge studies measured plasma levels of prolactin (a hormone released from the anterior pituitary in response to 5-HT stimulation), after administration of a 5-HT agonist, usually d-fenfluramine, and found the response to be blunted in personality disordered patients with impulsive aggression(Coccaro et al., 1996; Siever et al., 1993; New et al., 2004a; Soloff et al., 2003a), and sociopathy (O'Keane et al., 1992). More recent challenge studies using meta-chlorophenyl-piperazine (m-CPP) have shown similar findings (Paris et al., 2004; New et al., 2002). Cumulatively, these results have suggested that the neuroendocrine response is related to dimensional measures of impulsive aggression rather than to the BPD diagnosis *per se.*

Neuroimaging Studies and Circuitry

Although the 5-HT system has been implicated in the etiology of impulsive aggression, the exact nature of the dysfunction and the identities of the brain systems involved remain elusive. Likely brain regions include the orbital frontal cortex (OFC), which inhibits limbic and other subcortical regions and is part of the prefrontal cortex (PFC), the area in the brain that controls "higher" functions involving cognition, planning and the processing of memories and feelings. Other implicated brain regions are the anterior cingulate cortex (ACC), which assesses affective incoming stimuli critical to the initiation of aggression, and the adjacent ventral medial cortex (VMC). New et al. (2002) assessed 5-HT activity in several brain regions by comparing changes in regional glucose metabolism after m-CPP versus placebo in 13 impulsive aggressive patients and 13 age- and gender-matched controls. Impulsive aggressive patients, compared to normals, demonstrated decreased activation of inhibitory regions in the left anteromedial OFC. Moreover, patients but not controls showed deactivation of the ACC and instead showed activation of the posterior cingulate gyrus. These findings demonstrate differing patterns of brain activation in impulsive aggressive personality disordered subjects compared to controls.

Supporting this conclusion are other PET studies in impulsive aggressive and/or BPD subjects that have demonstrated blunted responses in the OFC, adjacent VMC, cingulate cortex (Siever et al., 1999; Schmahl et al., 2003; Soloff et al., 2003b) and dorsolateral prefrontal cortex (DLPFC) (Schmahl et al., 2003), and hypometabolism in the hippocampus and cuneus regions (Juengling et al., 2003). These important findings suggest that specific brain structures, including the ACC and areas of the frontal cortex, all of which are involved in 5-HT function, are implicated in impulsive aggression.

Turning to the relatively new field of molecular neurotransmitter studies, our understanding at the microscopic level of the serotonergic disturbances associated with impulsive aggression has yet to be worked out fully. Nevertheless, the scientific community knows much more now than it did even a few years ago, largely because of a relatively recent advance in PET scanning–the availability of radioactive "ligands" that bind to specific proteins that line nerve cell surfaces within the 5-HT system.

The proteins of greatest interest are the various "receptors," to which the 5-HT molecule binds and which then initiate its physiological effects and the "transporters," which scoop up and inactivate the neurotransmitter, thereby terminating its ability to bind to a receptor. Our newfound ability, through ligand PET scans, to take "snapshots" of 5-HT receptors and transporters in live humans has permitted unprecedented exploration of the pathophysiology of impulse dyscontrol. 5-HT transporters in the ACC have been found to be diminished in impulsive aggressive subjects as compared to normal controls (Frankle et al., 2005). An important subtype of 5-HT receptors, on the other hand, appears to be *increased* in non-clinical subjects with low harm avoidance, a plausible proxy for impulsivity (Moresco et al., 2002). Pilot data from our research group has found that that current impulsive aggressive behavior, directed at either self or others, is associated with increased numbers of this same receptor subtype (Siever et al., unpublished data).

Further investigations focusing on the different 5-HT receptor subtypes as well as on other neurotransmitters, including dopamine and gamma-aminobutyric acid (GABA), will be future paths of exploration. Although various agents, including catecholamines, opiates, androgens and adrenocorticotropins have been postulated to play a neuroregulatory role in impulsive aggressive behavior, it is unclear how these agents interact with serotonergic activation.

AFFECTIVE INSTABILITY
AND EMOTIONAL DYSREGULATION IN BPD

Phenomenology

Affective instability has been defined as "a predisposition to marked, rapidly reversible shifts in affective states that are extremely sensitive to meaningful environmental events" (Siever & Davis, 1991). Prominent BPD researchers have built on the affective instability model and defined the disorder as stemming from "emotional dysregulation" (Linhean et al., 1993). Emotional dysregulation captures many of the BPD diagnostic criteria, including affective lability, intense anger, chronic emptiness, and behaviors like suicide and self-mutilation that may reflect misguided efforts to modulate strong and aversive emotional states (McMain et al., 2001). Applying neurobiological correlates to Linehan's biosocial theory (Linehan, 1993), the two components of emotional dysregulation are: (1) heightened emotional responsivity, characterized by high sensitivity to emotional stimuli, and heightened emotional intensity, both of which are suggestive of amygdala hyperactivity; and (2) difficulties in effortful modulation of negative affect, implying hypoactivity of PFC regions that regulate limbic structures.

Heightened emotional responsivity is postulated to be biologically mediated, arising from genetic vulnerabilities and intrauterine and/or early childhood events, which then interact with an "invalidating" present-day environment to produce current symptomatology (Linehan et al., 1993). Support for this theory includes neuroimaging data demonstrating amygdala hyperexcitability in impulsive aggressive subjects (Donegan et al., 2003) and the multiple studies indicating high rates of childhood trauma and neglect in this population (Fossati et al., 1999; Goodman et al., 2004).

However, systematic study of emotional dysregulation in BPD has been limited, in part by the absence of a standardized measurement tool, the lack of a consensus definition of what constitutes emotional regulation and the difficulties inherent in separating emotion from its regulatory processes. Current conceptualizations of emotion regulation extend beyond the simple control of negative emotion to include the importance of: (1) awareness, identification, acceptance and modulation of emotions; (2) maintenance of goals in spite of emotionality and impulsivity; and (3) flexible choice of regulation strategies (Gratz & Roeme, 2004). Oschner and Gross (2005) similarly emphasize the differences between cognitive regulation (reappraisal, reinterpretation) and behavioral regulation (suppression).

Empirical research on emotional dysregulation and processing in BPD to date has included subjective reports of heightened affective responses to various emotional stimuli such as films, audiotapes, and pictures from the International Affective Picture System (IAPS) in most (Renneberg et al., 2005; Herpertz et al., 2000), but not all (Herpertz et al., 2001b) studies. More recently, studies using objective psychophysiological parameters including startle eye blink modulation (SEM), skin conductance and heart rate measures of emotional arousal have suggested physiological underarousal despite heightened subjective responses (Herpertz et al., 2001b; 2005). However, in our SEM study (Hazlett et al., 2007), use of BPD-specific emotional probes yielded the opposite response. BPD subjects, as compared to normal controls, demonstrated a *heightened* startle response to emotionally charged words, though they had diminished subjective ratings. One potential explanation for the discrepancy between our findings and those of other groups is that individuals with BPD may have heightened emotional reactivity and intensity to only particular types of emotional triggers (e.g., interpersonal domains). In the near future, the relationship between SEM and subjective measures of affective processing and emotional regulation will be studied to clarify the disconnect between subjective report and objective physiological response seen in our results.

Neuroendocrine Studies

Though it has been less intensively studied than the serotonergic system, the cholinergic system is also believed to play an important role in regulating affect. Depressive symptoms can be elicited with the administration of cholinomemetics (Janowsky et al., 1974). Procaine, a cholinergic agonist, has been shown to induce a high degree of dysphoria in BPD patients compared to those with affective disorder and normal controls (Kellner et al., 1987), and this response correlated with metabolic activation of the left amygdala in a PET study in normal controls (Kellner et al., 1996). The cholinomimetic, physostigmine, has been shown to produce significantly more depressive symptoms in BPD patients than placebo, and this effect was greater and more rapid that that seen in healthy controls (Steinberg et al., 1997).

The noradrenergic system has also been implicated in the affective instability of BPD (Gurvits et al., 2000). In healthy controls, a dysphoric response to dextroamphetamine, a catecholaminergic agent, correlated with measures of affective instability (Steinberg et al., 1997). Additionally, in a neuroendocrine challenge using clonidine, an alpha-2 agonist, the amount of growth hormone released correlated with a measure of irritability (a symptom related to affective instability), in BPD patients but not depressives (Coccaro et al., 1991). These data suggest the possibility of altered noradrenergic and cholinergic activity in BPD, though a more recent investigation studying BPD subjects only (Paris et al., 2004) did not support this premise. The neurobiology of affective instability remains unclear at present.

Neuroimaging Studies and Circuitry

Prefrontal Cortex: Davidson and colleagues (2000) propose a model for emotional modulation involving a circuit that includes the ACC, OFC, VMC and DLPFC. The affective component of the ACC has connections with the amygdala, OFC and other regions and is believed to be involved in the cognitive processing and evaluation of emotional stimuli, responses to conflict and regulation of emotional responses (Devinsky et al., 1995). Additionally, the OFC is posited to inhibit impulsive aggression by regulating the amygdala, while the DLPFC integrates emotions with cognition, and the VMC is involved in the general processing of emotions.

Use of structural and functional neuroimaging has revealed abnormalities in this same network of brain regions in BPD. Fluorodeoxyglucose (FDG) PET studies in BPD provide evidence for altered baseline metabolism in PFC regions (New et al., 2002; De La Fuente et al., 1997; Soloff et al., 2003a) and the ACC (New et al., 2002). Similarly, reductions in frontal and OFC volumes have been reported (van Elst et al., 2003; Hazlett et al., 2005). Furthermore, a magnetic resonance spectroscopy (MRS) study (van Elst et al., 2001) reported a 19% reduction of N-acetylaspartate (NAA) concentrations in the DLPFC in BPD compared with controls. There is general agreement that NAA depletion reflects neuronal dysfunction. Because the acquisition of high-quality MRS spectra for a single anatomical area is time-demanding, the authors noted that they were unable to assess possible reductions of NAA in the OFC and ACC.

Amygdala: While there is substantial literature in both animals and humans that implicates the amygdala in emotional processes, including the perception and production of emotion (reviewed by Davidson & Irwin, 1999), there is limited but growing data on the role of the amygdala in the emotional dysregulation of BPD. There have been three fMRI studies involving mood induction in BPD subjects. Herpertz and colleagues (2001a), using IAPS negative and neutral slides, demonstrated bilaterally elevated blood-oxygen-level-dependent (BOLD) response in the amygdala, fusiform gyrus (which processes complex visual features), the OFC and ACC in BPD (n = 6) but not control subjects. In a similar design, however, our research group found different patterns of activation, with BPD subjects (n = 11) showing activation in the ventrolateral PFC, while controls activated the DLPFC (Koenigsberg et al., 2004), suggesting that BPD subjects may require activation of alternative frontal regions to modulate negative emotion. A third study noted increases in left amygdala activation in BPD compared to controls during observation of slides of facial expressions (Donegan et al., 2003). Moreover, some of the BPD subjects reported having difficulty disambiguating, and even feeling threatened by, neutral faces, perhaps pointing to a mechanism for the effect of emotional dysregulation on interpersonal relationships, which are often disturbed in BPD (Donegan et al., 2003). Additionally, most (Driessen et al., 2000; van Elst et al., 2003), but not all (Rusch et al., 2003), structural MRI studies report significantly smaller amygdala volumes in BPD subjects compared to controls.

Structural abnormalities in either the PFC or amygdala are relatively nonspecific, but disturbance in both these regions simultaneously is much less common and might be a signature of BPD pathology. In one study, this frontolimbic pattern of volume loss in BPD patients included not only a decrease in size of the left OFC, the right ACC, the hippocampus and the amygdala, but also a correlation between the volumes of structures in the amygdala and the left OFC (van Elst et al., 2003). These and other findings have led to the categorization of BPD as a "dual-brain pathology" (Bohus et al., 2004) or "hyperarousal-dyscontrol syndrome" (Lieb et al., 2004), reflecting the importance of both a weakening of PFC inhibitory control and amygdala hyperreactivity in the neurobiology of the disorder. Treatment efforts to target this dysfunction have included a PET study by our research group (New et al., 2004), which found that 12 weeks of the selective serotonin reuptake inhibitor, fluoxetine, increased activation in the PFC.

FUTURE DIRECTIONS

Neurobiological research into this complex and multifaceted disorder has benefited from examining the simpler dimensions of impulsive aggression and affective instability separately. While substantial progress has been made in the arena of impulsive aggression and the hypothesized causative deficit in serotonergic activity, such a purported mechanism has not yet been identified for affective instability. Even in the case of impulsive aggression, the specific component(s) of the serotonin system implicated in the disorder has yet to be identified with any certainty.

The PFC, and especially the OFC, are underactive in personality-disordered patients with impulsive aggression, and these same regions exert an inhibitory control over aggressive behavior in normal people. For BPD individuals with impulsive aggression, these regions may not be recruited appropriately in response to serotonergic activation, with the result that the "brake" on aggressive responding does not function adequately.

The application of methodologies such as SEM and fMRI have only recently begun to aid in our understanding of the mechanisms of emotional dysregulation and the abnormal processing of emotion in BPD. Provisional findings have highlighted the role of the amygdala, whose apparent overactivity in BPD may contribute to the unstable affect central to the disorder.

In view of the evidence for paired dysfunction in both the regulatory regions of the PFC and at the level of emotional processing in the amygdala, "dual-brain pathology" (Bohus et al., 2004) or "hyperarousal-dyscontrol syndrome" (Leib et al., 2004) may be the neurobiological signature of BPD. Continued clarification of this underlying neurobiology will be essential for the development of more specific and effective pharmacological and psychological treatments for this widespread, sometimes crippling, disorder.

REFERENCES

Alnaes, R. & Torgersen, S. (1989). Clinical differentiation between major depression only, major depression with panic disorder and panic disorder only. Childhood, personality and personality disorder. *Acta Psychiatrica Scandinavica*, 79(4), 370-377.

Blais, M. A., Hilsenroth, M. J. et al. (1997). Content validity of the DSM-IV borderline and narcissistic personality disorder criteria sets. *Comprehensive Psychiatry*, 38 (1), 31-7.

Bohus, M., Haaf, B. et al. (2004). Effectiveness of inpatient dialectical behavioral therapy for borderline personality disorder: a controlled trial. *Behaviour Research and Therapy*, 42 (5), 487-499.

Breslow, R., Klinger, B. et al. (1993). Crisis hospitalization on a psychiatric emergency service. *General Hospital Psychiatry*, 15(5), 307-315.

Coccaro, E., Siever, L. et al. (1989). Serotonergic studies in patients with affective and personality disorders. *Archives of General Psychiatry*, 44, 573-588.

Coccaro, E. F., Bergeman, C. S. et al. (1993). Heritability of irritable impulsiveness: A study of twins reared together and apart. *Psychiatry Research*, 48 (3), 229-42.

Coccaro, E. F., Berman, M. E. et al. (1996). Relationship of prolactin response to d-Fenfluramine to behavioral and questionnaire assessments of aggression in personality disordered men. *Biological Psychiatry*, 40(3), 157-164.

Coccaro, E. F., Lawrence, T. et al. (1991). Growth hormone responses to intravenous clonidine challenge correlates with behavioral irritability in psychiatric patients and in healthy volunteers. *Psychiatry Research*, 39, 129-139.

Davidson, R. & Irwin, W. (1999). The functional neuroanatomy of emotion and affective style. *Trends in Cognitive Sciences*, 3(1), 11-21.

Davidson, R. J., Putnam, K.M. et al. (2000). Dysfunction in the neural circuitry of emotion regulation–a possible prelude to violence. *Science*, 289, 591-594.

De La Fuente, J. M., Goldman, S. et al. (1997). Brain glucose metabolism in borderline personality disorder. *Journal of Psychiatric Research*, 31 (5), 531-541.

Devinsky, O., Morrell, M. J. et al. (1995). Contributions of anterior cingulate cortex to behaviour. *Brain*, 118 (Pt 1), 279-306.

Donegan, N. H., Sanislow, C. A. et al. (2003). Amygdala hyperreactivity in borderline personality disorder: Implications for emotional dysregulation. *Biological Psychiatry*, 54(11), 1284-93.

Driessen, M., Herrmann, J. et al. (2000). Magnetic resonance imaging volumes of the hippocampus and the amgydala in women with borderline personality disorder and early traumatization. *Archives of General Psychiatry*, 57 (12), 1115-1122.

Fossati, A., Madeddu, F. et al. (1999). Borderline personality disorder and childhood sexual abuse: A meta-analytic study. *Journal of Personality Disorders*, 13 (3), 268-280.

Frankle, W. G., Lombardo, I. et al. (2005). Brain serotonin transporter distribution in subjects with impulsive aggressivity: A positron emission study with [11C]McN 5652. *American Journal of Pyschiatry*, 162 (5), 915-23.

Goodman, M. A., New et al. (2004). Trauma, genes, and the neurobiology of personality disorders. *Annals of the New York Academy of Sciences*, 1032, 104-16.

Gratz, K. & Roemer L. (2004). Multidimensional assessment of emotion regulation and dysregulation: Development, factor structure, and initial validation of the difficulties in emotion regulation scale. *Journal of Psychopathology and Behavioral Assessment*, 26(1), 41-54.

Gurvitz, I. G., & Koenigsberg, H. W. et al. (2000). Neurotransmitter dysfunction in patients with borderline personality disorder. *Psychiatric Clinics of North America*, 23 (1), 27-40.

Hamberger, L. K. & Hastings, J. E. (1986). Personality correlates of men who abuse their partners: A cross-validation study. *Journal of Family Violence*, 1 (4), 323-341.

Hansson, L. (1989). Utilization of psychiatric inpatient care: A study of changes related to the introduction of a sectorized care organization. *Acta Psychiatrica Scandinavica*, 79 (6), 571-578.

Hazlett E. A., Newmark, R., Haznedar, M. M., Lo, J. N., Speiser, L. J., Mitropoulou, V., Minzenberg, M., Siever, L. J., & Nussbaum, M. S. (2005). Reduced anterior and posterior cingulate gray matter in borderline personality disorder. *Biological Psychiatry*, 58, 614-623.

Hazlett E. A., Goodman, M., Roy, M., Carrizal, M., Wynn, J.K., Williams, W. C., Romero M., Minzenberg, M., Siever, L. J., & New, A.S. (2007). A dissociation between self-report and affective startle measures of emotion in borderline personality disorder. *Biological Psychiatry*, Jan 26, Epub ahead of print.

Herpertz, S., Dietrich, T. et al. (2001). Evidence of abnormal amygdala functioning in borderline personality disorder: a functional MRI study. *Biological Psychiatry*, 50 (4), 292-298.

Herpertz, S. C. & Koetting, K. (2005). Startle response in inpatients with borderline personality disorder vs. healthy controls. *Journal of Neural Transmission*, 112 (8), 1097-106.

Herpertz, S. C., & Schwenger, U. B. et al. (2000). Emotional responses in patients with borderline as compared with avoidant personality disorder. *Journal of Personal Disorder*, 14 (4), 339-51.

Herpertz, S. C., & Werth, U. et al. (2001). Emotion in criminal offenders with psychopathy and borderline personality disorder. *Archives of General Psychiatry*, 58 (8), 737-45.

Janowsky, D. S., & el-Yousef, M. K. et al. (1974). Acetylcholine and depression. *Psychosomatic Medicine*, 36 (3), 248-57.

Juengling, F. D., & Schmahl, C. et al. (2003). Positron emission tomography in female patients with borderline personality disorder. *Journal of Psychiatric Research*, 37 (2), 109-15.

Kellner, C. H., & Post, R. M. et al. (1987). Intravenous procaine as a probe of limbic system activity in psychiatric patients and normal controls. *Biological Psychiatry,* 22 (9), 1107-1126.

Ketter, T. A., & Andreason, P. J. et al. (1996). Anterior paralimbic mediation of procaine-induced emotional and psychosensory experiences. *Archives of General Psychiatry,* 53 (1), 59-69.

Koenigsberg, H. W., Guo, X., New, A., Goodman, M., & Prohovnik, I. (2004). An fMRI study of emotion processing in borderline personality disorder patients. *Biological Psychiatry,* 55, 89S.

Lieb, K., & Zanarini, M. C. et al. (2004). Borderline personality disorder. *Lancet,* 364, (9432), 453-61.

Linehan, M. (1993). *Cognitive behavioral treatment of borderline personality disorder.* New York: Guilford.

Linnoila, M., & DeJong, J. et al. (1989). Family history of alcoholism in violent offenders and impulsive fire setters. *Archives of General Psychiatry,* 46, 613-616.

Linnoila, M., & Virkkunen, M. et al. (1994). Serotonin, behavior and alcohol. In B. Jansson, H. Jornvall, U. Rydberg, L. Terenius, & L. Vallee (Eds.), *Toward a molecular basis of alcohol use and abuse.* Basel, Switzerland: Birkhauser Verlag.

Mann, J. J., McBride, & P. A. et al. (1992). Platelet and whole blood serotonin content in depressed inpatients: Correlations with acute and lifetime psychopathology. *Biological Psychiatry,* 32, 243-257.

McMain, S., & Korman, L. M. et al. (2001). Dialectical behavior therapy and the treatment of emotion dysregulation. *Journal of Clinical Psychology,* 57 (2), 183-96.

Mikolajczak J. & Hagen, D. Q. (1978). Aggression in psychiatric patients in a VA hospital. *Military Medicine,* 143 (6), 402-404.

Molinari, V., & Ames, A. et al. (1994). Prevalence of personality disorders in two geropsychiatric inpatient units. *Journal of Geriatric Psychiatry and Neurology,* 7 (4), 295-300.

Moresco, F.M., Dieci, M., Vita, A, Messa, C., Gobbo, C., Galli, L, Rizzo, G., Panzacchi, A., De Peri, L., Invernizzi, G., & Fazio, F. (2002). In vivo serotonin 5HT(2A) receptor binding and personality traits in healthy subjects: a positron emission tomography study. *Neuroimage.* 17 (3), 1470-8.

New, A., & Hazlett, E. et al. (2002). Blunted prefrontal cortical 18fluorodeoxyglucose positron emission tomography response to meta-chloropiperazine in impulsive aggression. *Archives of General Psychiatry,* 59 (7), 621-629.

New, A., & Trestman, R. et al. (2004). Low prolactin response to fenfluramine in impulsive aggression. *Journal of Psychiatric Research,* 38 (3), 223-30.

New, A. S., & M. S. Buchsbaum et al. (2004). Fluoxetine increases relative metabolic rate in prefrontal cortex in impulsive aggression. *Psychopharmacology,* 176 (3-4), 451-8.

O'Keane, V., & Maloney, E. et al. (1992). Blunted prolactin response to d-fenfluramine in sociopathy: Evidence for subsensitivity of central serotonergic function. *British Journal of Psychiatry,* 160, 643-646.

Ochsner, K. N. & Gross, J. J. (2005). The cognitive control of emotion. *Trends in Cognitive Science,* 9(5): 242-9.

Paris, J., & Zweig-Frank, H. et al. (2004). Neurobiological correlates of diagnosis and underlying traits in patients with borderline personality disorder compared with normal controls. *Psychiatry Research,* 121 (3), 239-52.

Renneberg, B., & Heyn, K. et al. (2005). Facial expression of emotions in borderline personality disorder and depression. *Journal of Behavior Therapy and Experimental Psychiatry*, 36 (3), 183-96.

Rusch, N., & van Elst, L. T. et al. (2003). A voxel-based morphometric MRI study in female patients with borderline personality disorder. *Neuroimage*, 20 (1), 385-92.

Sanislow, C. A., & Grilo, C. M. et al. (2000). Factor analysis of the DSM-III-R borderline personality disorder criteria in psychiatric inpatients. *American Journal of Psychiatry*, 157 (10), 1629-33.

Sanislow, C. A., & Grilo, C. M. et al. (2002). Confirmatory factor analysis of DSM-IVcriteria for borderline personality disorder: findings from the collaborative longitudinal personality disorders study. *American Journal of Psychiatry*, 159 (2), 284-90.

Schmahl, C. G., & Elzinga, B. M. et al. (2003). Neural correlates of memories of abandonment in women with and without borderline personality disorder. *Biological Psychiatry*, 54 (2), 142-51.

Siever, L. J. & Trestman, R. L. (1993). The serotonin system and aggressive personality disorder. *International Clinical Psychopharmacology*, 8 (Suppl 2), 33-39.

Siever, L. J., & Buchsbaum, M. et al. (1999). d,l- fenfluramine response in impulsive personality disorder assessed with 18F-deoxyglucose positron emission tomography. *Neuropsychopharmacology*, 20 (5), 413-423.

Siever, L. J. & Davis, K. (1991). A psychobiological perspective on the personality disorders. *American Journal of Psychiatry*, 148, 1647-58.

Siever, L. J. & Davis, K. L. (1991). A psychobiologic perspective on the personality disorders. *American Journal of Psychiatry*, 148, 1647-1658.

Skodol, A. E., & Oldham, J. M. et al. (2005). Dimensional representations of DSM-IV personality disorders: relationships to functional impairment. *American Journal of Psychiatry*, 162 (10), 1919-25.

Soloff, P. H., & Kelly, T. M. et al. (2003). Impulsivity, gender, and response to fenfluramine challenge in borderline personality disorder. *Psychiatry Research*, 119 (1-2), 11-24.

Soloff, P. H., & Meltzer, C. C. et al. (2003). Impulsivity and prefrontal hypometabolism in borderline personality disorder. *Psychiatry Research*, 123 (3), 153-63.

Steinberg, B. J., & Trestman, R. et al. (1997). Depressive response to physostigmine challenge in borderline personality disorder patients. *Neuropsychopharmacology*, 17 (4), 264-73.

Torgersen, S. (1994). Genetics in borderline conditions. *Acta Psychiatrica Scandinavica,* Suppl 379, 19-25.

Trull, T. J., & Useda, J. D. et al. (1998). Two-year stability of borderline personality measures. *Journal of Personal Disorders*, 12 (3), 187-97.

van Elst, T. L., & Hesslinger, B. et al. (2003). Frontolimbic brain abnormalities in patients with borderline personality disorder: a volumetric magnetic resonance imaging study. *Biological Psychiatry*, 54 (2), 163-71.

van Elst, L. T., & Thiel, T. et al. (2001). Subtle prefrontal neuropathology in a pilot magnetic resonance spectroscopy study in patients with borderline personality disorder. *The Journal of Neuropsychiatry and Clinical Neurosciences*, 13 (4), 511-4.

Verkes, R. J., & Van der Mast, R. C. et al. (1998). Platelet serotonin, monoamine oxidase activity, and [3H]paroxetine binding related to impulsive suicide attempts and borderline personality disorder. *Biological Psychiatry*, 43, (10), 740-6.

Virkkunen, M., & R. Rawlings et al. (1994). CSF biochemistries, glucose metabolism, and diurnal activity rhythms in alcoholic violent offenders, fire setters, and healthy volunteers. *Archives of General Psychiatry*, 51 (1), 20-27.

Watson, D. C. & Sinha, B. K. (1998). Comorbidity of DSM-IV personality disorders in a nonclinical sample. *Journal of Clinical Psychology*, 54 (6), 773-80.

doi:10.1300/J200v06n01_04

The Case of Joan

Ellen J. Safier
Perry Hoffman

Joan originally presented for treatment with her parents. Although she was 29 at the time of her referral, she was still dependent on her parents for financial support. She is the youngest of three children with an older sister and an older brother. Joan came to the first meeting accompanied by her parents.

A psychiatrist who had been treating Joan and managing her medications made the referral. Joan had left home after college. Her course was marked by unstable relationships, significant drug use, several brief hospitalizations, incidents of self-injury, a charge of assault related to an arrest while using drugs, and episodic employment. Joan returned home at the urging of her family, initially to live with her parents. Over time, the situation became so difficult that they helped her find an apartment with hopes that she would become more financially independent and take over payments.

Joan had been a very beloved child. She was bright and charming and extremely social. She loved performing and had been a good student according to her parents though she reported that school had always been difficult. Her grades dropped precipitously in high school and she began to use drugs more heavily as a way to medicate her increased depression and her sense of failure. During her years that Joan lived in another city, she maintained some ongoing contact with her family but much of the contact centered on the times of crisis when she was out of control and desperately in need of financial help or legal assistance.

[Haworth co-indexing entry note]: "The Case of Joan." Safier, Ellen J., and Perry Hoffman. Co-published simultaneously in *Social Work in Mental Health* (The Haworth Press) Vol. 6, No. 1/2, 2008, pp. 49-51; and: *Borderline Personality Disorder: Meeting the Challenges to Successful Treatment* (ed: Perry D. Hoffman, and Penny Steiner-Grossman) The Haworth Press, 2008, pp. 49-51. Single or multiple copies of this article are available for a fee from The Haworth Document Delivery Service [1-800-HAWORTH, 9:00 a.m. - 5:00 p.m. (EST). E-mail address: docdelivery@haworthpress.com].

Her return to the family home represented a real shift for the entire system. There was recognition on all sides that Joan's situation was becoming increasingly precarious and willingness on Joan's part to accept help and to more realistically appraise her current status with less of the kind of grandiose posturing that had characterized her description of herself. At the same time, the move exacerbated unresolved issues between her parents who understandably experienced her behavior in very different ways and had quite divergent views on providing support. It also opened up longstanding conflicts between Joan and her father, whom she had always perceived as quite critical and judgmental and as favoring her siblings over herself. Joan had a fairly well developed view of the difficulties that prevented her father from being more connected to her. She had less perspective on her own contribution to the friction and a kind of desperate hope that if her father could behave differently and accept her, that she would be able to live a more productive life and be less reactive and sensitive.

At the time of the referral, Joan had just started a new position as a sales clerk. She was humiliated at the thought of running into friends who were more successful and she also continued to medicate her anxiety and depression by nightly use of alcohol and marijuana. She made some attempt to curtail her alcohol use but was not at all committed to giving up marijuana and continued to spend whatever small amounts of money she made on drugs. She had several friends in her apartment but her relationships with them were stormy at best and she would frequently feel hurt or rejected by some small slight. The one area of progress was that she was taking significantly better care of herself. Her clothes were clean, she had begun going to a local gym on a regular basis to exercise and she began to take some small pleasure in preparing food for herself.

Joan's sister and brother were both successful in their respective fields. Her sister had trained as a photographer and was now traveling internationally for a well-known magazine. Her brother was married and had two young children. Joan would attend family dinners with her parents and siblings but these would often turn into shouting matches with Joan blaming her entire family for thinking she was a failure and for being unwilling to support her now or, in her mind, ever. The vehemence of her attacks, which often reflected her worst feelings about herself, would often precipitate retaliation from her father who would feel even more unappreciated and defeated.

Joan's psychiatrist's diagnoses included borderline personality disorder and polysubstance abuse. She was treated with Lexipro and had a prescription for Klonipin to help with anxiety. With regard to family history, Joan's father had a brother who had struggled through much of his life to maintain a job though he had been able to marry and have children. Joan had had several boyfriends over the years but she would frequently become obsessive in her thinking about them and her need for their comfort, and she would often drive them away.

At the start of treatment, Joan's goals were to help her parents understand her situation and be more supportive. She had a general wish to work but no real idea about how she would succeed and some sense that her parents ought to be able to support her if they really wanted to. She also had some beginning appreciation of the role that drugs and alcohol were playing in her life but at best an ambivalent commitment to abstinence or a 12-step program or to really tackling them directly. Joan's goals for herself were more nebulous. At times, she could talk about a wish to succeed at work and in relationships but the very activation of these hopes would result in a kind of dark despair about a situation that at times felt hopeless. Joan's parents were torn between their loyalty to their daughter and their wish to help her and their rage at feeling manipulated and abused by what they saw as her complete lack of responsibility. They all were aware of the diagnosis and had had some education about the kind of affective storms that Joan deals with but their knowledge often faded in the heat of the moment when her affect was most intense.

doi:10.1300/J200v06n01_05

BPD and the Need for Community:
A Social Worker's Perspective

Maureen Smith

SUMMARY. This chapter emphasizes the importance of a community/systems approach in managing the treatment of individuals with borderline personality disorder. The natural systems existing around patient, clinician and family are recognized, and we examine how working teams are built from these systems. The Borderline Center at McLean Hospital is used as an illustration of an organizational model that utilizes the concept of the "holding environment" (Winnicott, 1965) to provide comprehensive services to borderline patients and their families. As patients move through various levels of care and exhibit typical borderline symptomatology, the importance of communication and coordination on the part of the treatment team is highlighted. This chapter also will illustrate the essential ways in which patients, clinicians and families are able to join together in the treatment of this disorder, with special emphasis on the necessity of family involvement. We also will examine how the treatment teams provide the foundation for larger communities, which are critical to sustaining the ongoing work of its members. doi:10.1300/J200v06n01_06 *[Article copies available for a fee from The Haworth Document Delivery Service: 1-800-HAWORTH. E-mail address: <docdelivery@haworthpress.com> Website: <http://www.HaworthPress.com> © 2008 by The Haworth Press. All rights reserved.]*

[Haworth co-indexing entry note]: "BPD and the Need for Community: A Social Worker's Perspective." Smith, Maureen. Co-published simultaneously in *Social Work in Mental Health* (The Haworth Press) Vol. 6, No. 1/2, 2008, pp. 53-66; and: *Borderline Personality Disorder: Meeting the Challenges to Successful Treatment* (ed: Perry D. Hoffman, and Penny Steiner-Grossman) The Haworth Press, 2008, pp. 53-66. Single or multiple copies of this article are available for a fee from The Haworth Document Delivery Service [1-800-HAWORTH, 9:00 a.m. - 5:00 p.m. (EST). E-mail address: docdelivery@haworthpress.com].

KEYWORDS. Systems, community, family, collaboration

INTRODUCTION

John Gunderson, M.D., developed the Center for the Treatment of Borderline Personality Disorder at McLean Hospital in an effort to deliver psychiatric treatment targeted to the needs of individuals with BPD. Together with Edmund Neuhaus, Ph.D., director of the partial hospital program and George Smith, L.I.C.S.W., who directs the intensive outpatient service, we have developed a coordinated program linking appropriate modalities of treatment at graduated levels of care. Fortunately, as Gunderson has been a pioneer in the effort to bring families into the treatment of their relative with BPD, this program includes a prominent family component, which I have overseen since 1999. The Borderline Center is an attractive model for treatment of BPD in that it is interdisciplinary, multimodal, and interactive.

THE HOLDING ENVIRONMENT

A central feature of the Borderline Center is that it is rooted in a programmatic organization based on a systems approach, with a goal of creating collaborating communities composed of patient groups, clinical teams and families. Partial hospital, outpatient groups and family create the "holding environment" (Winnicott, 1965) necessary for borderline patients to feel sufficiently contained for growth to occur (Smith et al., 2001; Gunderson et al., 2006). This "holding" develops from participants' experience of themselves as part of a community; patients feel connected to each other as well as those who treat them. This patient community parallels the professional community, as well as that of the family. The mission of these communities is the symptom management and recovery of the borderline individual. Another equally important purpose of the community is to support those within it. This is particularly necessary when considering the burden BPD places on patient, treaters, and family alike. Furthermore, the thoughtful integration of these intertwining systems of patient, caregiver and family is essential when working with individuals with BPD. The challenge to providing such integration must be met with an appreciation of the importance of the "holding" functions of each of the communities.

SYSTEMS

MacFarlane's (2004) "Integrative Systemic Therapy" describes an effective application of the systems approach as implementing "a contemporary biopsychosocial model in a relational matrix." The advantage of this perspective is that it takes into account the multiple internal and external system influences on an individual and thus allows a broad range of effective interventions for promoting personality and relationship change. As stated by Magnavita (in press), "Personality is complex, and when it has become dysfunctional it represents a total system response from the microscopic (biological), intrapsychic (cognitive-affective-defense constellation), interpersonal (dyadic configurations), relational (triadic configurations), and the macro system (sociocultural influences)." A psychiatric treatment that can consider all these component sub-systems is desirable. At McLean's Borderline Center, we try to fulfill MacFarlane's and Magnavita's messages. We use a combined treatment approach incorporating individual psychotherapy, group work, skills training and a variety of family interventions. Our goal is to integrate all of these modalities in a fluid and flexible manner. These treatments are delivered in gradually diminishing intensity, from partial hospital throughout levels of outpatient care. Patients are given the opportunity to learn from Cognitive Behavioral Therapy (CBT), Dialectical Behavior Therapy (DBT), Mentalization Based Treatment (MBT), and psychodynamically oriented therapies.

TEAM BUILDING

As soon as there are two treaters on a case, you have a team, and it is possible to draw on the strength of a systems approach. Even the most difficult clinical situations are bearable when the responsibility is shared with another clinician with whom there is a good working relationship. When such collaboration occurs, the value of split treatments is evident to anyone who has treated individuals with the borderline patient's hallmark symptoms of suicidality, self-harm, splitting (devaluation and idealization), and emotional excesses. Gunderson notes: "The borderline patient's inability to manage anger towards needed caretakers helps account for the high frequency of dropouts, non-compliance with medications, use of suicide gestures as 'calls for help,' and, secondarily, for the high burden on therapists. When a second caretaker is present, there is readily available opportunity to express anger towards either without fear that the therapist's expected withdrawal or retaliation will leave them abandoned. When practiced well, split treatment will diminish the likelihood of dropouts and improve the alliance with treatment goals *as long as the treaters have an appreciation and respect for each other and for what each is providing"* (Gunderson, 2006, italics mine). Even in the two-person team, interaction and communication between the clinicians is crucial. It is always painful to find treaters playing into the devaluation of another on the team, but it is surprisingly easy to engage in, particularly by the one who is overvalued.

Our Borderline Center patients are likely to have a larger team consisting of some combination of the following: psychotherapist, group therapist, psychopharmacologist, skills coach, case manager, and family therapist. Coordination remains a challenge; no matter what the size of the team, it remains only as effective as its ability to collaborate. In addition to providing treatment for the patient, these working relationships also serve as the foundations of the larger communities, which are so important in sustaining the needed "holding environment."

COMMUNITY

In any treatment setting, it remains important to value the views of all staff members, including the front line workers who often have the least training but the most contact with the patients. We have various structures built into the partial and outpatient levels of care, which encourage clinicians and staff to discuss cases. There are specific weekly rounds on Borderline Center patients at both the partial hospital and intensive outpatient services. In addition, there are weekly group therapy supervisions, DBT consultation team meetings. and peer supervisory sessions for individual therapists. These group meetings are in addition to regular telephone contact among treaters. This ongoing communication, although time-consuming, can be as important for the success of treatment as what happens between the patient and any clinician in their discrete 50-minute hours. The modality of communication for the two-person team is typically the phone call, while the larger teams must rely on structures such as the meetings noted above, active use of voice mail group messages, conference calls and treatment reviews to keep the collaboration ongoing.

COLLABORATION

Outpatient staff meetings at the Borderline Center are similarly used for administrative, clinical and social purposes and provide the opportunity to build connections. An illustration of the effectiveness of this meeting follows.

Case Example

A young clinician who had just returned from family leave after the birth of his first child was panicky about his borderline patient's safety. The patient was paging him repeatedly throughout the night and was asking for multiple early morning appointments to help her manage her suicidal impulses. The clinician became sleep deprived and emotionally spent. Senior outpatient staff, to whom this patient was well known, helped the clinician look at how the patient might be feeling abandoned by his attention to his new baby and his time off. They also helped him recognize how feelings of guilt might be affecting his ability to set reasonable limits on her access to him. Staff shared memories of the overwhelming sense of responsibility of a new baby and the stress of those first months. The clinician appreciated being validated and cared for, but even more importantly was able to refocus on more appropriate boundaries.

While individual supervision could have addressed these issues, the team offers first-hand knowledge of the patient, multiple perspectives, and group support. Such help is built into the framework and does not require initiating a request for help. This is the strength that comes from a community of clinicians.

The administrative structures of rounds and other staff meetings supporting clinical teamwork are stable. However, the patient groups that form a large part of the treatment and holding environment are always being examined and improved, and ideally are flexible adaptable, as necessary. Patients begin with the full-time schedule of the partial hospital groups and transition after a few weeks to intensive outpatient. However, many factors can affect the stability of a treatment plan as a case unfolds and the system must deal with various challenges. Our partial hospital director, Ed Neuhaus has written: "A resilient (i.e., stable and flexible) program structure anticipates changes and withstands inevitable pressures. Now more than ever, systems and organizational structures providing care are mutable, and patients face obstacles other than their own as they strive to attain stability" (Neuhaus, 2005).

FINANCIAL ISSUES

The social worker is often needed to help patients and their families face financial obstacles to obtaining treatment. The variability of managed care coverage for treatment of BPD affects patients, families and clinicians alike. For example, at the Borderline Center we have found that anywhere from two to six weeks in our partial hospital can be the necessary time to establish goals, develop a plan, and form alliances with both patient and family. Based on "medical necessity," managed care companies typically approve one to two weeks. Thus, many individuals admitted to the Borderline Center will need to augment their insurance coverage to fulfill the initial clinical tasks.

Case Example

Mrs. Jones contacts the Borderline Center, desperately seeking specialized treatment for her daughter, who is currently recovering from a serious suicide attempt. Fearing her daughter's life is at stake, Mrs. Jones states "money is no problem" and is annoyed at discussions of the limited coverage her insurance offers. She agrees to pay "whatever is necessary to get the best possible care," minimizing concerns about possible out-of-pocket expenses and refusing to consider other alternatives. After her daughter begins the program, the insurance company, as expected, decides they will pay only a portion of the costs. Outraged, Mrs. Jones begins a battle with her insurance company and complains to staff that she cannot sustain the cost of her daughter's treatment. Meanwhile, the daughter, who initially engaged well in treatment, begins to decompensate as she feels the stress from her family's financial pressures.

In times of crisis, parents will do anything to get the care they believe their child needs and it is difficult, especially for parents new to the mental health system, to understand the complexities of insurance coverage. At the time of this writing, the diagnosis of BPD alone, as an Axis II diagnosis, is not sufficient to obtain authorization from insurers for treatment. It is the co-morbid Axis I diagnosis (most often depression and/or anxiety) on which claims are processed. The additional diagnosis of BPD may be of use only as a way of explaining treatment resistance to insurers. It is the clinical team's mandate to articulate the patient's treatment plan, but that is only the beginning. Establishing the cost of the patient's treatment, clarifying questions about insurance funding, and sorting out the possibilities of family contribution are complex and time-consuming tasks. Moreover, this task must often be revisited every time a patient moves from one level of care to another. Establishing the financial possibilities and a viable treatment plan depend upon collaboration of the treaters and family and is an illustration of the critical importance of having the family as part of the working team.

THE FAMILY SYSTEM

Historically, the families of individuals wit BPD have been blamed, vilified, and held responsible by clinicians who relied solely on the patient's report. As we have come to understand this disorder, we now recognize that devaluation, distortion and the negative filter with which borderline individuals view their lives often skew their reports. Caring, well-intentioned parents can struggle to come to terms with the clinical assumption that they have abused their child in some way. For such families, it is important to note that Gunderson states in the BPD Brief (revised 2006) that while physical or sexual abuse has been reported as present in 70% of patients with BPD, much research has shown that such abuse experiences are neither necessary nor sufficient to cause BPD. He goes on to say that relatively few people who have been physically or sexually abused develop the borderline disorder and roughly half develop without any psychiatric disorder.

In the families that I work with, there are inevitably complaints levied against them by their borderline relative. Patients often report the traumatic effects that derive from common sources, such as multiple family moves, academic pressures, loss of significant others, failed friendships, or bullying. Parents often note that the borderline patient's siblings demonstrated greater resilience in the face of these same life challenges. Parents can be angry, alienated, or bewildered by accusations of neglect or abuse their child has made about them to clinicians.

Case Example

The parents of one borderline patient recalled their history of being rudely shunned by ER staff after delivering their daughter for care. This happened so often through years of recurring crises that they ruefully joked that they must have had a reputation in local emergency rooms of being "Mr. and Mrs. Ogre." They felt humiliated and angry, but until their daughter was accurately diagnosed with BPD when she was 30 years old, they did not know how to manage the situation. Since adoles-

cence, she had been diagnosed with an eating disorder, for which they had funded extensive treatment and had continued to support her financially and emotionally throughout her 20s. The ER visits occurred invariably around breakups with boyfriends and concurrent financial problems. Until the recurrent crises became understood in the context of her typically borderline struggles with relationships, her parents often were seen as a major cause of the daughter's problems. After adjusting her treatment for BPD, the parents became involved in ways that were more productive and joined with their daughter in a shared goal of a more functional life.

In times of crisis, borderline patients may be ambivalent about asking for help. Families can thus be over- or under-involved. An angry, enraged patient, who constantly criticizes her parents' every action, can intimidate and cause such a parent to be wary of stepping in; conversely, a needy, dependent patient who openly seeks input from her parents on every matter may inspire such a parent to be intrusive. We believe patients usually need the support of their family even when they deny it, and that the family usually needs the support of the treatment team even when they do not seek it. It is always true that at times of psychiatric crisis, the family is most in need of compassion, rather than criticism from professionals.

FAMILY INVOLVEMENT

Our approach to families begins by actively recruiting their involvement. We tell them that often the success or failure of whatever we do depends on their becoming knowledgeable about the disorder and making adjustments in their ways of responding. The Multiple Family Group, (Gunderson, Berkowitz, & Ruiz-Sancho, 1997) remains a core element of our program. The work of Perry Hoffman and Alan Fruzzetti has further incorporated DBT skill building into this educational model through the development of "Family Connections," a consumer led multiple-family education group (Hoffman et al., 2005). At its best, psychoeducation is the least threatening, most empowering and non-blaming of interventions. In addition to information on the disorder, we also give families guidelines about how to interact with their family member and materials for improving communication skills.

A clinician's initial contact with a patient's family often begins during a time of crisis or hospitalization when family members bear their own multitude of pain and grief. It is most effective for a member of the clinical team to reach out and offer information and education as a way of supporting the family. The clinician should inquire about the family's perspective on the presenting problem. This helps establish that they have valuable information to share and that their views and concerns matter. This can be accomplished in the context of history taking at intake, discharge planning or at any time in early treatment. As treatment proceeds, so does the need for continued alliance building.

Treatment works better for patients when their families understand the clinical rationale and are supportive of it. It is important to be sensitive to the fact that parents can feel displaced, devalued, or marginalized by treaters, especially when their BPD offspring is enthralled by an idealized therapist. For example: "Dr. A is the first person I can really talk to. She understands me." The parent hears: "You, on the other hand, are impossible to talk to and you don't understand." Parents can feel a complicated mix of relief and rejection when their offspring is intensely connected to a therapist. Alternatively, there is the challenge of a patient who devalues the therapist to the family: "Dr. A is an idiot; he does paperwork during our sessions and isn't helping me at all!" The parent thinks: "This doctor sounds incompetent; she should switch to someone else." Thus, families can engage in a split, or inadvertently sabotage a treatment if they are not included in an appropriate way, such as being invited to attend periodic administrative meetings or conjoint meetings with the individual therapist and family treater. This is a critical step in engaging the family system and minimizing the potential for a failed treatment. It is also a way to continue the psychoeducational process.

MULTIPLE FAMILY GROUP

The Multiple Family Group (MFG) is an efficient and cost effective professionally led intervention for family members. We developed the MFG as a vehicle to promote change within the family system. Family members learn about the diagnosis, practice communication skills to enhance their relationships and learn ways to modify the home environment to support recovery. As families commit to changing their own behavior, they join the treatment and support the concept that the entire system must change, not just the patient. Groups meet twice a month for one and a half hours; there are about six families in each group. The groups are ongoing and families remain in them for as long as they are useful. This can range from a few months to a few years, with most continuing for at least a year. It is a great benefit to have "veteran" families in the group, who can offer sage advice and the comfort of shared experience to new members. As our program is composed of a large proportion of young adults, the groups are primarily made up of parents.

There is a strong focus on ongoing education and skill building. Validation, active listening and the teaching of counter-intuitive parenting skills, in addition to updates regarding most recent advances in research and treatment, are all a part of the Multiple Family Group. Parents can begin to see that the type of parenting they learned from their upbringing may be having a negative effect on their offspring with BPD. They must learn how to respond with sensitivity to issues around abandonment, fear of success, and criticism if they are to make positive changes in the home environment. They begin to see how the pressuring and nagging that might work with their other children only alienates and angers their borderline child. Parents can learn how to become less judgmental and to listen with curiosity and openness to their child's experience. They can learn to accept that they cannot force their adult child to behave as they believe he or she should, even when they are correct.

Actively listening without defensiveness can be difficult and frustrating, and thus it is critical that the supportive setting of the group is also a place for family members to vent their negative feelings and grieve their lost dreams without censure. Parents who feel overwhelmed by their own child's problems are invariably able to offer reassurance and encouragement to the next parent. The group is often the only place where family members are comfortable fully disclosing the more horrible details of their adult children's desperate lives. Fathers, in particular, have bonded with one another in the painful struggle to understand suicidality and self-harm. They seem to share the belief that they should be able to protect their children and solve their problems. They empathize with each other's heavy-handed attempts to do so. At one group, a big, brawny father broke down in sobs, revealing to the group that he had refused to look at his daughter's self-inflicted wounds in the emergency room: "She wanted me to see what she had done, but I wouldn't. I could not. She's still my baby girl." It was the first time he had allowed himself to weep, and it was a powerful moment. What followed was a more candid discussion of how self-mutilation affected the other parents, and the challenges they faced in dealing with this behavior.

It is also helpful for spouses to see other couples struggle with the marital conflict and divisiveness that is nearly universal as a result of parenting a child with BPD. We emphasize the importance of spouses working together and supporting each other. Members applaud each other's efforts and commiserate around their mistakes. As the group is ongoing, the skills learned are often driven by the behaviors the families are currently dealing with, so the clinician must be flexible and versatile in the content of the skills taught. The Multiple Family Group is a powerful way of empowering the family system, an effective clinical service, and a vehicle for advocacy. I have seen the MFG, along with Family Connections, provide the core community so essential for families faced with such burden. Some family members have gone on to join together in raising awareness and sensitivity to BPD by joining regional groups such as the New England Personality Disorder Association (NEPDA), the National Education Alliance for Borderline Personality Disorder (NEA-BPD), and by attending national conferences on mental health issues.

FAMILY WORKSHOPS

As part of our effort to keep families informed about the latest advancements in the understanding and treatment of BPD, we have developed a program of monthly presentations by various experts in the field. These free evening workshops include a lecture and a discussion period when questions can be posed to the speaker. NEPDA joins us in running the program and serves refreshments after the discussion to encourage families to connect and socialize. This is yet another way to foster a sense of community is fostered which, in turn, expands both social networking and the psychoeducational process.

FAMILY THERAPY

We introduce family therapy only when both patients and family members have developed communication skills, such as active listening and validation. Otherwise, the sessions tend to be contentious and often are counterproductive. One very effective modality is the use of conjoint sessions that include the patient, patient's therapist, family and family therapist. This allows the patient to feel supported, even coached in what he or she wants to bring up or work on during the session and it gives the therapist a great opportunity to observe the patient in the context of the family relationships. The patient and family see the individual and family therapist working as a team, including modeling problem solving and managing differences. Just as patients remain in their other treatment modalities during the course of family therapy, we believe that parents who are in family therapy should remain in the Multiple Family Group. It provides reinforcement for the guidelines, an opportunity to practice their skills and deepens their awareness of their roles in the family system. It also provides necessary support. The following case vignette illustrates the value of the MFG and the necessity for a collaborative team.

Case Example

Jane was an attractive 20-year-old college dropout hospitalized for slashing her arms while drunk. She did not allow her parents to be present during the intake and allowed them only minimal information about her condition, which included an extensive history of prior cutting, alcohol and drug use. A diagnosis of BPD was established and Jane was referred to a partial program, and her very anxious parents were referred to me.

Jane's parents came to see me for psychoeducation and began attending the Multiple Family Group. The parents were bewildered as they discovered more about her psychiatric symptoms, particularly her self-loathing and self-mutilation. While staying connected to her family and the church, Jane was described as a rebel, who pushed limits and had a "dark" side. Jane endorsed the diagnosis of BPD and worked hard to convince her family that she was doing well. After leaving the partial hospital, Jane continued in individual therapy with an outside (non-McLean) therapist and also attended an evening DBT skills group.

Over the next year, Jane had a number of admissions for suicidality and substance abuse but did not allow the inpatient team to disclose relevant clinical details to her family. The parents were told only the most basic information, as the inpatient staff felt bound by HIPPA regulations to respect Jane's privacy. Therefore, while Jane was not openly oppositional, and appeared very compliant, remorseful and concerned about her family, she controlled information about her hospitalizations and deflected any open communication among inpatient team, her individual therapist, DBT therapist and her family.

The parents, impressed by Jane's sadness and distance, became increasingly uneasy about how she was managing. Yet Jane continued to reassure them that all was well. In the parents' Multiple Family Group, we decided that I should share the family's concerns with the DBT leader. This began the process of team building. When I did, the DBT leader noted that the DBT group also had similar concerns about Jane, and she contacted the individual therapist to request a team meeting. The therapist discussed the request with Jane, who refused, saying she would be "ganged up on." Initially the therapist supported her refusal, which alarmed both the DBT leader and me. Discussions began with the therapist about the importance of creating a more effective, unified treatment. Jane finally agreed to meet, but then barely survived a near lethal overdose of heroin shortly before the team meeting was to occur.

During the following inpatient admission Jane's treatment turned around. Her clinicians and family joined firmly together and insisted that her treatment needed to be more open and coordinated. Eventually Jane accepted this unified position. It was clear Jane was desperately trying to hide her "dark side" from her respectable family. She had a hidden life where she embraced dangerous substance abuse and other extremely risky behaviors, which, for the most part, she had kept out of her treatment.

LEGAL ISSUES

In addition to highlighting the importance of collaboration, this case illustrates the legitimacy of using a clinical override. In the case of patients who are financially and emotionally dependent on their families, their refusal to allow their family access to relevant information will make meaningful treatment impossible. The clinician in charge of such a case has the right to override the right to privacy of a patient if it is deemed clinically imperative. It often seems reasonable and may seem necessary to allow patients over 18 to keep their lives private from their parents, but clinicians do such patients a disservice when honoring that legal privilege is not in the patient's best interest. Jane's impulsive, self-destructive drug use needed to be brought to light, rather than kept a shameful secret, so that she could engage in a more authentic, effective treatment. Only when such patients are able to see that their treaters and their family can tolerate all the "bad" sides of themselves, can they begin to do the same. When patients interview at the Borderline Center, our team approach, including family involvement, is emphasized as a condition of treatment.

CONCLUSION

The rich social work tradition of service to the community and the family has proved to be particularly significant in managing the treatment of BPD. Respecting and utilizing the intersecting systems in an individual's life invites creative approaches and shared energy. It is both lonely and dangerous to go it alone, especially when the therapist is dealing with a disorder that is essentially one of alienation and isolation. Working as a team allows those involved to share both the burden of BPD and the satisfaction that comes from witnessing borderline individuals regaining control over their lives. Building communities where patients, clinicians and families are supported and educated, can sustain recovery and growth. Furthermore, these communities can then promote organizations such as NEPDA, NEA-BPD and NAMI, who go on to raise public awareness of the need for research and funding for BPD.

Acknowledgments

The author would like to thank John Gunderson, MD for his thoughtful help and inspiration; and George Smith, LICSW, James Hudson, MD and Karen Caplan, LICSW, for their review of the manuscript.

REFERENCES

Gunderson, J.G., Berkowitz, C., & Ruiz-Sancho, A. (1997). Families of borderline patients: A psycho educational approach. *Bulletin of the Menninger Clinic*, 61 (4), 446-457.

Gunderson, J.G. (2001). *Borderline Personality Disorder: A Clinical Guide*. Washington, DC: American Psychiatric Press.

Gunderson, J.G. (2006 revised). *The BPD Brief: An introduction to borderline personality disorder*. New England Personality Disorder Association.

Gunderson, J.G. (2006). Competing perspectives on psychotherapy of borderline personality disorder: *The case of Ellen*. Unpublished.

Hoffman, P., Fruzzetti, A., Buteau, E., Neiditch, E., Penney, D., Bruce, M., Hellman, F., & Struening, E. (2005). Family connections: a program for relatives of persons with borderline personality disorder. *Family Process*, 44:217-225.

MacFarlane, M. M. (Ed.) (2004). *Family treatment of personality disorders: Advances in clinical practice*. New York: Haworth Clinical Practice Press.

Magnavita, J.J. *Personality-guided realtionship theory: A component system model*. Washington, D.C.: American Psychological Association (in press).

Neuhaus, E. (2006). Fixed values and a flexible partial hospital program model. *Harvard Review of Psychiatry*, 14:1.

Smith, G., Ruiz-Sancho, A., & Gunderson, J.G. (2001). An intensive outpatient program for patients with borderline personality disorder. *Psychiatric Services*, 52:4.

Winnicott, D.W. (1965). *The Maturational Process and the Facilitating Environment*. New York: International Universities Press.

doi:10.1300/J200v06n01_06

Borderline Personality Disorder and Hospitalization

Freda Baron Friedman

SUMMARY. This chapter reviews and discusses the issues and controversies related to the hospitalization of suicidal patients with a diagnosis of borderline personality disorder. It highlights the challenges faced by both the clinical staff and a prototypical patient during a hospitalization. Included are a discussion of the transference and counter-transference that arise during inpatient treatment, the stressors on the staff as well as on the patients themselves. The chapter offers suggestions for enhanced in-hospital treatment, including increased collaborative decision-making, clear and realistic short- and long-term goals for patient and family, and increased supervision and ongoing education of staff. doi:10.1300/J200v06n01_07 *[Article copies available for a fee from The Haworth Document Delivery Service: 1-800-HAWORTH. E-mail address: <docdelivery@ haworthpress.com> Website: <http://www.HaworthPress.com> © 2008 by The Haworth Press. All rights reserved.]*

KEYWORDS. Borderline personality disorder, hospitalization, controversies about treatment, suicide, suicidal ideation, transference and counter-transference, staff/nursing stressors

INTRODUCTION: TWO CASE STUDIES

Amy came to her Tuesday afternoon therapy session and reported that she had cut herself that same morning with a kitchen knife, creating

[Haworth co-indexing entry note]: "Borderline Personality Disorder and Hospitalization." Friedman, Freda Baron. Co-published simultaneously in *Social Work in Mental Health* (The Haworth Press) Vol. 6, No. 1/2, 2008, pp. 67-84; and: *Borderline Personality Disorder: Meeting the Challenges to Successful Treatment* (ed: Perry D. Hoffman, and Penny Steiner-Grossman) The Haworth Press, 2008, pp. 67-84. Single or multiple copies of this article are available for a fee from The Haworth Document Delivery Service [1-800-HAWORTH, 9:00 a.m. - 5:00 p.m. (EST). E-mail address: docdelivery@haworthpress.com].

a three inch-long horizontal cut that had bled for half an hour. Amy had decided it didn't need stitches, and indeed, by the time she arrived at her session, the wound had stopped bleeding. She also reported to Dr. B, her therapist, that she had stopped feeling like cutting and really was ok now. This morning she had been upset with her boyfriend and his plans to go away for the weekend with his brother; now, she had made plans with someone and had made up with her boyfriend.

Still, Dr. B. was very concerned and wanted to hospitalize Amy because of the cutting. In the two months she had worked with Amy, this was the third time she had cut herself. The therapist felt that Amy was at risk this weekend, what with the boyfriend away, and the therapist planning to leave town herself. She posed the concern to Amy, who said "It makes no sense to hospitalize me now for cutting myself this morning . . . I absolutely have no urge to cut myself now and feel much more in control. I can put my knives away, call my friend if I'm upset and I'll be ok." Dr. B. was not so sure.

What she knew about Amy was that she had been in therapy for the past 10 years with about five different therapists. She had been hospitalized several times before for suicidal ideation and cutting, but had not previously demonstrated any severe life-threatening behaviors . . . not yet, thought Dr. B. Amy had some stability in her life now: her own apartment, a responsible job for the past few years and a declining credit card balance. Although her relationships tended to be rocky, this current boyfriend relationship had been lasting significantly longer than previous ones. She had stopped drinking several months ago and attended AA irregularly, but usually at least once a week.

Amy's therapist was in a quandary. She knew that Amy definitely didn't want to go into the hospital. A coerced admission would affect their working relationship. At the same time, Dr. B. had had a traumatic experience with another patient, Monica, several months earlier and was inclined to be much more conservative and cautious.

Monica, an off-again, on-again long-term patient of Dr. B's, had had bouts of depression and anxiety. Once every few weeks, she would call in sick, stay in bed all day, withdraw from friends and sink into depression, hopelessness and suicidal ideation. But the next day, she'd pull herself together, carefully and expertly apply her makeup and go out to dazzle colleagues and clients. For the past few weeks, Monica had been experiencing increasing difficulty concentrating at work and was having more feelings of insecurity about her work and her relationship with her partner. She had been spacing out her medications so that they would last longer and had recently cancelled several appointments with Dr. B.

Monica's psychiatrist decided to hospitalize her briefly for medication re-evaluation and adjustment. Her only previous hospitalization, some 20 years ago for similar issues, had been followed by several decades of fairly solid functioning and stability. Monica was hospitalized this time for three days, having adjusted quickly and well to a new medication regime. She had a therapy session the next day with Dr. B and reported that she was definitely feeling better and was ready to resume work on a more consistent basis.

Forty-eight hours later, Monica took a near-lethal dose of Tylenol and alcohol and then called a good friend to say she wasn't feeling well. She was taken to another hospital, at her insistence, and stabilized via the Intensive Care Unit. Within several days, Monica began agitating for immediate discharge, insisting that she was "totally better," and that she would avoid the trigger to her suicide attempt [contact with her mother]. She participated actively in therapeutic groups on the unit, and appeared to be stabilized within a week. The multidisciplinary staff was quite divided about keeping or discharging Monica. There were those who felt she wasn't stable enough to keep herself safe and there were those who felt that Monica was chronically unstable and would not benefit from further hospitalization when she so clearly wasn't willing to stay. Insurance coverage limitations and family pressure also tipped the scales in favor of discharge. The disagreements about Monica's care created significant tension for the unit staff, particularly since Monica was relentless in her requests to be discharged. Dr. B. felt wary about having Monica discharged so soon.

Patients like Amy and Monica are not uncommon among the population of people with severe symptoms of borderline personality disorder. According to many researchers in the field of BPD, 2-3% of the population in this country meet criteria for BPD. Their use of mental health services in this country is strikingly large: they represent about 10% of all individuals who utilize outpatient mental health clinic services. Even more striking, they account for 15 to 20% of all psychiatric hospital admissions (APA, 2000).

The issues of hospitalization for such patients are complex and multifaceted. These include: controversy about the role of hospitalization for patients such as Amy and Monica; the benefits and hazards of hospitalization, factors that influence effective treatment and that work against it; obstacles to treating such patients; guidelines for helping to ensure more effective treatment; and effective adjuncts or alternatives to hospitalization. A discussion of these issues is the focus of this chapter.

WHY THE HIGH RATES OF HOSPITALIZATION?

The suicide potential for BPD is among the highest in the psychiatric population. One out of 10 chronically suicidal patients with BPD will eventually commit suicide (Paris, 2004). This outcome is not generally or readily predictable (Paris, 2004). Even higher is the level of suicidal ideation for many people with BPD; it is chronic, fairly persistent and occurs with startling frequency. For people with BPD who are accustomed to fending off emotional flooding, suicidal ideation often becomes a deeply ingrained "coping mechanism." Many also engage in behaviors that are potentially self destructive in order to fend off this flooding, numb themselves, or to distract themselves from unbearable emotional pain. This combination of high rates of suicidal ideation coupled with high rates of suicidal and parasuicidal behavior, leads many clinicians, families and clients themselves to seek what they may perceive as the protection of a hospital unit. Patients like this are often hospitalized to protect them from further self-harm.

In reality, however, hospitalization is often not the treatment of choice for such patients. First, this protection is often illusory. An inpatient treatment is of unproven value for suicide prevention and can often produce negative results. The patient may settle down quickly in a contained environment, but not develop the strength and resiliency to manage life's stressors outside the hospital any better than before admission. Hospitalization may give a false sense of security to patient, treaters and family. The patient's intra- and interpersonal difficulties may be exacerbated in the intense environment of an inpatient unit and these may weaken the tenuous hold the patient may have had prior to admission.

Second, it may well be that such patients are hospitalized more for the benefit of the therapist, family or supportive involved friends than for the patient herself. The person or people who are the patient's supports may have been dealing with a barrage of crisis-laden phone calls and/or self-destructive behaviors during the previous days or weeks. They are often terrified that they will do the "wrong thing" in trying to support and help the person in crisis. They may be burned out, or feeling helpless after sleepless nights and worried days. For such a person, for her treaters, and certainly for her family and friends, life feels like a high stakes roller coaster with no predictable or consistent twists and turns. The only predictable pattern is the unpredictability: functioning well one minute, falling apart the next. With hospitalization of their client or loved one, there is the sense of insured safety, as well as some respite from the terror of anticipating a tragedy.

Third, it is surprisingly difficult to determine when a client with BPD is, and is likely to remain, at such a high level of risk of severe harm to herself or another. The lability and volatility that often typifies someone with severe symptoms of BPD makes periods of suicidal ideation frequent. To distinguish between chronic suicidal ideation and active suicidal ideation is a risk that many clinicians feel ill advised or ill equipped to take.

THE CONTROVERSY OVER HOSPITALIZATION

It is because of these and many other reasons that hospitalization is an issue of considerable debate among clinicians and researchers in the BPD field. A review of the literature (Paris, 2004; Rosenbluth, 1987; Vijay, 2007) indicates that hospitalization is still an unresolved issue and that guidelines for when to hospitalize someone with BPD are implemented inconsistently. Those who advocate hospitalization join with Glenn Gabbard's comment: "When the patient is extremely suicidal, hospitalization is necessary, but most patients with BPD can do well with a structured outpatient program involving individual and group therapy and medication."

The hospital is viewed as "a part of the therapeutic tools available" (Gabbard, 2001) for the treatment of these individuals and should serve to contain a crisis, specify a diagnosis and to prepare and reinforce a rapid return in their community. Intensive day treatment has increasingly become an evidence-based treatment alternative to full admission (Paris 2004).

The American Psychological Association Practice Guidelines for treatment of patients with BPD identify the following indications for brief hospitalization:

- Imminent danger to others
- Loss of control of suicidal impulses or serious suicide attempt
- Transient psychotic episodes associated with loss of impulse control or impaired judgment

- Symptoms of sufficient severity to interfere with functioning, work or family life that are unresponsive to outpatient treatment and partial hospitalization

For extended inpatient hospitalization, the APA indicates the following guidelines:

- Persistent and severe suicidality, self destructiveness or non-adherence to outpatient treatment or partial hospitalization
- Co-morbid refractory Axis I disorder (e.g., eating disorder, mood disorder) that presents a potential threat to life

The indicators for partial hospitalization, under APA Guidelines, are:

- Dangerous, impulsive behavior unable to be managed with outpatient treatment
- Nonadherence to outpatient treatment and a deteriorating clinical picture
- Complex comorbidity that requires more intensive clinical assessment of response to treatment
- Symptoms of sufficient severity to interfere with functioning, work or family life that are unresponsive to outpatient treatment

When these guidelines are followed, the individual with BPD is hospitalized for three primary reasons:

- To protect the patient against him/herself and/or to protect him/her from hurting someone else
- To remove the patient from his home and/or work environment, which is serving as a toxic trigger for unmanageable feelings and behaviors
- To ensure that the patient will have only one concern, i.e., his health, rather than to be overwhelmed by multiple unmanageable relationships or responsibilities

WHAT HAPPENS DURING INPATIENT TREATMENT?

While there is no "typical" picture of hospitalization for a patient with severe BPD, the initial goals of all inpatient treatments are similar: to stabilize the patient and to provide a secure environment. The degree to which the inpatient treatment is designed to meet the specific needs and the psychological profile of the patient depends on many factors, whether treatment is individualized, the length of stay, and the specialized training of the staff.

At one end of the broad continuum of BPD inpatient treatment is the intensive, specialized intervention program that includes several supplementary and intertwined components: hospitalization and an attached specialized inpatient psychotherapeutic program, individual psychotherapy (psychoanalytic or dialectical behavioral therapy), followed by outpatient intensive partial hospitalization with supervised therapeutic living arrangements, followed by outpatient psychiatric management, transitional planning and follow-up. The focus is on somatic treatment with neuroleptics, individual and group psychotherapy, family or couples therapy, psychoeducation, and rehabilitation with work and living skills. At the other end of the continuum are short-term and crisis units utilizing aggressive psychopharmacology, rapid assessment and intervention, and several groups in relapse prevention, stress management and medication management. Transition planning is often limited to ensuring that the patient has a follow up appointment following discharge with a previous or new clinician for therapy and, if necessary, psychopharmacological management. In between these two extremes are the more typical inpatient offerings for people with BPD: one to four weeks, depending on the patient's insurance, financial resources, availability of treatment, and the patient's commitment to treatment. Results of such treatment are also mixed. While it may be an excellent way of helping stabilize the client, hospitalization is usually too short to attain significant changes.

The most effective inpatient facilities for BPD are highly structured environments that seek to stabilize a patient and prepare the patient for more productive treatment in a less restrictive environment. Clinicians familiar with such programs (Butler, 2007), in discussion with this author, emphasize that the goals of such programs should include:

- Providing brief hospitalization and rapid return to the community, provided that there is effective treatment in the community (Maslar, 2007);
- Helping the patient learn how to use long-term treatment more effectively;
- Providing a spectrum of services that will connect patients to fully qualified outpatient clinicians;

- Providing interventions that lead to decreasing acting out behavior;
- Clearly identifying of targeted interventions that address those behaviors;
- Fostering acceptance among the staff and the patient of the magnitude of the therapeutic task;
- Fostering more effective interpersonal relationships; and
- Providing a family component, especially for children and adolescents, in order to help parents to establish a validating environment at home.

In previous decades, these goals were more attainable. There were a number of specialized units geared specifically for an all-BPD patient population. Inpatient lengths of stay lasted from 1-3 years. Intensive treatment occurred on the unit, and some patients truly benefited from the containment and the nurturing of interpersonal relationships. Of course, the disadvantage was that the transition to outpatient life was often excruciatingly difficult, and at times patients had to be rehospitalized repeatedly in order to be able to benefit from an intense level of outpatient treatment.

A variety of issues led to plummeting inpatient lengths of stay, which decreased from a few months to a few weeks, and then to a few days. These shifts were influenced by the increased use of psychopharmacology as the mainstay of treatment; other factors included pressures to reduce costs, make inpatient units more responsive to external demands, speed up decision making and the treatment process, and involve the patient in treatment planning in accord with regulatory demands. Over the last decade, the hospital treatment of the difficult-to-treat patient has become ever more challenging because of these demands (Munich, 2003). At the same time, the growing demand for evidence-based treatments has put pressure on the treatment team to look at outcomes. In the past, treatment for BPD has lacked evidence of efficacy and its theory has not generally been backed by developmental studies.

The evidence-based treatments with measurable outcomes for difficult-to-treat patients with BPD now fall into the area of cognitive-based approaches, particularly Dialectical Behavior Therapy, and psychodynamically based approaches founded on the central concept of mentalization (Bateman & Fonagy, 2004). Linehan's DBT approach has proved to be highly effective on a number of measures to reduce hospitalization, rehospitalization, and morbidity (Linehan, 2006). Bateman and Fonagy's psychodynamically based treatment has also shown to be effective in reducing morbidity (Fonagy & Bateman, 2006; Munich 2003). Both treatments are introduced on inpatient units initially, with a focus on more concentrated treatment in intensive partial hospitalization programs. In both models, treatment is based on a team approach. In the Linehan model, the consultation team is an essential component to provide support and dialectical coherence to the therapist(s). In the Bateman and Fonagy model, the patient is an integral member of the team. The model, currently in use at the Menninger Clinic (Munich, 2003), includes the following components:

- The staff members are more available for flexible therapeutic interventions, working actively in liaison with the individual and family therapist when those modalities are prescribed.
- All disciplines provide the team with significant information about the patient's life, providing a fuller picture of the patient's behaviors and the positive and negative consequences of treatment interventions.
- The patient's presence on the team and in the treatment meeting creates a situation that resembles the nuclear family. Ideally, the patient is in the presence of a unified and coherent group who can provide the "good-enough" measure of safety, holding and attunement, can agree and disagree comfortably in front of the patient, can work together to ascertain what the most relevant problems are, and can discuss what is involved in starting or restarting a treatment process.
- With the patient present, the team is encouraged to think out loud about and compromise on medication trials and effectiveness, progress in various psychosocial treatments, interpersonal and milieu issues and therapeutic passes and impasses.
- The decision-making process is demystified, the patient is more involved, the processes are more interactive, and the various sectors of the unit's treatment system are synchronized.

THE "CHALLENGING PATIENT"

Despite the many changes in the actual treatment for BPD over the decades, some aspects of care have not changed. One that has persisted over time is the concept of the "difficult patient." The therapeutic staff, most often the nursing staff who are generally on the "front lines" of treatment on inpatient units, describe individuals diagnosed with BPD as among the most challenging patients encountered in their practice (Bland & Rossen, 2005; Cleary, Siegfried & Walter, 2002; Deans & Meocevic, 2005; Gallop, Lancee, & Garfinkel, 1989; Wong, 1983; Fraser & Gallop, 1993; Pavlovich-Danis, 2004). These studies emphasized specific client behaviors that nurses personally found to be problematic. These included: stalking behavior; bringing weapons onto the unit; using threatening behaviors in session; suicidal behavior; manipulative behavior and behaviors that created uncertainty for the staff regarding their roles, especially in connection with issues surrounding responsibility for the client behavior (Laskowski, 2001). Another study of inpatient psychiatric nurses noted that difficult patients were labeled as such because they challenged the professional and personal competence of the nurses (May & Kelly, 1982). Other challenging behaviors reported in the literature are unstable interpersonal relationships, unstable moods, manipulation, and splitting (Gallop et al., 1989; Greene & Ugarriza, 1995; Piccinino, 1990).

How the concept of the "challenging patient" plays itself out on the hospital unit is highlighted by Monica's recent hospitalization and how she and the staff experienced it.

When Monica was admitted to the inpatient unit following her overdose, she was flooded with feelings of shame about her actions, as well as anger at herself, her mother and others. So after she had had her stomach pumped and was free of the overdose medications, she felt much more controlled and sounded much more rational. The staff members were trying to do what they do best to help clients who have recently been suicidal, and offered supportive but firm and consistent limits. Monica responded at times with understanding and appreciation. At other times, she reacted as though these efforts were unhelpful, wrong or even threatening. With Nick, one of her favorite male mental health workers, she was cooperative about curfews and phone restrictions. She occasionally opened up to him about some of her conflicts with her mother and other family members. But with Natalie and several other female nursing staff members, Monica was often angry, sarcastic and dismissive. She often complained to Nick about Natalie and other female staff.

Everyone felt angry. Monica firmly believed that Natalie had no idea what she was thinking or feeling. "I'm the patient, and the staff should be smart enough and trained enough to know what's bothering me. They are acting like I should be acting in a healthy, normal way . . . If I could express my every thought and feeling like they want me to, I wouldn't be in the hospital." Monica was trying to preserve her sense of safety in the only way she knew how when she was under extreme stress by using the same off-putting coping skills that had caused her problems elsewhere in her life. Natalie and her staff were angry and frustrated because Monica would not communicate directly with them, and often attacked what Natalie and the other nurses felt they were best trained and qualified to do. Nick began feeling more and more stressed because he was caught in the middle between Monica and many of his co-workers. They accused him of being manipulated by Monica, of only seeing one side of her and of not supporting his team members. As the tension built, the communication decreased between Nick and his colleagues, and the interactions between Monica and the inpatient staff became increasingly polarized.

When admitted to the hospital, many BPD patients are in a state of acute crisis or regression, and often present to the therapeutic staff with aggressive or self-destructive behavior. A borderline patient's internal difficulties and conflicts are often transferred to the inpatient staff, who are called upon to deal with the patient's dysregulated emotions and behavior and to set limits in the service of creating a safe and stable environment. These efforts, though caring and appropriate, may trigger in newly admitted patients a variety of extreme reactions: hostility, neediness, demands for special favors and relationships. Typically, the BPD patient under these circumstances will idealize some staff and demonize others, shifting frequently to the opposite sentiments and behavior. The impact of this behavior on the staff is enormous. Staff describe experiencing a wide range of feelings in working with patients with BPD on an inpatient unit, including frustration, anxiety, fear, guilt, helplessness, anger and other visceral feelings (Laskowski, 2001).

BPD patients are often complex and perplexing to the treatment team members. Although each patient is unique and different from others, the characteristics they share may include certain co-morbidity disorders that may be in an acute stage, such as anorexia, bulimia, addiction to substances, alcohol, gambling, or other extreme behaviors. There may also be new and emerging problems, such as cognitive impairment, the presence of multiple medical diagnoses that overlap symptomatically, and the use of multiple medications that increase the risk of side effects. The families and/or caregiver support systems of these patients may themselves be overwhelmed, adding yet another layer of complexity to the care. Perhaps as a result of working with patients who can present such challenges, mental health nurses report high levels of stress and burnout (Rees & Smith, 1991).

At the same time, many individuals with BPD report feeling angry, and even traumatized and victimized, as a consequence of hospitalization. When admitted, many BPD patients are in a state of acute crisis or regression and often present to the therapeutic staff with aggressive or self-destructive behavior. Their hospitalization may follow a real or perceived rupture in an important relationship with family or a personal or professional significant other. Accordingly, the patient may be feeling panic, despair, emptiness, anger or shame caused by this rupture, often related to unrealistic demands or expectations of others (Bowers & Park, 2001).

Not surprisingly, considering the tendency of patients with BPD to experience strong but often polarized feelings, some suicidal patients report positive feelings about some aspects of hospitalization. One group of BPD patients who were placed on special observation status because of suicidal risk reported that this inpatient intervention helped them feel safe and that the interactions with the observers helped to restore their hope (Pitula & Cardell, 1996). Another group reported that dysphoria, anxiety, and suicidal thoughts were reduced when the observing nurses engaged in positive interaction (Fletcher, 1999). The process of constant observation also elicited negative reactions, including a lack of privacy, poor interaction with the staff observer, perceptions of being treated like a prisoner, and frequent changes of staff (Pitula & Cardell, 1996; Jones, Lowe & Ward, 2000; Jones et al., 2000). Similar patients reported experiencing a mixed bag of positive (feeling understood and accepted) and negative (feeling isolated, degraded, coerced) reactions. Whether these experiences were seen as positive or negative depended on the behavior of the nurse (Jones et al., 2000).

TRANSFERENCE AND COUNTERTRANSFERENCE IN THE TREATMENT

During treatment, an individual with BPD often experiences an intensification of feelings that originated with earlier parental caretakers. This process of transference occurs when the person experiences an emotional reaction to someone based on unconscious drives and feelings that originated earlier in life. In the intensity of an inpatient setting, many of these original relationships are reconstructed with staff members. The patient once again experiences intense feelings of love, hate, anger, and fear. This re-enactment of strong emotional conflicts within the parental relationship is transferred to the relationship with nursing staff and can evoke the same intense countertransference reactions from staff members resulting from their own developmental experiences.

It has been suggested that a diagnosis of BPD will influence the level and quality of care and interaction that staff have with patients (Deans & Meocevic, 2005; O'Brien, 1998). Countertransference reactions by the staff affect the patient's treatment because of their ability to distort or even destroy the therapeutic relationship. Some authors in the psychiatric literature (Steiger, 1967; Steiger & Hirsh, 1965) have recognized the complexity of the health care provider-client relationship and have suggested that clients themselves are never difficult; rather the treatment is difficult or the person doing the treating is having difficulty. Even more so, the primary challenge for both patient and staff relates to the nature of their interpersonal difficulties and inability to express their feelings effectively.

Perhaps the most frequently seen scenario involves a patient who is hospitalized against his or her will. Under those circumstances, the patient is likely to be less than totally cooperative and is often unwilling to participate in the therapy offered. Such a patient is likely to be resistant and interfere with treatment on many levels. These reactions do not occur in a vacuum; they affect the staff who are trying to treat them as well. A cycle of mutual frustration often is set up, with patient and therapeutic staff working at cross purposes with and against each other.

OTHER CHALLENGES TO HOSPITALIZATION

The involvement of a caregiver and/or family members in the treatment of a patient with BPD is particularly challenging for many interdisciplinary teams (Smith & Schultz, 2000). Often the discharge plans fail to take into consideration the benefits or liabilities of involving outside family/caretaker supports, particularly if the adult client has strong preferences about the degree of involvement they wish others to have in their post hospitalization life. When a patient is discharged in stable, functioning condition, it is frustrating, puzzling and discouraging to everyone involved to readmit the same person in a decompensated state shortly after discharge.

There are a number of issues that complicate the stabilization and maintenance of BPD patients during hospitalization and following discharge. These are inherent in many patients' attitudes towards their own treatment and illness, and family members may share these attitudes:

- Denial–not accepting the patient's level of impairment and need for supervision and assistance;
- Resistance–failing to sustain supportive care needed to promote optimal function following discharge;
- Divergent opinions on care needs and options–unrealistic expectations about the patient's ability to function or failure to adapt routines to promote functional capacity; and
- Indifference–failing to make arrangements for follow-up care or treatment, despite having decision-making authority and capability.

Monica's experience on the unit during her first and second hospitalization yield many insights into the challenges of her treatment.

During the first brief three-day hospitalization, Monica withheld significant information from staff in order to avoid a more prolonged hospitalization. She didn't tell them about her previous hospitalization and difficulties and minimized her job difficulties and interpersonal stressors with her boyfriend. Unstable though her mood was, she was able to figure out what she thought the staff wanted to hear, and worked hard to be "the best " patient on the unit. This was a skill nurtured since childhood to avoid punishment from her volatile alcoholic parents. She complimented staff, used her charm and sense of humor to good advantage to win over staff and other patients. She used her habitual caretaking skills, offering to help other patients and accommodating staff's needs.

During her second hospitalization, Monica was unable to contain her affect as effectively. She tried to be cooperative, but angered easily when she felt her needs were not being met. She did open up to a male member of the therapeutic staff about her intense attachment and dependency on her outpatient female therapist. She sought him out and always thanked him profusely for the attention he tended to give her, sometimes at the expense of other patients. When other members of the therapeutic staff heard about this relationship, Monica sensed that they began to avoid her. She asked the favored male nurse about this and he confirmed that the staff members were trying to remain neutral and establish boundaries so that she would not begin to feel overly attached to them and to the unit

Monica felt hurt and betrayal, by both the male staff member and the other staff with whom she had had contact. This quickly led to anger alternating with shame. Her determination to leave the unit became intense. Instead of using interactions with staff and her assigned therapist to explore this in depth, she went underground with those feelings, believing that if she revealed too much, her discharge would be postponed. She reverted to "best patient" mode and now that she was slightly stabilized, she was able to maintain it. On discharge, however, she quickly returned to her old patterns of numbing by cutting, smoking pot, and drinking alcohol. It was only when she returned to individual therapy that she was able to begin exploring these destructive behaviors.

ENHANCING HOSPITAL CARE FOR BPD PATIENTS

Given the problems Monica experienced and the previous discussion of challenges to treatment, there are a number of practices that should be an essential part of inpatient care, especially for those who are seriously ill with BPD symptoms. It is essential to elicit an understanding of patients' perceptions of their problems and the way they prioritize their problems and goals (Pollack & Cramer, 2000). These goals may vary widely from one patient to another, depending on the severity of symptoms and the origins of dysregulation, attachment and developmental difficulties. The more insightful and stable patients may be interested in and capable of acquiring an understanding of their emotional instability while still in the hospital. Others may be primarily focused on basic stabilization, particularly if the length of stay is very limited. Still others may show a low motivation for self-awareness; rather, they focus primarily on their strong need to be taken care of by the therapist or the therapeutic staff. Their inability to be satisfied and soothed by others–and by themselves–presents an obstacle for establishing a psychotherapeutic relationship. In situations such as these, the beginning work of hospitalization is to help patients become more aware of their difficulty in self-soothing and to help them develop this skill.

Another aspect of improved care is to involve the patient and the health care team in collaborative decision-making. Some of the recent modifications in treatment of BPD symptomatology in inpatient and partial hospitalization programs include team meetings that involve the patient throughout the course of treatment (Munich, 2004). These meetings address issues such as identification of progress, challenges, and the risks and benefits of various treatment approaches.

Patients and staff need to be clear about what the treatments involve and realistic about short-term and long-term outcomes. Often, when patients don't see changing occurring rapidly enough, they may become discouraged and resist continuing the potentially helpful strategies they have begun to develop. Staff, on the other hand, may be discouraged at seeing a patient revert to old behaviors, even though they appeared to be becoming more emotionally regulated and/or connected interpersonally. It is critically important to help both patients and staff to accept the "one step forward-half a step backward" momentum patterns of change.

Another essential component of improved hospital treatment involves supervision and ongoing education of the staff. A study of 20 registered psychiatric nurses (Laskowski, 2001) showed that these nurses were skilled at integrating knowledge enabling them to quickly connect and stay connected with BPD patients and responding empathically to their patient needs. Support for the inpatient staff also involves helping them become attuned to their own emotional responses to patients, particularly those patients with BPD who "push their buttons." This critical component enables the staff to remain calm and to use their own responses purposefully and therapeutically.

REFERENCES

Bateman, A. & Fonagy, P. (2004). *Psychotherapy for borderline personality disorder: Mentalization-based treatment.* Oxford: Oxford University Press.

Bland, A. R. & Rossen, E.K. (2005). Clinical supervision of nurses working with BPD Issues. *Mental Health Nursing*, 26, 507-517.

Bowers, L. & Park. A. (2001). Special observation in the care of psychiatric patients: A literature review. *Issues in Mental Health Nursing*, 22, 769-786.

Butler, C. Personal communication. Feb. and Mar., 2007.

Cleary, M. Siegfried, M., & Walter, G. (2002). Experience, knowledge and attitudes of mental health staff regarding clients with a borderline personality disorder. *International Nursing Journal of Mental Health*, 1 (3), 186-191.

Deans, C. & Meocevic, E. (2006). Attitudes of registered psychiatric nurses towards patients diagnosed with borderline personality disorder. *Contemporary Nurse*, 21, 43-49.

Fletcher R. F. (1999). The process of constant observation: Perspectives of staff and suicidal patients. *Journal of Psychiatric and Mental Health Nursing*, 6 (1), 9-14.

Fonagy, P. & Bateman, A. W. (2006). Mechanisms of change in mentalization-based treatment of BPD. *Journal of Clinical Psychology*, 62 (4), 411-30.

Fonagy, P., Gergely, G., Jurist, E., & Target, M. (2002). *Affect regulation, mentalization and the development of the self.* New York: Other Press.

Fraser, K. & Gallop, R. (1993). Nurses' confirming/disconfirming responses to patients diagnosed with BPD. *Archives of Psychiatric Nursing*, 7 (6), 336-341.

Gabbard, G. & Kay, J. (2001). The fate of integrated treatment: Whatever happened to the biopsychosocial psychiatrist? *American Journal of Psychiatry*, 158, 1956-1963.

Gallop, R., Lancee, W., & Garfinkel, P. (1989). How nursing staff respond to the label "Borderline Personality Disorder." *Hospital and Community Psychiatry*, 40 (8), 815-819.

Haslam-Hopwood, G.T.G. (2003). The role of the primary clinician in the multidisciplinary team. *Bulletin of the Menninger Clinic*, 67, 5-17.

Horwitz, L., Gabbard, G., Allen, J., Freiswyk, S., Colson, D., Newsom, G. & Coyne, L. (1996). *Borderline personality disorders: Tailoring the psychotherapy to the patient.* Washington, DC: American Psychiatric Press.

Johnson, M. E. & Hauser, P. M. (2001). The practice of expert psychiatric nurses: Accompanying the patient to a calmer personal space." *Issues in Mental Health Nursing*, 22, 651-668.

Jones J., Lowe, T. & Ward, M. (2000). Psychiatric inpatients' experience of nursing observation. A pilot study. *Mental Health Care*, 4 (4), 125-129.

Jones, J., Ward, M., Wellman, N., Hall, J. & Lowe, T. (2000). Psychiatric inpatients' experience of nursing observation: United Kingdom perspective. *Journal of Psychosocial Nursing*, 38 (12), 10-12.

Laskowski, C. (2001). The CNS and the difficult patient. *Issues in Mental Health Nursing*, 22, 5-22.

Linehan, M. M., Comtois, K. A., Murray, A. M., Brown, M. Z., Gallop, R. J., Heard, H. L., Korslund, K. E., Tutek, D. A., Reynolds, S.K., & Lindenboim, N. (2006). Two-year randomized controlled trial and follow-up of dialectical behavior therapy vs. therapy by experts for suicidal behaviors and borderline personality disorder. *Archives of General Psychiatry*, 63 (7), 757-66.

Linehan, M. (1993) Cognitive behavioral treatment of borderline personality disorder. New York: Guilford Press.

Maslar, M. Personal communication. Feb. and Mar., 2007.

May, D. & Kelly, M. (1982) Chancers, pests and poor wee souls: Problems of legitimization in psychiatric nursing. *Sociology of Health and Illness*, 4, 279-301.

Munich, R. (2003). Efforts to preserve the mind in the contemporary hospital treatment. *Bulletin of the Menninger Clinic*, 67 (3), 167-186.

O'Brien, L. (1998). Inpatient Nursing Care of Patients with Borderline Personality Disorder: a review of the literature. *Australian/New Zealand Journal of Mental Health Nursing,* Dec., 7(4): 172-183.

Pavlovich-Danis, S. J. (2004). On the border-borderline personality disorder. *Nursing Spectrum*, 5 (3), 16-18.

Paris, J. (2004). Is hospitalization useful for suicidal patients with borderline personality disorder? *Journal of Personality Disorders*, 18 (3), 240-247.

Piccinino, S. (1990). The nursing care challenge: Borderline patients. *Journal of Psychosocial Nursing*, 28 (4), 22-27.

Pitula, C. & Cardell, R. (1996). Suicidal inpatients experience of constant observation. *Psychiatric Services*, 47 (6), 649-651.

Pollack, L. E. & Cramer, R. D. (2000). Problems of people hospitalized for bipolar disorder. *Issues in Mental Health Nursing*, 21, 765-768.

Rees, D. W. & Smith, S. D. (1991). Work stress in occupational therapists assessed by the occupational stress indicator. *British Journal of Occupational Therapy*, 54 (8), 289-294.

Rosenbluth, M. (1987). The inpatient treatment of the borderline personality disorder: A critical review and discussion of aftercare implications. *Canadian Journal of Psychiatry*, 32 (3), 228-37.

Severinson, E. & Hummelvoll, J. K. (2001). Factors influencing job satisfaction and ethical dilemmas in acute psychiatric care. *Nursing and Health Sciences*, 3, 81-90.

Smith, M. & Schultz, S. K. (2000). Managing perplexing patients. *Issues in Mental Health Nursing*, 26, 47-63.

Steiger, W. (1967). Managing difficult patients. *Psychosomatics*, 8 (6), 305-308.
Steiger. W. & Hirsh, H. (1965). The difficult patient in everyday medical practice. *Medical Clinics of North America*, 49 (5), 1449-1465.
Streicker, S. Personal communication, Feb. and Mar., 2007.
Swenson, C., Sanderson, C., & Dulit, R. (2001). The application of dialectical behavior therapy for patients with borderline personality disorder on inpatient units. *Behavioral Science and Medicine*, 72 (4), 307-24.
Vijay, N. R. & Links, P. S. (2007). New frontiers in the role of hospitalization for patients with personality disorders. *Current Psychiatry Reports*, 9 (1), 63-7.
Waldon, M. Personal Communication, Feb. and Mar., 2007.
Wong, N. (1983). Perspective on the difficult patient. *Bulletin of the Menninger Clinic*, 47 (2), 99-106.

doi:10.1300/J200v06n01_07

Borderline Personality Disorder and Adolescence

Alec L. Miller

Deborah Neft

Nira Golombeck

SUMMARY. This chapter addresses many of the potential challenges clinicians face when working with adolescents with BPD. First, we present the diagnostic issues related to an adolescent population. Second, we review issues related to the families, peers, and larger systems (e.g., schools) that reciprocally influence the adolescent and the treatment. Third, we discuss specific treatment concerns and propose solutions, including how to effectively manage therapists' own reactions to working with this population. Many of the clinical vignettes and suggested interventions in this chapter derive from our experience working in an outpatient adolescent Dialectical Behavior Therapy (DBT) program. As described later in this book, DBT is an evidence-based treatment effective for suicidal multi-problem individuals with promising data published with suicidal adolescents diagnosed with borderline features (Rathus & Miller, 2002). doi:10.1300/J200v06n01_08 *[Article copies available for a fee from The Haworth Document Delivery Service: 1-800-HAWORTH. E-mail address: <docdelivery@haworthpress.com> Website: <http://www. HaworthPress.com> © 2008 by The Haworth Press. All rights reserved.]*

[Haworth co-indexing entry note]: "Borderline Personality Disorder and Adolescence." Miller, Alec L., Deborah Neft, and Nira Golombeck. Co-published simultaneously in *Social Work in Mental Health* (The Haworth Press) Vol. 6, No. 1/2, 2008, pp. 85-98; and: *Borderline Personality Disorder: Meeting the Challenges to Successful Treatment* (ed: Perry D. Hoffman, and Penny Steiner-Grossman) The Haworth Press, 2008, pp. 85-98. Single or multiple copies of this article are available for a fee from The Haworth Document Delivery Service [1-800-HAWORTH, 9:00 a.m. - 5:00 p.m. (EST). E-mail address: docdelivery@haworthpress. com].

Available online at http://swmh.haworthpress.com
© 2008 by The Haworth Press. All rights reserved.
doi:10.1300/J200v06n01_08

KEYWORDS. Adolescence, multi-problem borderline personality disorder, dialectical behavior therapy

INTRODUCTION

Normal adolescence is a time of growth in physical, cognitive, social and emotional domains, each with characteristic challenges and changes. Puberty, increasing cognitive abilities, identity formation, social maturation, and struggles for autonomy are all part of normal adolescent development. For most adolescents, the difficulties faced are challenging but endurable. However, for those with borderline personality disorder, adolescence is an entirely different experience, one that feels increasingly intolerable and significantly impairs the quality of life for the adolescent and possibly for others close to him or her.

As with adults, adolescents with BPD have a cascading series of problems typically initiated by their inability to regulate emotions. These adolescents live with unstable emotions and frequently are unable to control their anger, sadness, anxiety, and shame. Feeling perpetually overwhelmed by emotions leaves them unable to identify specifically what they are feeling and thinking. Many of these teens feel more discouraged and empty than their peers, regardless of what skills and extracurricular activities they are proficient at. They are exquisitely interpersonally sensitive, often misinterpreting the rest of the world as not liking them. Consequently, their relationships with schoolteachers, parents, and peers suffer tremendously. Fears of abandonment by their few loved ones abound, frequently resulting in self-harm to prevent people from leaving. Both suicidal behavior and non-suicidal self-harm are often behavioral solutions to unwanted emotions. Other common "behavioral solutions" to their emotional swells include substance abuse, disordered eating, dissociation, and violent behaviors. Emotional, behavioral, interpersonal and self-dysregulation often adversely impact adolescents' cognitive capacities. Although intellectually intact, many of these emotionally vulnerable teens are unable to attend and concentrate in school and on their homework, resulting in impaired academic functioning. This often triggers the family to perceive them as "not trying hard enough" which causes more emotional dysregulation–and the cycle continues. Without treatment, many of these adolescents are at risk for worsening mental health issues, academic and social problems, as well as chronic self-injury and even suicide.

DIAGNOSTIC ISSUES

As a result of to the commonly held belief among mental health professionals that personality is still evolving during adolescence, there has been a reluctance to diagnose personality disorders in this age group. From our clinical experience, both on psychiatric inpatient units and outpatient clinics, many multi-problem adolescents meet criteria for a personality disorder but are diagnosed and treated only for Axis I disorders. When Axis II criteria are ignored, many adolescents may not receive specific treatment for their dysfunctional behaviors, or worse, receive inappropriate treatments. These oversights could exacerbate serious problems, including suicidality, delinquency, academic failure, social dysfunction, and substance abuse (Kernberg, Weiner, & Bardenstein, 2000). Once engrained, these behaviors are more difficult to treat later in life, and their long-term consequences can be devastating.

Regarding the "age debate," the DSM-IV-TR states that "Personality disorder categories may be applied to children or adolescents in those relatively unusual instances in which the individual's particular maladaptive personality traits appear to be pervasive, persistent, and unlikely to be limited to a particular developmental stage or an episode of an Axis I disorder . . . To diagnose a personality disorder in an individual under 18 years of age, the features must have been present for at least one year" (APA, 2000, p. 687). The critical elements of this definition are that the identified BPD behaviors are severe enough such that the behavioral manifestations persistently interfere with an adolescent's daily functioning over the course of one year or longer. Assuming a comprehensive clinical assessment is conducted, the DSM-IV definition permits the diagnosis of BPD for adolescents; however, it does remain vague, leaving much to clinical judgment.

Given the clinical nature of this chapter, we will not provide a thorough review of the empirical literature highlighting the support for the existence of BPD in adolescents. In sum, however, a recent review by Miller, Muehlenkamp, and Jacobson and found that the prevalence, reliability, and validity of BPD in adolescent samples are adequate and largely comparable to those found among adults. This comparability alone may suggest that BPD operates in a similar fashion and has a similar course regardless of age and developmental period. Studies also indicate clearly that while there is a legitimate subgroup of severely affected adolescents for whom the diagnosis remains stable over time, there appears to be a less severe subgroup that moves in and out of the diagnosis. Thus, the rate of diagnostic stability of BPD in adolescents is comparable to that of adults, and a select few symptom criteria have consistently emerged as significant predictors of BPD retention. Consequently, one implication is that it may be beneficial to conceptualize personality disorders in adolescents using a dimensional/continuous rather than categorical approach, since a dimensional approach may account for the developmental variability and the heterogeneity found among adolescents.

We strongly believe that mental health practitioners should formally assess for personality disorders, both categorically and continuously, when working with adolescents. Regardless of the presence of a full-fledged disorder, symptoms of BPD in adolescents, even if fewer than five, may accurately reflect significant distress and dysfunction (e.g., suicidality, self-cutting, identity disturbance, academic failure, social dysfunction, and substance abuse) that requires intervention. By considering the diagnosis of BPD, many more adolescents may receive appropriate treatment for their BPD symptoms, and hopefully fewer will develop an ingrained and refractory pattern of dysfunctional behaviors.

CHALLENGES IN TREATING THE ADOLESCENT WITH BPD

In contrast to treating adults, mental health professionals working with adolescents typically need involve the adolescents' family, their peers, and the larger systems within which the adolescent is engaged.

Interacting with Families

Adolescents with BPD often have relatives with emotional problems. A recent study conducted by Bradley, Jenei, and Westen (2005) found that a negative childhood family environment (i.e., unstable, low warmth), as well as parental psychopathology and a history of childhood abuse, all predict the diagnosis of BPD. Teenagers with BPD often grow up in environments that tend to be reciprocally invalidating (Linehan, 1993). It is important to note, however, that some teens with BPD hail from "ordinary" families that may not start as invalidating, but become inadvertently invalidating and desperate over time due to the "poorness of fit" between the child's and the parents' temperaments. A seemingly benign example might be a hyperactive five year-old boy poorly matched in temperament with a mother who is subdued and likes things slow and quiet. Over time, the child's behavior may exacerbate the en-

vironment just as the environment may exacerbate the individual's behavior.

Clinicians working with adolescents face the added challenge of simultaneously attempting to involve and treat the family members who
may have their own share of emotional dysregulation, despair, anxiety,
and even burnout. They will need to strike a balance between treating
both the adolescent and his/her family without becoming the individual
therapist for other family members. We encourage clinicians to spend
time with parents individually and in family sessions to achieve several
functions: (1) to teach them positive parenting strategies (e.g., how to
provide positive reinforcement and effective punishment); (2) to provide the parents with considerable validation of how difficult it is for
them as well as for their adolescent (e.g., "I know you are both doing the
best you can in this moment, and despite your best efforts, things are not
going as you'd like them to go . . . and that is extremely frustrating"); (3)
to offer appropriate praise for their efforts (e.g., "I really appreciate
your efforts in therapy, and I believe it will help your daughter in the
long run"); and (4) to help with case management issues (e.g., school
enrollment, health insurance applications). Again, one challenging aspect of achieving these functions is to avoid becoming the parents' therapist and to offer them referrals if they need their own therapy. In order
for the therapeutic alliance with the adolescent to be preserved, it is important for the clinician to reassure the parents in words and actions that
his or her primary clinical responsibility is to the adolescent. Typically,
we suggest that clinicians resist the urge to meet alone with family
members. When family sessions are indicated, it is best to meet first
with the adolescent alone, and to bring the parent in for the second half
of the session or to have the entire family present for the whole session. This is an effective method for strengthening the alliance with the
adolescent, while keeping contact with the parent in a structured manner. Confidentiality parameters need to be reviewed on a regular basis.

Another frequent therapeutic challenge that arises with families is the
ineffective and often negative communication style between the adolescent and their primary caretakers. As the literature suggests, many of
our adolescent clients and their families engage in invalidating interactions. Many of our patients report that their feelings, thoughts, and
behaviors are often not understood and/or are discounted by family
members, teachers, (sometimes therapists), and other important persons
in their lives. This invalidation may be obvious and direct (e.g., "You
have no reason to be upset, why can't you just snap out of it?") or seemingly benign and meant with the best intentions (e.g., "You're young

and they'll be other fish in the sea, so don't worry about him."). One of the consequences of experiencing pervasive invalidation over time is that the individual is likely to internalize the invalidating comments (e.g., "I am so stupid," or "I shouldn't get so upset about this."). Some of the long-term consequences of self-invalidation are feeling unsure of what one is feeling or thinking in the moment, lacking confidence in one's own judgment, having trouble setting realistic expectations and goals for oneself, and often thinking in depressive and punitive ways about oneself. Sadly, in a reciprocal fashion, some families become more emotionally dysregulated, self-invalidating, and doubt their own capacity to function effectively as caretakers.

Learning how to validate others and oneself is one of the hardest skills both for adolescents and parents to acquire and, therefore, a difficult task for the therapist. Many families in crisis come to therapy sessions wanting to start solving problems immediately, and they embark on a laundry list of things that need to be "fixed." Therapists need to resist the urge to dive into solving family problems until all parties involved are taught how to validate one another effectively. Once validation is taught and practiced in session, then problem solving can begin. One of the authors (DN) can remember a teenager and her mother effectively validating each other's feelings in session (e.g., Mother: "I understand that you really want to go to this party, yet I worry about your safety." Adolescent: "I get that you're worried about me, Mom, though I'll be fine at the party and promise to be home early."). Later that night the therapist was paged by the adolescent who was emotionally dysregulated and about to engage in self-harm due to a conflict she had with her mother over the same issue that was riddled with invalidating statements (e.g., Mother: "You'd have to be crazy to want to go to this party–there's no way I'm letting you go!" Adolescent: "You don't care about me at all and never let me do anything!"). This example illustrates that emotions can quickly inhibit the use of effective validation skills, and that other treatment strategies need to be used during these episodes. In fact, many of the adolescents and their parents *can* improve their communication style over time with a lot of skills training, coaching and practice of validation.

Interaction with Peers

While there are many potential peer-related issues to discuss, one of the most common and problematic is that of contagion and copycat behavior among teens who self-harm. The adolescents in our outpatient program often seek ideas on how to reduce their isolation, fit in with their peers, and decrease their negative feeling states. As a result, they are especially susceptible to a phenomenon known as social or behavioral contagion. Contagion can be defined as bursts of self-injury among several people that occur successively within a statistically significant period of time (Walsh, 2006). The majority of our self-harming patients have friendship circles made up of other teenagers who cut and contemplate suicide. In fact, we sometimes receive multiple referrals from the same school counselor reporting what seems to be a "cutting epidemic" in school. Contagion episodes are thought to develop as a way for adolescents to communicate distress, to punish others, or to bring about action (Walsh, 2006). Cutting may also be learned by imitation or modeling. Our patients often say that they first contemplated cutting themselves because "I saw it in a movie" or "I saw my friend do it." The question then becomes: How can we offer our patients alternative ways of dealing with problems when they are regularly exposed to ineffective coping models?

As part of our DBT skill-building treatment program, we have clear rules forbidding adolescents from describing any specific details of their self-injurious behaviors in front of other teenagers; rather, we encourage such discussions in individual therapy settings. Our rationale is consistent with research suggesting that contagion is exacerbated by description of self-injurious methods, discussion of positive feeling states while injuring, and other graphic portrayals (Gould, Jamieson, & Romer, 2003; Jamieson, Hall Jamieson, & Romer, 2003; Whitlock, Powers, & Eckenrode, 2006). By monitoring the details of disclosure in public settings, we help prevent romanticizing, reinforcing, or encouraging self-injury. Further, we seek to behaviorally reinforce more adaptive coping styles and educate family members, teachers, and school counselors on how to do the same.

Systems (Schools, Healthcare, etc.)

Beyond individual, family and group therapy, case management may become a critical component of the treatment, especially when working with adolescents diagnosed with BPD. Often, multiple agencies and systems are involved in the lives of these adolescents because of the high-risk nature of their behaviors, the potentially dysfunctional environments in which they live, and the likelihood of co-morbid mental, medical and academic problems beyond the BPD diagnosis. Therefore, it is important and helpful to be in regular contact with all of the relevant parties in these systems (e.g., school administrators, teachers, pediatricians, intensive case managers, and child protective services caseworkers) in order to be able to obtain and provide information about academic problems, high-risk behaviors (e.g., suicidal ideation, self-harm, drug use, risky sexual behavior, restricted eating), and plans for behavioral emergencies. One of the challenges of maintaining communication with these outside parties is the preservation of the therapeutic alliance with the adolescent, as well as with the family members, particularly around issues of confidentiality.

In the first therapy session with an adolescent and family, clinicians should emphasize the importance of maintaining confidentiality between the therapist and the adolescent. At the same time, however, teens are told that confidentiality will be broken if crises arise that suggest they may do something imminently dangerous or life threatening to themselves or someone else. Moreover, efforts are always made to include the adolescent in discussions of emergency planning with other agencies. For issues that are less crisis-oriented and are more typical of case management (e.g., applying to a GED program, getting health insurance, etc.), or behavioral plans to enhance attendance at school, we try to balance direct consultation with other agencies with encouragement of the adolescents to communicate directly with the agencies. This provides the adolescent an opportunity to practice interpersonal skills, as well as to learn how to advocate for him or herself and to build a sense of self-efficacy and accomplishment.

As a consequence of the high frequency of sexual and physical abuse and neglect reported by adolescents with BPD, clinicians may find it necessary to enlist state child protective agencies in order to adhere to their state laws regarding child protection. These agencies are sometimes, but not always, helpful in intervening with adolescents and families. Although every attempt is made to continue to preserve the therapeutic relationship with both the adolescent and the family, when an allegation of abuse or neglect is reported, the clinician is often fraught with anxiety about their reactions. In addition, the adolescent is often afraid of being removed from the home and feels guilty about getting a family member "in trouble." In our experience, the adolescents and their families are often able to re-engage in treatment with the same therapist who reported the incident, and trust is often re-established. It is helpful to remind the adolescent (and for each therapist to remind him or herself) that, above all, the job of the therapist is to act in the patient's best interest while also following state law.

TREATMENT CONCERNS AND PROPOSED SOLUTIONS IN WORKING WITH ADOLESCENTS WITH BPD

Adolescents in general are a challenging population to engage and retain in treatment. Studies have found rates of dropout among adolescent outpatient samples ranging from 33% to 77% (Armbruster & Fallon, 1994; Dierker et al., 2001; Trautman, Stewart, & Morishima, 1993). It remains unclear exactly which factors contribute most to these alarming statistics. Likely contributors are the lack of self-referral, the reliance on family members to attend treatment, and the stigma associated with treatment among their peers. In addition, the severity of the psychopathology may influence the noncompliance of adolescent patients. Teenagers diagnosed with BPD who often have numerous coexisting problems, including suicidal and self-injurious behaviors, and whose families are also crisis-driven, are particularly difficult to engage and sustain in treatment. However, Dialectical Behavior Therapy (DBT) with its numerous commitment strategies outlined in the treatment protocol, is uniquely effective at engaging these patients in treatment (Linehan, 1993). For example, if a patient is late or non-compliant with therapy homework, the therapist enlists the patient in a behavioral analysis to establish the reason for this behavior, its consequences, and the solutions that may discourage this behavior in the future.

ENLISTING FAMILIES IN THE THERAPY

Numerous studies have demonstrated the importance of parental involvement in and attitudes towards therapy in increasing treatment compliance and effectiveness among adolescent patients (Hawley & Weisz, 2005; Morrissey-Kane & Prinz, 1999; Nevas & Farber, 2001). The very same DBT commitment strategies used with teens are also employed with their family members in an effort to "get a foot in the door" and strengthen their motivation and commitment to participate in treatment (Miller, Rathus, & Linehan, 2007. Family therapy sessions are intended to generate support for all members, strengthen and generalize a range of behavioral skills, and solve family problems. Another modality of treatment intended to engage family members is the multi-family skills training group. The primary function of this group is for the adolescent to acquire and strengthen a new set of behavioral skills. A secondary function of the group is for the family members to acquire and strengthen the same set of skills and to have the adolescent and family share the same therapeutic experience and language.

The skills taught in DBT correspond directly to Linehan's reorganization of DSM-IV BPD symptoms (Linehan, 1993a). According to this reorganization, the symptoms fall into areas of dysregualtion across five domains (Miller et al., 2007). The areas of dysfunction and the corresponding skill modules follow:

Problem Areas	Skills Modules
1) Self Dysregulation	Core Mindfulness Skills
2) Interpersonal Dysregulation	Interpersonal Effectiveness Skills
3) Behavioral and Cognitive Dysregulation	Distress Tolerance Skills
4) Emotional Dysregulation	Emotion Regulation Skills
5) Adolescent-Family Dilemmas	Walking the Middle Path Skills

The first four skills modules are described elsewhere (Linehan, 1993b). The fifth module, "Walking the Middle Path," was developed specifically for teens and family members to address all of their non-balanced thinking and behavior. These skills involve learning about principles of behavior change, validation, and finding the middle path between common dialectical dilemmas in these families. Adolescents with BPD, along with their parents and therapists, commonly vacillate and become polarized along various dimensions, including three prominent dimensions common among our population: (1) excessive leniency versus authoritarian control; (2) pathologizing normative behaviors, versus normalizing pathological behaviors; and (3) fostering dependency, versus forcing autonomy (Miller, Rathus & Linehan, 2007). These dilemmas taught in the group are further discussed in family sessions to assist parents and teens in changing their extreme behavioral patterns into a more balanced lifestyle.

Just as teens are instructed to call their therapists for coaching when in distress between sessions, family members in the multi-family skills group are instructed to call the skills group leaders for telephone consultation for purposes of skills generalization.

THE THERAPISTS' OWN REACTIONS

Some of the largest potential obstacles in working effectively with this population are the attitudes and beliefs held by inexperienced, naïve, poorly trained, or burned-out therapists and their supervisors,

and programs providing the actual treatment. "Refer out" is a common response when we ask the question, "How do you treat an adolescent with
borderline personality disorder?" This reluctance to treat BPD adolescents may stem from some therapists' pejorative attitudes toward persons
with a BPD diagnosis; they may think of them as angry, out of control,
manipulative, and unresponsive to treatment. Other therapists have strong
feelings of incompetence in treating these patients given the emotional
dysregulation and high-risk behaviors that commonly occur among this
population. Looking back after years of working with BPD adolescents,
one of the authors (NG) can still remember her first reactions:

> *I did not sleep during my first month working as a therapist at the
> Adolescent Outpatient DBT Program. I often sat awake at night,
> with my pager strategically placed under my pillow to assure that I
> would not miss a call, should it come. The way I saw it, I had just
> become a caretaker to several self-injuring, high suicide-risk,
> multi-problem teens and had little-or-no treatment experience up
> to that point. Needless to say, I was terrified. I feared that my pa-
> tients would cut themselves despite their commitment not to; I
> feared that they would page me and I would not be able to help
> them; or worse yet – that they would not call for my assistance and
> that they would kill themselves in a bout of emotional pain. I re-
> member the concern and disappointment I experienced in learning
> that one of my patients cut herself again, as well as the guilt I felt
> for not having been able to prevent it. I can also recall tremendous
> frustration when I felt as if I was working from crisis to crisis, with
> my work and home-life disrupted by calls to and from my patient's
> family members, school counselors, child protection workers, and
> hospital personnel. I felt irritation and sometimes full-blown an-
> ger at family members who did not follow through with the teen-
> ager's appointments, at entire systems that did not protect the
> child from further danger, and at the patient for placing herself in
> harm's way. There were times when I felt isolated when acting in
> the best interest of my patient elicited objections by her, her family
> members, and other important system workers. I was horrified
> when I learned that though my patient had denied cutting herself,
> she had in fact been self-injuring for two weeks. After all, she was
> an outpatient and our work together was based on trust.*

These reactions are documented here in order to validate the feelings
of clinicians who are just beginning their work with borderline adoles-

cents. Working with teenagers who are prone to intense emotional reactivity, and who engage in a range of high-risk behaviors including suicide attempts, cutting, eating disorders, risky sex, or drug use, can certainly cause apprehension. After all, there is a lot at stake. The added complexities of adolescence, characterized by parent-child struggles over independence, can often exacerbate the problems. These factors contribute to the aversive reactions we see repeatedly from those who are treating adolescents with BPD. Clinician responses are emotional (e.g., anger, fear, burn-out), physiological (e.g., racing heart, sweating, fatigue), cognitive (e.g., "She's going to kill herself and it will be my fault for not having helped her."), and behavioral (e.g., coming late to or canceling sessions, avoiding returning phone calls, abandoning the patient) (Walsh, 2006). There are, however, various strategies to use when working with adolescents with BPD that can help reduce negative feelings, improve attitudes, and counter the therapists' therapy-interfering behaviors. Use of these strategies can further treatment efficacy and enhance both therapists' and patients' quality of life.

First, every clinician needs a support system. It is essential to assemble a strong team of clinicians to whom the therapist can turn with questions, grievances, and problems. Within the framework of DBT, we provide weekly emotional support and supervision to therapists in team meetings. The function of these meetings is to treat the therapist so that he or she can help the teenager and the family. Just as we try to encourage our teenagers to seek out social support and positive influences, so too do we encourage our colleagues to seek out similar assistance. In this way, we aim to reduce feelings of isolation and despair and increase feelings of hopefulness and confidence.

The biosocial theory (Linehan, 1993) of the patient's problems is another aspect of DBT that aims to decrease therapist burnout and improve relationships between therapists, patients, and families. Concept- ualizing the family's problems as a result of the transaction between the teen's biological emotional vulnerabilities and an environment that may be exacerbating these problems can foster an atmosphere of acceptance and understanding. This theory promotes effective compassion and a non-judgmental stance among therapists toward the adolescents and family members with whom they work. Assuming that our patients, their family members, school personnel, other systems workers, and even we as therapists, are doing the best we can at any given moment, enables us to think and act in ways that foster better rapport and promote healthier therapeutic responses. We also encourage therapists to use many of the skills and other DBT strategies that we teach our patients and their families: using self-soothing and distraction skills in times of distress; formulating plans based on the realities of situations rather than on situations we would have wished for; generating alternative ideas to replace some of our more distorted thoughts; reaching compromises rather than digging in our heels; and learning to tolerate and even accept negative emotions. These are some of the many strategies that can be used when treating this population.

Recently, a patient walked into one author's office (NG) and exclaimed, "I'm angry at you, I don't want to be here, and I'm not telling you why." Even after years of experience and training, her immediate reactions have not changed. She continues to be aware of some feelings of fear and frustration. The difference now is that her initial anxious and frustrated reactions are tempered by hope, self-efficacy, and an assortment of skills. She has better means to manage her anxiety and to act wisely in difficult situations. Having the tools and support necessary to address challenging situations can help make the treatment of adolescents with BPD more rewarding and can foster a more positive treatment outlook for patients and therapists alike.

REASONS FOR HOPE

Clinicians who provide treatment for adolescents with BPD and their families need to be formally educated and supervised with the most up-to-date treatment research and techniques for this population. Based on pilot data and our clinical experience (Miller et al., 2007), we believe that DBT offers enormous hope. The plight of the borderline adolescent needs to be understood within the framework of family, school, peers, and various other systems. An empathic stance that considers these adolescents' emotions and behaviors within the context of their biological make-up and their environments is essential. The more skillfully a clinician can assess the adolescent with BPD, conceptualize the case, and relate to the teenager and family, the more effective the therapeutic process will be. We urge all clinicians who work with this population to obtain training and supervision in DBT, which is a promising comprehensive treatment approach for adolescents with borderline personality disorder. Information regarding training opportunities can be obtained from www.behavioraltech.com and the National Education Alliance for Borderline Personality Disorder (NEA-BPD).

REFERENCES

American Psychiatric Association. (2000). *Diagnostic and statistical manual of mental disorders, Fourth Edition, Text Revision.* Washington, DC: American Psychiatric Association.

Armbruster, P. & Fallon, T. (1994). Clinical, sociodemographic, and systems risk factors for attrition in a children's mental health clinic. *American Journal of Orthopsychiatry,* 64, 577-585.

Bradley, R., Jenei, J., and Westen, D. (2005). Etiology of borderline personality disorder: Disentangling the contributions of intercorrelated antecedents. *The Journal of Nervous and Mental Disease,* 193 (1), 24-31.

Dierker, L., Nargiso, J., Wiseman, R., & Hoff, D. (2001). Factors predicting attrition within a community initiated system of care. *Journal of Child and Family Studies,* 10, 367-383.

Gould, M., Jamieson, P., & Romer, D. (2003). Media contagion and suicide among the young. *American Behavioral Scientist,* 46, 1269-1284.

Hawley, K. M. & Weisz, J. R. (2005). Youth versus parent working alliance in usual clinical care: Distinctive associations with retention, satisfaction, and treatment outcome. *Journal of Clinical Child and Adolescent Psychology,* 34 (1), 117-128.

Jamieson, P., Hall Jamieson, K., & Romer, D. (2003). The responsible reporting of suicide in print journalism. *American Behavioral Scientist,* 46, 1643-1660.

Kernberg, P. F., Weiner, A. S., & Bardenstein, K. K. (2000). *Personality Disorders in Children and Adolescents.* New York: Basic Books.

Miller, A. L., Rathus, J. H., & Linehan, M. M. (2007). Dialectical behavior therapy with suicidal adolescents. New York: Guilford Press.

Miller, A. L., Muehlenkamp, J. J., & Jacobson, C. M. (Under review). A review of borderline personality disorder in adolescents.

Morrissey-Kane, E. & Prinz, R. J. (1999). Engagement in child and adolescent treatment: The role of parental cognitions and attributions. *Clinical Child and Family Psychology Review,* 2 (3), 183-198.

Nevas, D. B. & Farber, B.A. (2002). Parents' attitudes toward their child's therapist and therapy. *Professional Psychology: Research and Practice,* 32 (2), 165-170.

Rathus, J. H. & Miller, A. L. (2002). Dialectical behavior therapy adapted for suicidal adolescents. *Suicide and Life-Threatening Behaviors,* 32 (2), 146-157.

Trautman, P. D., Stewart, N., & Morishima, A. (1993). Are adolescent suicide attempters noncompliant with outpatient care? *Journal of the American Academy of Child and Adolescent Psychiatry,* 32, 89-94.

Walsh, B. (2006). *Treating self-injury: A practical guide.* New York: Guilford Press.

White, C. N., Gunderson, J. G., Zanarini, M. C., & Hudson, J. I. (2003). Family studies of borderline personality disorder: A review. *Harvard Review of Psychiatry,* 11 (1), 8-19.

Whitlock, J. L., Powers, J. L., & Eckenrode, J. (2006). The virtual cutting edge: The internet and adolescent self-injury. *Developmental Psychology,* 42, 1-11.

doi:10.1300/J200v06n01_08

An Evidence-Based Approach to Managing Suicidal Behavior in Patients with BPD

Joel Paris

SUMMARY. This review will suggest an evidence-based approach to managing suicidal patients with borderline personality disorder (BPD). Many principles currently used in practice have little basis in empirical data. And some approaches used to manage chronic suicidality, particularly the emphasis on "safety," may actually be counter-productive. doi:10.1300/J200v06n01_09 *[Article copies available for a fee from The Haworth Document Delivery Service: 1-800-HAWORTH. E-mail address: <docdelivery@ haworthpress.com> Website: <http://www.HaworthPress.com> © 2008 by The Haworth Press. All rights reserved.]*

KEYWORDS. Suicidality, borderline personality disorder, personality disorders

SUICIDAL BEHAVIORS IN BPD

Patients with BPD make multiple suicide attempts, gestures, and threats (Soloff et al., 2000). These behaviors are often brought on by a breach in an intimate relationship (Gunderson, 2001). The most common scenario is an impulsive but non-lethal overdose, carried out in circumstances in which rescue is likely. Self-mutilation, particularly

[Haworth co-indexing entry note]: "An Evidence-Based Approach to Managing Suicidal Behavior in Patients with BPD." Paris, Joel. Co-published simultaneously in *Social Work in Mental Health* (The Haworth Press) Vol. 6, No. 1/2, 2008, pp. 99-108; and: *Borderline Personality Disorder: Meeting the Challenges to Successful Treatment* (ed: Perry D. Hoffman, and Penny Steiner-Grossman) The Haworth Press, 2008, pp. 99-108. Single or multiple copies of this article are available for a fee from The Haworth Document Delivery Service [1-800-HAWORTH, 9:00 a.m. - 5:00 p.m. (EST). E-mail address: docdelivery@haworthpress.com].

Available online at http://swmh.haworthpress.com
© 2008 by The Haworth Press. All rights reserved.
doi:10.1300/J200v06n01_09

wrist-cutting, is also common in BPD (Gerson & Stanley, 2002), but this is not suicidal behavior. Cutting has a different purpose from an overdose; instead of providing escape from a difficult situation, cutting functions as a means of regulating dysphoric affects (Leibenluft et al., 1987; Brown et al., 2003), and can take on some of the characteristics of an addiction (Linehan, 1993).

The term "suicidal," used often in practice, is ambiguous. It can refer to people who think about suicide, to attempters with low intent, to self-cutters who have no real suicidal intent, or to people who make life-threatening attempts. In most cases, clinicians use the term to describe patients who are troubled enough to consider ending their lives. But these thoughts have little value for predicting completion. The reason is that suicidal ideation is common, while suicidal attempts are much less so, and completed suicide is quite a rare event (Paris, 2006).

We also need to distinguish between acute suicidality, in which patients suffer from an acute mental illness (such as melancholic depression) that drives temporarily intense suicidal intentions, vs. chronic suicidality, in which patients consider (and/or attempt) suicide over many years. Some of the diagnoses associated with acute suicidality respond to treatment interventions (such as drugs and electroconvulsive therapy) that can be usefully carried out in a hospital. In contrast, chronic suicidality, in which patients consider suicide as an option over years, and make multiple attempts, requires a completely different strategy.

The mantra of "safety" has been used to describe a need to prevent patients from harming themselves. However, there is little evidence that we know how to make patients safe. Every mental health clinician is taught to prevent suicide in patients who think about killing themselves or make attempts. But we cannot prevent events we cannot predict. Moreover, treating chronically suicidal patients as if they were always in danger reinforces cycles of repeated emergency room visits and hospitalizations that are unproductive and interfere with therapy. Management of these patients has been impaired by a focus on preventing suicide.

SUICIDE PREVENTION AND SUICIDE COMPLETION

It has never been shown that prevention of suicide in patients with chronic ideation is possible. It is also very difficult to predict who will complete suicide, even for acutely suicidal cases. While patients who make repeated attempts are statistically more at risk for completion (Zahl & Hawton, 2004), only a minority will actually end their lives (Goldney, 2000).

Suicide attempters and completers are, by and large, two different populations (Beautrais, 2001). While about one in 20 people make a suicide attempt sometime during their life, the overall ratio of attempts to completions is about 1/500 (Welch, 2001). Moreover, completers tend to be older, male, use more lethal methods, and to die on the first attempt; attempters tend to be younger, female, use less lethal methods, and to survive (Maris et al., 2000).

Attempts to predict completed suicide in individuals within clinical populations have been unsuccessful. Two large-scale studies (Goldstein et al., 1991; Pokorny et al., 1983) followed populations of patients admitted to hospital to determine who eventually completed suicide. The researchers applied algorithims based on established risk factors in the literature, but failed to predict any individual case of suicide.

Many risk factors (psychiatric diagnosis, previous attempts, lack of social supports) have a statistical relationship to completion (Maris et al., 2000), but none of them helps us to identify particular patients at risk. Again, completed suicide is a rare event, and algorithims based on these risk factors produce a large number of false positives. For this reason they are not clinically useful.

FOLLOW-UP STUDIES OF SUICIDE IN BPD

Long-term follow-up studies of patients with BPD have yielded important findings as how often, and even more important, *when* suicide completion takes place. Statistically significant relationships with standard risk factors have been found, such as substance abuse (Stone, 1990) and previous attempts (Paris et al., 1989). However, given the number of false positives, this information could not have been used in any practical way to predict completion in individual patients.

As for when suicide occurs, in a 15-year follow-up of patients with BPD, Stone (1990) found that the mean age at completion was 30. In a 27-year old follow-up study (Paris & Zweig-Frank, 2001), the mean age at suicide was 37, with a standard deviation of 10. Thus, few completions occur at the point when patients are most threatening in their suicidality, i.e., when they are in their 20s. Instead, suicide occurs later in the course of illness, generally in patients who have undergone a series of unsuccessful treatments (Paris, 2002). Thus, while most patients with severe personality disorders improve over time (Paris, 2003; Zanarini et al., 2002), suicide completion will occur in those who have failed to recover from their condition. The practical implication is that the patients who are most at risk for killing themselves constitute a group that differs in important ways from those who present in emergency rooms and clinics with threats and attempts.

IS THERE ANY VALUE TO HOSPITALIZATION?

Admission to a hospital ward has been the traditional approach to suicide prevention. The American Psychiatric Association Guidelines for the Treatment of Borderline Personality disorder (Oldham et al., 2002) offer hospitalization as a recourse but present no evidence base for this recommendation. Nonetheless, hospitalization is common in patients with BPD. The most important driver is that in an emergency setting, psychiatrists worry that patients may commit suicide if sent home. Ironically, that sequence of events has never been documented. And in nearly 40 years of practice, I cannot identify a single case where a patient with BPD killed him/herself after being sent home from an emergency room.

The rationale for hospital admission is based on the concept that suicidal patients require "safety." But in what way is the hospital environment truly "safe?" Suicide is far from impossible on a ward, and some patients (with psychosis or melancholia) will kill themselves in spite of all precautions. Moreover, in patients with BPD, hospital wards tend to reinforce the very behavior they attempt to control. The more the patient threatens suicide, the more attention the staff provides, and the longer is the stay in hospital. Patients who are afraid of discharge, having to return to a difficult life on the outside, only need to report increased suicidality in order to delay discharge. In spite of nursing procedures designed to reduce risk, such as removing sharp objects from the patient's possession, wrist-slashing tends to escalate on a ward. This pattern can also lead to repeated hospitalizations (Paris, 2002), and some patients become worse when admitted (Dawson & MacMillan, 1995). Linehan (2003) has suggested wryly that if a patient must be hospitalized, the ward environment should be made as unpleasant as possible.

A patient who recovered from BPD (Williams, 1998) published a brief article in *Psychiatric Services* describing how repetitive hospital admissions made her worse: "Do not hospitalize a person with borderline personality disorder for more than 48 hours. My self-destructive episodes–one leading right into another–came out only after my first and subsequent hospital admissions, and after I learned the system was usually obligated to respond." She went on to say, "When you as a service provider do not give the expected response to these threats, you'll be accused of not caring. What you are really doing is being cruel to be kind. When my doctor wouldn't hospitalize me, I accused him of not caring if I lived or died. He replied, referring to a cycle of repeated hospitalizations, 'That's not life.' And he was 100% right!" (Williams, 1998, p. 174). Many experts on the treatment of personality disorders (Linehan, 1993; Kernberg, 1997; Paris, 2002; Livesley, 2003; Gunderson, 2003) agree with her views. It has even been suggested that one of the few benefits of managed care in the United States is to discourage admissions of patients with severe personality disorders.

Another reason for hospitalizing patients is the therapist's fear of litigation if a suicide should occur. However, as Gutheil (1992) has pointed out, clinicians who choose not to hospitalize patients can adequately protect themselves by keeping careful records documenting the reasons for their decision, by obtaining consultations, and by involving the family in the treatment plan.

We need to sort out rational and irrational reasons for admission. The most common reasons why patients with BPD are hospitalized are psychotic episodes, serious suicide attempts, suicidal threats, and self-mutilation (Hull et al., 1996). In a brief psychosis, one can at least provide specific treatment (neuroleptic medication) to control symptoms. The hospitalization of a patient after a life-threatening suicide attempt may also have some value; even if no active treatment is conducted in hospital, a brief admission can provide an opportunity to assess precipitating factors and review treatment plans. The purpose of hospitalization is less clear for suicidal threats, minor overdoses, or self-mutilation. There is no specific treatment to offer on the ward that cannot be provided in another context. Often, the patient is only monitored and observed. And since outside life is interrupted, patients have no opportunity to learn or practice behavioral skills.

Hospitalization has also been used to carry out specialized forms of psychotherapy for patients with severe personality disorders (Kernberg, 1987). This approach died out with the advent of managed care, although it is still used in Europe, where there are fewer restrictions on the expense of a hospital stay. The concept is to provide more intensive therapy in a controlled environment.

However, the utility of using full hospitalization to carry out specialized psychotherapy has not been demonstrated. Such interventions can equally be carried out in day hospitals, as has been shown by several groups (Bateman & Fonagy, 1999, Piper et al., 1999; Chiesa et al., 2002). Day hospitals have all the advantages of a ward (opportunity for intensive management within a structured environment) without the disadvantages of full admission (regression in patients who are cut off from their ordinary life during the course of the hospitalization). And patients may have a better outcome if a brief hospitalization is followed by a period of day treatment (Chiesa et al., 2002).

Thus, day treatment offers an evidence-based alternative to hospital admission. The main problem is that day hospitals tend to have waiting lists and are therefore hard to access. Moreover, many locations lack this option. This is unfortunate, given the evidence base for the effectiveness of day treatment, first developed more than 60 years ago. Many psychiatrists also are dependent on hospital beds because specialized outpatient clinics are either unavailable or have long waiting lists.

CHRONIC SUICIDALITY

When patients are chronically suicidal, sometimes for years on end, we need to apply a different set of therapeutic principles than those applied to depressed patients who do not have personality disorders (Schwartz et al., 1974; Fine & Sansone, 1990; Paris, 2002b).

Kernberg (1984) suggests that chronic suicidality requires patience rather than action. He notes (1984, p. 261) that he might state he "would feel sad but not responsible if the patient killed himself," but would avoid unusual measures to prevent completion, and would routinely inform the family of his management plan. This rationale is similar to that of Rachlin (1984), who pointed out that attempts to save lives in suicidal patients may only succeed in depriving patients of their quality of life.

Clearly, it is difficult to conduct effective therapy in a situation of constant turmoil. An excessive focus on an illusory goal of suicide prevention actually prevents therapists from doing their job. When clinicians feel forced to do almost anything to prevent completion, the therapeutic relationship becomes characterized by "coercive bondage" (Hendin, 1981), in which the patient controls the behavior of the therapist, and the quality of the patient's life becomes compromised by this concern.

Ultimately, treatment has to help patients deal with real life issues. When clinicians spend too much time worrying about suicide completion, this process becomes derailed. Maltsberger (1994) has described the acceptance of chronic suicidality as a "calculated risk," although we do not really know whether a significant risk is involved. In any case, therapists should focus less on responding to threats and more on understanding the distress that lies behind them, while refocusing the patient to work on resolving life problems.

AN APPROACH TO THE MANAGEMENT OF SUICIDALITY IN BPD

There is evidence for the efficacy of Dialectical Behavior Therapy (DBT) (Linehan, 1993), and Mentalization-Based Treatment (MBT) (Bateman & Fonagy, 2004) in BPD. Both are effective in reducing both self-mutilation and suicide attempts. DBT is conducted in an outpatient setting and Linehan (1993) has specifically advised against hospitalization. MBT, which was originally tested in a day hospital setting, has recently undergone trials in outpatient clinics (Fonagy, 2004). Other psychotherapeutic methods, including schema therapy (Young, 2002) and Transference-Focused Psychotherapy (TFP) (Clarkin et al., 2003) are also undergoing clinical trials in outpatient settings.

The approach recommended here is consistent with the concepts behind these evidence-based approaches, as well as with the views of other experienced therapists (Kernberg, 1997; Livesley, 2003; Gunderson, 2003). The key principle is to maintain the overall structure of treatment, even in the face of suicidal threats. The reason is that psychotherapy needs to provide a predictable structure for these patients. No matter how strongly that structure is challenged, it needs to be retained.

Evidence-based methods of therapy, such as DBT, are conducted entirely in an outpatient setting. Once a week therapy remains the most useful way to manage patients. When suicide is threatened, providing extra sessions (or even telephone contact in a crisis) should not be carried out automatically, as doing so changes the structure of therapy. While DBT (Linehan, 1993) does offer telephone contact, it consists of a 5-10 minute coaching session, and is not provided if the patient acts out.

Similarly, we should be cautious about responding to a crisis by changing (or asking someone else to change) a patient's medication. While psychopharmacology has its role in the treatment of severe personality disorders, the evidence suggests that most of the drugs that have been used (specific serotonin reuptake inhibitors, low dose neuroleptics, and mood stabilizers) have ameliorative properties, but do not lead to remission of the underlying disorder (Soloff, 2000). The best demonstrated effect of these agents is a reduction in impulsivity (Paris, 2003). The effects are generally marginal, and most patients need only one drug. The mainstay of treatment for BPD remains psychotherapy.

Suicidality, like any other symptom, is a phenomenon to be understood, and therapists need to develop strategies to deal with it. Linehan (1993) applies the principle of "behavioral analysis" to suicidal ideas and behavior, which focuses on explaining the circumstances in which they arise, and developing alternate solutions to the life problems that underlie these symptoms. Gunderson (2001) and Livesley (2003) describe similar approaches.

Since most patients with BPD show a gradual pattern or recovery, therapists should not be unduly anxious about long-term outcome. Ultimately, suicidality is part and parcel of BPD. Clinicians need to understand that it "comes with the territory."

REFERENCES

Bateman, A. & Fonagy, P. (1999). Effectiveness of partial hospitalization in the treatment of borderline personality disorder: A randomized controlled trial. *American Journal of Psychiatry*, 156, 1563-1569.

Beautrais, A.L. (2001). Suicides and serious suicide attempts: Two populations or one? *Psychological Medicine*, 31, 837-45

Black, D.W., Blum, N., Pfohl, B., & Hale, N. (2004). Suicidal behavior in borderline personality disorder: Prevalence, risk factors, prediction, and prevention. *Journal of Personality Disorders,* 18(3), 226-239.

Brown, M.Z., Comtois, K.A., & Linehan, M.M. (2002). Reasons for suicide attempts and nonsuicidal self-injury in women with borderline personality disorder. *Journal of Abnormal Psychology*, 111, 198-202.

Dawson, D. & MacMillan, H.L. (1993). *Relationship management of the borderline patient: From understanding to treatment.* New York: Brunner/Mazel.

Fine, M.A. & Sansone, R.A. (1990). Dilemmas in the management of suicidal behavior in individuals with borderline personality disorder. *American Journal of Psychotherapy*, 44, 160-171.

Fonagy, P. (2004). An update on BPD treatment evaluation research in England. Presented to the NIMH International Think Tank for the More Effective Treatment of Borderline Personality Disorder, Lincthinum, MD, July 2004.

Gerson, J. & Stanley, B. (2002). Suicidal and self-injurious behavior in personality disorder: Controversies and treatment directions. *Current Psychiatry Reports*, 4, 30-8.

Goldney, R.D. (2000). Prediction of suicide and attempted suicide. In K. Hawton, K. van Heeringen (Eds.), *The international handbook of suicide and attempted suicide* (pp. 585-596). New York: John Wiley.

Goldstein, R.B., Black, D.W., Nasrallah, A., & Winokur, G. (1991). The prediction of suicide. *Archives of General Psychiatry*, 48, 418-422.

Gunderson, J.G. & Phillips, K.A. (1991). A current view of the interface between borderline personality disorder and depression. *American Journal of Psychiatry*, 148, 967-975.

Gunderson, J.G. (2001). *Borderline personality disorder: A clinical guide*. Washington, DC: American Psychiatric Press.

Gutheil, T.G. (1992). Suicide and suit: liability after self-destruction, in D. Jacobs (Ed.), *Suicide and Clinical Practice* (pp. 147-167). Washington DC: American Psychiatric Press.

Hellinga, G., Van Luyn, B., & Dalewijk, H. J. (Eds.) (2002). *Personalities: Master clinicians confront the treatment of borderline personality disorder*. Amsterdam: Boom.

Hendin, H. (1981). Psychotherapy and suicide. *American Journal of Psychotherapy*, 35, 469-480.

Hull, J.W., Yeomans, F., Clarkin, J., Li, C., & Goodman, G. (1996). Factors associated with multiple hospitalizations of patients with borderline personality disorder. *Psychiatric Services*, 47, 638-641.

Leibenluft, E., Gardner, D. L., Cowdry, R. W. (1987). The inner experience of the borderline self-mutilator. *Journal of Personality Disorders*, l, 317-324.

Linehan, M. M. (l993). *Cognitive behavioral therapy of borderline personality disorder*. New York: Guilford.

Maltsberger, J. T. (1994). Calculated risk in the treatment of intractably suicidal patients. *Psychiatry*, 57, 199-212.

Maris, R. W., Berman, A. L., & Silverman, M. M. (2000). *Comprehensive textbook of suicidology*. New York: Guilford.

Oldham, J. M., Gabbard, G. O., Goin, M. K., Gunderson, J., Soloff, P., Spiegel, D., Stone, M., & Phillips, K. A. (2001). Practice guideline for the treatment of borderline personality disorder. *American Journal of Psychiatry*, 158, Supp, 1-52.

Paris, J. (2002a). Implications of long-term outcome research for the management of borderline personality disorder. *Harvard Review of Psychiatry*, 10, 315-323.

Paris, J. (2002b). Chronic suicidality in borderline personality disorder. *Psychiatric Services*, 53, 738-742.

Paris, J. (2003). *Personality disorders over time*. Washington, DC: American Psychiatric Press.

Paris, J. (2004). Half in love with easeful death: the meaning of chronic suicidality in borderline personality disorder. *Harvard Review of Psychiatry*, 12, 42-48.

Paris, J., Brown, R., & Nowlis, D. (1987). Long-term follow-up of borderline patients in a general hospital. *Comprehensive Psychiatry*, 28, 530-535.

Paris, J., Nowlis, D., & Brown, R. (1989). Predictors of suicide in borderline personality disorder. *Canadian Journal of Psychiatry*, 34, 8-9.

Paris, J. & Zweig-Frank, H. (2001). A twenty-seven year follow-up of borderline patients. *Comprehensive Psychiatry*, 42, 482-487.

Piper, W. E., Rosie, J. S., & Joyce, A. S. (1996). *Time-limited day treatment for personality disorders: Integration of research and practice in a group program.* Washington DC, American Psychological Association.

Pokorny, A. D. (1982). Prediction of suicide in psychiatric patients: Report of a prospective study. *Archives of General Psychiatry,* 40, 249-257.

Rachlin, S. (1984). Double jeopardy: suicide and malpractice. *General Hospital Psychiatry,* 6, 302-307.

Schwartz, D. A., Flinn, D. E, & Slawson, P. F. (1974). Treatment of the suicidal character. *American Journal of Psychotherapy,* 28, 194-207.

Soloff, P. (2000). Psychopharmacological treatment of borderline personality disorder. *Psychiatric Clinics of North America,* 23, 169-192.

Soloff, P. H., Lynch, K. G., Kelly, T. M., Malone, K. M., & Mann, J. J. (2000). Characteristics of suicide attempts of patients with major depressive episode and borderline personality disorder: A comparative study. *American Journal of Psychiatry,* 157, 601-608.

Stone, M. H. (1990). The fate of borderline patients. New York: Guilford.

Welch, S. S. (2001). A review of the literature on the epidemiology of parasuicide in the general population. *Psychiatric Services,* 52, 368-75.

Williams, L. (1998). A "classic" case of borderline personality disorder. *Psychiatric Services,* 49, 173-174.

Yen, S., Shea, M. T., Sanislow, C. A., Grilo, C. M., Skodol, A. E., Gunderson, J. G., McGlashan, T. H., Zanarini, M. C., & Morey, L. C. (2004). Borderline personality disorder criteria associated with prospectively observed suicidal behavior. *American Journal of Psychiatry,* 161, 1296-1298.

Zahl, D. L. & Hawton, K. (2004). Repetition of deliberate self-harm and subsequent suicide risk: Long-term follow-up study of 11,583 patients. *British Journal of Psychiatry,* 185, 70-75.

Zanarini, M. C., Frankenburg, F. R., Hennen, J., & Silk, K. R. (2003). The longitudinal course of borderline psychopathology: 6-year prospective follow-up of the phenomenology of borderline personality disorder. *American Journal of Psychiatry,* 160, 274-283.

doi:10.1300/J200v06n01_09

Dialectical Behavior Therapy

Cedar R. Koons

SUMMARY. This chapter provides an overview of Dialectical Behavior Therapy (DBT), an evidence-based outpatient treatment developed for suicidal women with borderline personality disorder (BPD), and since adapted for other settings and populations. The chapter introduces the biosocial theory of the etiology of BPD and how DBT addresses each aspect of the disorder. It further describes the theoretical foundations of DBT in behaviorism, Zen and dialectics. The reader learns about DBT structures of treatment and what client behaviors are targeted in each stage of treatment. Finally, the chapter uses a clinical case example to illustrate how a therapist would get started with a new client using DBT. doi:10.1300/J200v06n01_10 *[Article copies available for a fee from The Haworth Document Delivery Service: 1-800-HAWORTH. E-mail address: <docdelivery@ haworthpress.com> Website: <http://www.HaworthPress.com> © 2008 by The Haworth Press. All rights reserved.]*

KEYWORDS. Dialectical behavior therapy, borderline personality disorder, emotion dysregulation, invalidation

INTRODUCTION

Dialectical Behavior Therapy (DBT) is an evidence-based treatment for borderline personality disorder, developed by Marsha M. Linehan,

[Haworth co-indexing entry note]: "Dialectical Behavior Therapy." Koons, Cedar R. Co-published simultaneously in *Social Work in Mental Health* (The Haworth Press) Vol. 6, No. 1/2, 2008, pp. 109-132; and: *Borderline Personality Disorder: Meeting the Challenges to Successful Treatment* (ed: Perry D. Hoffman, and Penny Steiner-Grossman) The Haworth Press, 2008, pp. 109-132. Single or multiple copies of this article are available for a fee from The Haworth Document Delivery Service [1-800-HAWORTH, 9:00 a.m. - 5:00 p.m. (EST). E-mail address: docdelivery@haworthpress.com].

Available online at http://swmh.haworthpress.com
© 2008 by The Haworth Press. All rights reserved.
doi:10.1300/J200v06n01_10

Ph.D, and colleagues (1993a, 1993b) at the University of Washington, and described in a book and treatment manual. Linehan, a behaviorist, was working with chronically suicidal, self-injurious women and found that these severely disordered, multi-problem individuals did not respond well to standard behavioral treatment. They were impulsive, had mood instability, problems with a sense of self and with relationships, and could look thought disordered under emotional stress. These factors, combined with suicidal and non-suicidal self-injurious behaviors contributed to treatment dropout and frequent inpatient admissions. Most met criteria for borderline personality disorder (BPD).

Linehan theorized that the common factor underlying all these behaviors had to do with regulation of emotion. These individuals experience stronger than usual emotions and have trouble controlling emotional behavior. They also try to avoid emotions in problematic ways, such as with alcohol or drugs. This central problem, *emotion dysregulation*, contributes to all the other problems. For example, emotion dysregulation is a direct cause of mood swings and problematic anger behavior. Emotion dysregulation prompts suicidal and self-injurious behavior as well as other high-risk behaviors and is a factor in impulsivity. Emotion dysregulation contributes to relationship dysregulation, resulting in intense, unstable or chaotic relationships. With these individuals, emotion dysregulation can cause problem thinking, including dichotomous thinking, paranoia, dissociation and hallucinations. Finally, chronic emotion dysregulation results in problems with the sense of self and feelings of emptiness.

THE BIOSOCIAL THEORY

Where does emotion dysregulation originate? Linehan theorized that borderline personality disorder developed as the result of a pronounced biological vulnerability to emotion, transacting over time with a learning history characterized by pervasive invalidation. This theory seeks to explain the etiology and maintenance of BPD, and also guides therapists in the way they understand and treat many of the problems they encounter interacting with BPD patients.

The biological component of the biosocial theory refers to the temperament of the individual who develops BPD. These individuals could be called *emotionally vulnerable* in that (1) they have a low threshold of emotional activation; (2) their emotions reactions are extreme; and (3) the biological arousal associated with emotion is slow to subside, making the individual more vulnerable to the next event that prompts emotion. For example, a stimulus in the environment, such as a co-worker making a critical comment about one's messy desk, might cause mild anger in the non-disordered person while prompting rage in the person with BPD. The non-disordered person would probably recover in 24 hours or less. The person with BPD might ruminate about the comment for days or even weeks, re-experiencing the initial emotion and powerful secondary emotions and being more vulnerable to other stressors as a result.

Emotional vulnerability alone, however, is not enough to produce the disorder. To produce emotion dysregulation, vulnerability to emotions must be combined with an inability to regulate emotions once they are activated. The ability to regulate emotions is a learned behavior that basic research tells us is made up of several important skills. These include: (1) directing attention away from upsetting stimuli; (2) regulating physiological arousal, such as using deep breathing to reduce heart rate associated with fear or anger; (3) avoiding urges that result in mood-dependent behavior, such as not skipping work because of shame; and (4) continuing to pursue goals not related to current mood. People can learn to manage even very vulnerable temperaments if they are taught the necessary skills. Unfortunately, individuals who develop BPD, in addition to their problems with emotion vulnerability, also have problematic learning histories. The social settings that contribute to their problems are called "the invalidating environment."

An invalidating environment is one in which a person's private experiences, such as emotions, preferences, sense of pain, as well as their observable behaviors are *pervasively* dismissed, criticized or attributed to negative traits. This invalidation takes place repeatedly and over time. Invalidating environments provide little if any recognition of the validity of a person's needs or feelings, and do not provide instruction in how to regulate emotions or solve problems. Instead they attribute the difficulties in problem solving to negative characteristics of the person with the problem, such as lack of motivation, while also over simplifying what is needed to solve the problem. In addition, invalidating environments respond unhelpfully to demands placed upon them. When demands are at an appropriate level of intensity the environment may ignore them, thereby extinguishing moderate asking behavior. When the intensity of the demand escalates, however, the environment may punish, or, intermittently reinforce an elevated level of demand.

The invalidating environment, while not teaching the skills needed to regulate emotions, teaches some other very unhelpful things. By invalidating private experiences, the environment teaches the individual not to trust or respect their own inner experiences as valid, but to look to others to explain to them what they think or feel. As a result, individuals may not know how to label their own emotions, let alone regulate them. By over simplifying problem solving, the environment encourages unrealistic self-expectations, perfectionism and the tendency to become hopeless and self-invalidating in the face of difficult problems. Finally, when environments routinely ignore appropriate levels of request and intermittently reinforce escalated demands, the individual is shaped to go back and forth from inhibition of emotions to extreme displays of emotion, behavior that is very ineffective in most settings.

The biosocial theory explains not only the etiology of BPD, but also its maintenance. For example, treatment environments often function as invalidating environments, as do many school and work environments. Even very skillful individuals may have great difficulty coping with these environments when they are vulnerable because of being tired or sick. When therapists understand the biosocial theory they are less likely to stigmatize individuals with BPD. And since so many problematic client behaviors arise out of the interaction of biological vulnerability with pervasive invalidation, therapists become adept at attending to what is needed to help their borderline clients unlearn maladaptive behaviors and learn new, more helpful ways to manage themselves and their environments.

THE THREE FOUNDATIONS OF DBT

DBT is constructed from three very different branches of knowledge, each contributing useful principles to its foundation. Behaviorism contributes the technology of change, Zen contributes the technology of acceptance, and dialectics contributes a worldview and a striving for balance between acceptance and change.

Behaviorism

DBT is a behavioral therapy in that it seeks to understand how maladaptive behaviors are learned and to replace maladaptive behaviors with new, more skillful behaviors. Whether behavior is observable or private, it is influenced by the modeling and conditioning available in the environment.

Modeling in DBT is used in both individual therapy and in skills training. The model presented is not one of having perfected skillful behavior; rather, it is a coping model. As in other cognitive and behavioral therapies, DBT does not attempt to cultivate a transferential relationship. The therapeutic relationship is a real relationship between equals, at the same time that it is bound by all ethical and professional guidelines. Therapists model skills use in their own life circumstances, while not burdening clients with problems they have not resolved. DBT also encourages the client to use other helpful models, such as individuals who have overcome great adversity to achieve a worthwhile life. These models can counteract maladaptive models such as parents, siblings, other patients, etc., and help the client learn new behaviors.

Conditioning in DBT is undertaken through examining specific instances of behavior in their full contexts (including the emotions, urges, thoughts and bodily sensations associated with the antecedents and consequences), and then choosing and implementing solutions to change problematic associations, stimuli and responses as they occur. The DBT therapist works collaboratively with the client to undertake these behavior and solution analyses, and to see how certain patterns tend to repeat themselves. Together, they discover how, in the presence of certain stimuli, the client is likely to feel, think, and experience; these experiences then lead to certain actions or non-actions, which have consequences that may be rewarding, punishing or neutral. For example, a client's cutting often might occur as a response to a specific emotion, such as shame. The emotion is so overwhelming that there is an urge to seek relief. Cutting brings that brief sense of relief, but is nearly always followed by a sense of hopelessness and more shame. This understanding can help a client to understand that to change the cutting behavior, he or she will need to learn to tolerate the emotion of shame and begin to see the relief that cutting brings as something to be avoided. DBT also uses conditioning to construct a treatment environment where adaptive behavior of the client is rewarded and maladaptive behavior is not rewarded. For example, for a client who finds an extra session rewarding, the therapist is careful to offer it primarily for adaptive behavior, such as before a job interview, not solely because she is feeling suicidal.

Zen

Zen principles are another foundation of DBT that inform the skills curriculum as well as therapist's attitudes toward clients and treatment. Zen emphasizes the wisdom inherent in each individual. DBT translates this principle as "wise mind," a synthesis of information gathered from the emotions with information gathered from the facts. When wise mind is sought, one's awareness in informed by something more than the sum of emotions and facts, and includes intuition, the middle path, or wisdom. Access to wise mind is central to the use of most of the other DBT skills. Therapists are also encouraged to practice mindfulness in order to improve their skills as therapists and their interactions with their team.

To get to wise mind, DBT offers the core mindfulness skills, which derive from Zen. These include the "what skills" (observe, describe and participate) and the "how skills" (non-judgmentally, one-mindfully and effectively). Observe and describe instruct the student to notice what is just as it is and describe a situation, using just the facts in the here and now. To participate is to enter fully into the experience of the moment, to throw oneself into acting while in contact with wise mind.

The first "how skill" is to adopt a nonjudgmental stance, the student must eschew describing things, people, or events as good or bad, instead focusing on the facts of the issue at hand and the consequences. For example, rather than calling a boss "hateful," the individual looks at the fact that the boss required him to stay late at work and miss a child's school performance and did not apologize. While the individual may still feel highly distressed, the nonjudgmental stance allows for some access to wise mind. In addition to not judging others, DBT emphasizes non-judgment of the self and of the behavior of judging.

The skill of "one-mindfully" directs one to focus all of one's attention on one thing at a time, rather than allowing the mind to wander to go on autopilot. This allows the individual to slow down and notice what is, to reduce emotional arousal and accept the situation. Finally, the skill of "effectively" is used to help the individual adopt a course of action that is in concert with his or her goals and avoids impulsive urges, such as being vengeful, righteous or self-sabotaging. Being effective·includes doing what works, playing by the rules and keeping focused on the desired outcome.

The mindfulness skills are crucial for anyone who is experiencing a lot of pain, since the circumstances, attitudes and behaviors contributing to the pain are unlikely to change quickly, or may be exceedingly difficult to change. Therefore, acceptance of reality, a central tenet of Zen, can be seen as a necessary skill to endure the change process.

Dialectics

Dialectics is a western philosophical tradition that postulates that truth is found in the struggle of opposites. In contrast to absolute truth, dialectical truth proceeds from an argument between a thesis and its antithesis and moves toward synthesis. In DBT, the fundamental dialectical dilemma is that between an individual's profound and urgent need to change behaviors that are destroying her life and her equally compelling need to accept herself and her situation in the moment as she is. The struggle between these two opposites will inform the entire treatment course. For example, as a client gives up cutting (thesis) she may find she copes less well for a while and drinks more (antithesis) but over time will learn enough distress tolerance to sustain abstinence from both (synthesis). However, as she gives up her problem behaviors and is no longer in crisis (thesis) she will find her isolation intolerable (antithesis) and will have to confront her social anxiety (synthesis).

Dialectics stand in contrast to the dichotomous thinking characteristic of persons with BPD, as well as the systems that treat them. Dialectics see everything as connected to everything else, and in a constant state of transaction or struggle. For example, at the therapist consultation meeting two therapists disagree about whether or not a client is "doing the best she can" in skills group, or needs to do better. The individual therapist insists that the client has at least been showing up to group and cannot be expected to do better right now. The skills trainer says that the client consistently comes late with no homework and gets angry when confronted. The two therapists struggle and the team highlights "both/and" rather than "either/or." Finally, the individual therapist is influenced to help the client with homework in individual therapy and to address timeliness with her. She remembers to tell the team that the client has recently gone off her ADD medication. Hearing about the medication change, the skills trainer becomes more accepting and promises to notice any skillful behaviors the client does demonstrate, for example, if she progresses from being 20 minutes late to being 10 minutes late.

Adopting a dialectical worldview is the prerequisite for the DBT consultation team and is essential for it to function effectively. Any position taken on an issue is likely to generate an equally convincing opposite position. Polarity is a natural fact of life. But rather than "split" on these difficult issues, or rush to a watered down compromise, a dialectical world view promotes a more thoughtful search for "what is left out of this picture?" Often, the piece left out can be crucial for the treatment issue at hand.

Dialectics function throughout DBT to help balance acceptance strategies, primarily validation (see below), with change strategies, primarily behaviorism. DBT also uses dialectics to manage the style of the therapist, balancing a more accepting, reciprocal style with a more change-oriented or irreverent style. Dialectics also inform the balance with which the therapist intervenes on the client's behalf as a case manager. In this case, the emphasis is on consulting with the client on how to interact with her environment, as opposed to intervening in the environment on behalf of the client. Finally, DBT offers some specific "dialectical strategies," described in detail in the treatment manuals, which are used to move the client toward a synthesis, including the use of metaphor, entering the paradox with the client, allowing natural change, and playing devil's advocate.

STRUCTURE OF TREATMENT

Standard DBT is an outpatient treatment that uses four primary modes to deliver the functions of comprehensive treatment. The modes include individual therapy, skills training, the therapist consultation meeting, and telephone consultation, which is available to the client between sessions for coaching on skills use. The functions of treatment include enhancing motivation (individual therapy), increasing skills for the client (skills training), increasing skills for the therapists and skills trainers (therapist consultation), and generalizing skills to the environment (telephone consultation). DBT recognizes that important treatment functions are also provided by agents outside the standard DBT team, including the pharmacotherapist and the clinic administrator. Pharmacotherapy, like individual therapy, can enhance motivation and increase the potential for skillful behavior. The clinic administrator plays a role in structuring the delivery environment so that it is conducive to effective treatment, for example, by providing paid time for team consultation.

Individual Therapy

In standard DBT, the individual therapist is in charge of treatment and attends to client motivation to remain in and progress through treatment and addresses anything that is interfering with treatment. The individual therapist elicits from the client his or her goals and establishes the agenda according the client's stage of treatment. In at least one 50-minute session per week, the individual therapist keeps the treatment focused on the target hierarchy, reinforces the use of skillful behaviors and establishes a strong, effective relationship. The individual therapist also provides the telephone coaching as needed to help the client use skills in daily life, both to avoid suicidal and self-injurious behavior and to repair any perceived rifts in the therapeutic relationship between sessions.

Skills Training

Skills training is usually provided in a class with two co-teachers, which meets for approximately two hours each week, to cover the skills curricula, assign and review homework assignments. The skills are taught in four modules, Mindfulness, Distress Tolerance, Emotion Regulation and Interpersonal Effectiveness. The Mindfulness module, described above, is two weeks in length and is repeated at the beginning of each of the other modules. The remaining three modules last about eight weeks each. Most clients go through the entire cycle at least twice in order to over-learn skills; this process takes approximately one year.

Therapist Consultation

The therapist consultation includes all the therapists and skills trainers treating a specific cohort of clients. This meeting is held weekly to allow therapists time to consult on their clients and apply DBT principles to solve any problems arising in treatment. The function of the team meeting is to enhance the therapist's capacity to treat effectively. Toward this end, specific agreements are made and referenced regarding the DBT way to consult. These include the adoption of a dialectical philosophy of treatment and a willingness to look first for the most empathic explanation of a client or colleague's behavior. DBT encourages therapists to acknowledge first their own fallibility and that of their team colleagues. Therapists agree to observe their own limits with clients in each different context and need not be consistent with all their clients or with other colleagues. Finally, therapists are encouraged to observe their own limits with clients and also to be willing to stretch limits from time to time as needed in the context of treatment.

Telephone Coaching

DBT offers between-session telephone coaching for clients to (1) reduce suicide crises and self-harm behavior; (2) increase generalization of skills; and (3) repair rifts in the therapeutic relationship that could interfere with between session functioning. Telephone coaching is *not* therapy on the phone, and contacts are typically brief and focused on using skills to get through the crisis without engaging in maladaptive behavior. Clients are instructed to call the therapist *before* they engage in their problem behavior and are forbidden to call for 24 hours after they engage in self-injurious behavior; this avoids giving therapeutic contact that might reinforce the behavior. The role of telephone contact in DBT is similar to *in vivo* behavioral therapy and is balanced by team consultation and by the limits of the individual therapist. The management of this mode of treatment is described by Linehan (1993b) and also by Ben-Porath and Koons (2005).

Stages of Disorder

DBT structures treatment for borderline clients based on the severity of their behaviors, and treats those behaviors in a specified order called a target hierarchy. There are four stages of treatment each with its specific goals and treatment targets. The overarching goal of DBT is "a life worth living."

Stage one of treatment is characterized by pervasive behavioral dyscontrol. Stage one behaviors threaten life, health, the functioning of a therapeutic relationship and a basic quality of life. In stage one, the goal is getting behavior under control, building connectedness to care givers, and learning behavioral skills. Thus, stage one targets first any intentional life threatening or self-harming behavior. This includes suicidal or homicidal thoughts, plans or attempts, and suicidal or non-suicidal intentional self-injurious behavior. The second target for stage one is any behavior that interferes with therapy, such as nonattendance, nonpayment, noncompliance with medications, or hostile behavior directed at the therapist. The third target of stage one is any behavior interfering with an adequate quality of life, such as homelessness, drug or alcohol abuse or dependence, binging and purging, or being in a violent relationship. The final target of stage one is learning and using behavioral skills to replace maladaptive behavior.

Stage two is characterized by "quiet desperation." While clients are no longer in behavioral dyscontrol, they still exhibit problematic emotional inhibition, and symptoms of post- traumatic stress. In stage two, clients are often quite numb and miserable, even though they are able to use many skills and are no longer engaging in high-risk behaviors. The targets of stage two include decreasing symptoms of post-traumatic stress and increasing emotional experiencing. Stage two also targets increasing acceptance of traumatic events in the past, acceptance of emotions and acceptance of the self. It is important to note that the work of stage two cannot be undertaken with clients who lack the skills to manage exposure to extreme emotion without engaging in the chaotic behaviors of stage one. Effective treatment of common co-morbidities, such as depression, anxiety and OCD, can accelerate in stage two.

Stage three clients have achieved a life worth living, but continue to have ordinary problems of living. Stage three targets such common problems as decreasing interpersonal conflicts, coping with chronic health issues, and increasing a sense of mastery. Stage three clients use many behavioral skills in a variety of contexts and are capable of expressing a wide range of emotions. They do not look significantly different from other clients seen in CBT, except perhaps for their painful pasts and their emotional vulnerability.

Stage four deals with increasing the capacity for joy and freedom. Clients who have struggled for many years with BPD and have arrived at stage four often have a desire to express their newfound sense of self and their values more fully in their relationships and communities and desire more joy and meaning. They may be quite wise and skillful and often have as much to teach as to learn.

CORE STRATEGIES OF DBT

Given the enormous challenges of treating these severely disordered, multi-problem clients, it is not surprising that the armamentarium of DBT is large and varied. For the purposes of providing an overview, this chapter will address only the core strategies, which are problem-solving (change) and validation (acceptance). These two strategies are expressed and kept in balance by means of dialectical, stylistic and case management strategies, which will not be covered in this chapter. Commitment strategies will be illustrated in the case study.

Problem Solving

As mentioned above, the tools of DBT problem solving come from behavioral and cognitive therapies, and from protocols of other evidence-based treatments. DBT problem solving begins with behavioral assessment. First, the problem is defined as a specific behavior that either needs to increase (such as showing up at work) or decrease (such as yelling at a family member), or appear in the right place and time (such as saying no to unreasonable requests). Once the behavior is defined, it is analyzed to gain insight into where and when it is most likely to occur and what are the most likely variables that control it. For example, does the client fight with her mother, feel fear, cut in response to fear, feel calmer and then hide the cuts from her mother? Or does she fight with her mother, feel rage, cut and then show the cut to her mother, who soothes her? In both cases the cutting behavior is at once a response to a stressor and an attempt to get a desired consequence. Yet in each case, the therapist would proceed differently to solve this problem. Once all the factors influencing the problem are understood, the therapist and client can work together to find solutions. These might include learning new behavioral skills, changing disordered thinking, changing the associations between stimuli in the environment, and changing the reinforcing or punishing consequences of problem behavior. DBT therapists need to be adept at getting and maintaining commitment to behavioral change, and at teaching what clients need to learn to deal with the many issues that present during therapy.

DBT is a principle-driven therapy that employs protocols of other evidence-based treatments as needed. For example, a client in DBT who had been raped in adolescence might need exposure treatment (an evidence-based protocol) for his or her trauma. DBT principles indicate this would not be appropriate until stage two of treatment, once any life-threatening, therapy-interfering or quality of life-interfering behaviors were under control and the client had mastered sufficient skills to deal with the distress of exposure. DBT therapists are encouraged to learn as much as possible about effective treatment of such commonly co-occurring disorders as depression, panic, OCD, disordered eating, and substance abuse.

Validation

In order to balance the emphasis on change, DBT uses validation strategies. The therapist looks at the client's behavior, feelings and thoughts for what can be confirmed, corroborated, or highlighted as having validity. In her treatment manual, Linehan has compared finding validity in client behavior to looking for a "nugget of gold in a bucket of sand." Sometimes it can be very difficult to find something valid in behavior that is clearly maladaptive. DBT teaches that it is always possible to validate clients' emotional pain, their difficulty in using skills, and the feeling that they are very far from where they would like to be. Just listening to what clients are saying about their experience, awake to all the unspoken aspects but without adding interpretations, is very validating for most clients.

Since the biosocial theory informs about how temperament and learning history can prompt maladaptive responses, the therapist can often confirm what is understandable behavior in that context. For example, given that a client's father often belittled his son as "effeminate," it is understandable that when an authority figure at work teased him about the neatness of his attire he felt rageful and wanted to quit his job. In this circumstance, the therapist is validating that given the client's problematic learning history, his reaction of rage is understandable. Far more validating would be a comment that any man whose boss commented in a teasing fashion about his attire might feel anger, given the homophobia common in the workplace. In the latter instance, the therapist manages to find a way to communicate a much less conditional validation. Rage in either case is still probably an overreaction, and it is still unlikely that quitting one's job, based on this instance alone, would be considered a valid response.

Validation creates a context of understanding in which the therapist can move toward problem solving. For example, a client threatens to leave her husband because she saw him laughing with his former girlfriend in the parking lot at church. The client became jealous, and rageful and threatened to make him move out. The therapist wants to address her client's impulsive threat. She also wants to focus on skills the client can use to regulate her anger and help her check the facts about whether or not her jealousy is justified. However, if she goes immediately to problem solving, the therapist runs the risk that the client will feel misunderstood. The client might feel the need to communicate even more forcefully how jealous and angry she truly is. If the therapist begins by validating that the client is very upset, and that given that she and her husband have not been getting along well, it is understandable that she would feel jealous to see him interacting warmly with a former girlfriend, the client can feel heard and understood. Her emotional arousal might then decrease and she might become more willing to participate in problem solving around how to handle her emotions of jealousy and rage.

Now that we have an overview of treatment, we turn our attention to how DBT would be provided in the treatment of a 29 year-old woman who is still dependent on her parents and who presents with a history of self-harm behavior, recent hospitalizations, a history of assault, significant drug use, underemployment and unstable relationships.

CASE EXAMPLE

To address the case of Joan, it is helpful to understand how a DBT therapist–let us call her Barbara–might conduct the first four sessions. Relatively speaking, the first four sessions of DBT are crucial to instilling hope in clients who have had multiple therapeutic failures, getting the client committed and motivated to do the hard work ahead, and establishing a collaborative and balanced therapeutic relationship.

Joan has been referred for DBT to a private, nonprofit agency, where a team of six therapists and two interns provide DBT and other evidence-based treatment. Joan comes for her intake, where she fills out some clinic forms and releases, and completes some self-report assessments to establish a baseline against which to measure progress. She then meets with the intake intern who explains clinic policies and gives her an overview of the DBT agreements for treatment. These agreements will be reviewed later by the individual therapist as part of the commitment process. The intern conducts a semi-structured interview to confirm the BPD diagnosis and uncover any co-morbid diagnoses. When the assessment is complete, the intern brings Joan's case to the DBT team meeting. Barbara has an opening and calls Joan to set up their first meeting.

Barbara meets Joan prepared to focus on the six primary tasks of the first four sessions. These include: (1) orienting Joan to what to expect in individual therapy, skills group and telephone coaching; (2) gaining initial commitment to work on reducing and eliminating suicidal and self-injurious behaviors and behaviors that will interfere with therapy; (3) gaining commitment to participate in each aspect of treatment; (4) assessing the stage of treatment and the specific relevant targets; (5) orienting to and preparing the diary card (see Appendix); and (6) establishing the groundwork for a therapeutic relationship based on specific agreements and assumptions. Throughout these initial sessions, Barbara will be attending to how Joan reacts to her, and how she reacts to Joan. She will focus on establishing a warm and straightforward relationship.

Session One

Barbara initially meets Joan with her parents, but after a quick orientation to what DBT can offer Joan, Barbara asks the parents to leave. She explains that they will be invited to a later session once Joan herself is in commitment, to learn more about DBT and how they can help Joan.

It is made clear to the parents that if they need additional support, a referral will be provided for them.

Commitment and Goals: Once the parents have left, Barbara begins by asking how much Joan wants therapy herself, versus how much her parents want her in therapy. Barbara briefly explores Joan's relationship with her parents, keeping the biosocial theory in mind. It is clear to her that Joan's interest in therapy is somewhat limited but that she knows she has to attend to continue to get support from her parents.

Joan wants her parents to understand her and how hard life is for her. After some probing by Barbara, Joan also admits she'd like to be independent of her parents, but fears it is impossible. She is even afraid to say it lest her parents hear and withdraw support. "They can afford right now to support me, but I don't think they want to." Barbara says that she thinks gaining independence is a great goal and that she and DBT can help with that, but it will take time. Meanwhile, Joan will need her parents' support and will have to learn to interact with them more effectively. Joan agrees that she would like to do that but doubts that changing her behavior will help much. Barbara knows that gaining independence from her parents will be a struggle for Joan because of the long pattern of dependency and the parents' tendency to reinforce Joan's crisis behaviors with more support.

Barbara tells Joan that the overarching goal of DBT is "a life worth living" and asks Joan what that would look like for her. Joan said she would like to have a boyfriend and maybe go back to school to become a veterinary technician, but she is pretty vague about her level of interest in her goals and about how she might attain them. Barbara accepts Joan's goals with enthusiasm and then begins to explore what behaviors Joan feels might be getting in the way of her goals. Joan mentions conflict with her parents, drugs, and alcohol, and Barbara adds self-harm and keeping the option to suicide open. Barbara orients Joan to the concept of learning new ways to manage her emotions using the skills of the DBT curriculum. Barbara also discusses the DBT assumptions about clients and about treatment, including that clients are doing the best they can but need to do better. Joan is interested in how both of these can be true.

Barbara shares with Joan the research on DBT and her own clinical experience with how the treatment has helped others with similar problems. Joan expresses some interest. As Barbara conducts this initial session she is modeling a dialectical stance, keeping Joan a little off balance as to what to expect and encouraging Joan to consider her options very carefully. Barbara outlines for Joan how difficult the process of therapy is likely to be and how long it will take. Barbara discusses the importance of coming to weekly sessions, attending a weekly group, and learning lots of new ways to deal with her emotions, including accepting the feelings in the moment. Joan, though she might have arrived quite ambivalent about DBT is now more than a little curious. She likes Barbara's "let's get down to business" attitude and figures Barbara might really understand how hard therapy is for her. She secretly believes she cannot give up self-harm. And, Joan is very wary about the skills group piece. (She doesn't do groups!) But she won't say anything about that just yet. Joan wants to hear more and says she will commit to four sessions to decide.

Targeting: Barbara makes note to return to the commitment strategies, but now turns her attention to a history of the events leading up to treatment. She knows Joan is in stage one but needs to explore Joan's targets. Barbara asks whether or not Joan is still engaging in self-harm behavior and whether or not she considers suicide an option. Joan says she mainly self-harms after fights with her parents but has not done so in the last week. She says she wants to keep the option to kill herself open, but is not currently feeling suicidal. Joan has not been hospitalized in six months. Barbara asks for commitment to work on staying alive during at least the first year, and also to work on reducing self-harm behavior. Barbara highlights that these two commitments are necessary for DBT to proceed. Joan commits to staying alive for one month, until she decides whether or not she wants to do this treatment. She is not willing to commit to eliminating self-harm, but expresses interest in reducing it.

Session Two

In session two, Barbara summarizes what they accomplished in session one and highlights what she hopes to accomplish today. For her part, Joan wants to talk about a problem with one of her friends. Barbara sets the agenda: they will revisit commitment, discuss the specific problems that are getting in the way of Joan's goals, and begin making the diary card. After that, Joan can talk about her issue. Barbara asks about their one-month commitment to stay alive and reduce self-harm. Joan renews it willingly and even says she's been thinking she really doesn't want to kill herself at all, at least not today.

Target One: Barbara conducts a "pattern behavior analysis" of Joan's self-harm behavior, looking at the frequency of this behavior, the intensity of the urges and actions, the duration of the urges and actions, and how the behavior has typically manifested itself. She discovers that

Joan's self harm behavior almost always functions as a relief valve, and that even though Joan feels shame about the behavior and fears that it could escalate, she doesn't feel she can give it up. Barbara acknowledges Joan's shame and fear and instills hope that through the use of DBT skills Joan will be able to reduce and eliminate self-harm, replacing it with new, more adaptive behaviors that will give some relief from emotional pain. Barbara validates Joan's concern that if she stops cutting her suicidal thoughts might become worse and explains why DBT insists on eliminating both. Barbara remains aware through this process of its exposing nature and adopts a matter of fact tone of inquiry, careful not to introduce any emotion which could be activating or reinforcing. Barbara tells Joan she wants her to begin to see self-harm and keeping the option to suicide open as her "mortal enemy" rather than as a relief valve, and uses a metaphor to help Joan grasp this paradigm shift: "It as if you are lost at sea with your emotions and you are very thirsty. You have only a little bit of water until it rains, which it will do, and you can catch more in your sail. You have to ration your water, and if you do you will survive. But you keep feeling tempted to drink seawater. You know if you drink seawater it will moisten your mouth and relieve your thirst for a moment. But then your thirst will get so much worse and eventually drinking seawater will kill you. That is how self-harm works for you." Joan is very attentive to this metaphor and for the first time is ready to acknowledge that she wants to eliminate self-harm. Barbara accepts this commitment and then briefly describes some of the skills Joan will learn to replace self-harm as a strategy.

Barbara also inquires into Joan's assault history. Joan tells her that the incident happened four years ago under the influence of crack cocaine and that she had a great deal of shame about it. "I'm much more likely to hurt myself than anyone else," Joan says, "but my boyfriend accused me of being a crack whore." Joan denies using cocaine in the past two years. "Since I moved back home, I don't even know where to get it."

Target Two: Barbara then introduces the concept of "therapy-interfering behavior" and inquires into what behaviors of Joan's might get in the way of therapy. Joan readily admits that attendance, filling out the diary card and doing homework will be hard for her and that in the past she has gotten kicked out of therapy for not coming to sessions or calling to cancel. Barbara reminds Joan about the clinic attendance and cancellation policies and about the DBT attendance rule: that she is not allowed to miss four sessions in a row of either individual therapy or skills training. Barbara tells Joan that working on reducing this behavior will be of crucial importance and will make a huge difference in treatment. Joan agrees to work on reducing her therapy interfering behavior but asks Barbara for understanding about how hard it will be. Barbara introduces Joan to the concept of telephone coaching and to how they will use it in therapy. "One way I think we will be using the telephone is that I might call you to coach you to get to individual therapy or to skills group if I think you are not coming. How will you feel about that?" Joan admits that she will not want to come to group and might start avoiding. She feels that if Barbara called her it would only make her angry. Joan also says she cannot imagine "bothering" Barbara with a phone call. Barbara highlights for Joan how calling for coaching in DBT is actually skillful behavior and makes note to revisit the protocol in the next session. By now it is time to assign the final 15 minutes to Joan's interpersonal problem. Barbara helps Joan decide what to do with a friend who wants to borrow her car. As they work on Joan's difficulties with saying no, Barbara highlights for Joan how she will learn skills to manage situations exactly like this in skills group.

Session Three

Behavior and Solution Analysis: Joan arrives to session 10 minutes late to her 9:00 a.m. appointment. Barbara immediately conducts a behavior analysis of the lateness behavior and then a solution analysis. Joan, who has always been late to appointments, expresses surprise that Barbara gets so "uptight" about it. Barbara uses irreverence to disclose her limits with Joan saying, "You are right. I get uptight about anything that will interfere with our work together! And I want you to get uptight, too!" Joan laughs and feels validated by Barbara's concern. She says she will work on being on time by not staying out late the night before therapy and by setting her alarm.

Barbara elicits Joan's concerns about participating in the group and uses commitment strategies to build her willingness. Barbara knows that Joan is already becoming attached to her and somewhat hopeful and feels she can use that to leverage Joan's attendance in the group. Barbara has already put Joan on the waitlist for an evening group and knows that she could start in three weeks

Target Three: Barbara is ready to explore target three with Joan, that is, behaviors that decrease the quality of life. She inquires first into Joan's alcohol and drug use and finds out that when Joan comes home from work she usually has a glass or two of wine and smokes marijuana.

She also has used ecstasy, cocaine and methamphetamine in the past but denies current use. Joan says she has some willingness to eliminate alcohol she has no willingness to eliminate cannabis. Barbara explores Joan's willingness to participate in AA and Joan says she is unwilling to attend. Barbara says, "It will be really hard to give up alcohol. Are you sure you are ready?" Joan says, "If I can still smoke, I'll be okay. I really don't like alcohol as much as weed." Using a shaping strategy, Barbara leaves cannabis alone for now and focuses on the possibility of eliminating alcohol. "Let's see if you can cut out alcohol," Barbara says. "Just don't come to therapy stoned. We will put cannabis on the diary card to monitor how much you are using." Joan agrees.

Target-Relevant Emotions and Behaviors: The two then explore what emotions and events are most likely to contribute to Joan turning to suicidal thoughts, self-harm or substance-abusing behavior. Joan says that conflict with her father, feelings of inferiority toward her siblings, and conflicts with peers are directly related to her suicidality and linked to her drug and alcohol use. She admits to Barbara that she feels a lot of anger and self-loathing whenever these issues arise. Barbara suggests they put anger and self-loathing on the diary card. Joan agrees.

Orienting: Relationship of Targets and Goals: Barbara turns her attention to Joan's new job and to how success at work will take Joan toward her goals. The final area of the diary card, then, will be for attending work, not only showing up, but staying for her full shift and staying on task. Joan comments on how all the targets now on the card are connected because drug use, anger, self-loathing and even self-harm contribute to not succeeding at her job. She states that it will be hard to keep the diary card because just looking at it will remind her of what a loser she is. Barbara validates the exposing nature of the card and points out that "thinking I am a loser" is one of Joan's targets! The two laugh at this, and Barbara explains how each time she does the card the shame will decrease a little. After Barbara gets commitment from Joan to fill out the card daily, she spends the last five minutes of the session checking in with Joan about how she is feeling. "Pretty good, I guess," Joan says, "This therapy is definitely different from what I've had before. I feel like you know what is up with me. I don't want to get on your bad side!" Barbara says, "I like getting to know you. I like how honest you are with me. I feel pretty hopeful." She smiles, "No, you don't want to get on my bad side! But don't worry, I'll teach you how not to do that!"

Session Four

Shaping: Joan is on time to her fourth session but doesn't have her diary card. "I did do it," she says, "I just forgot it." Barbara hands her a blank copy and says, "I'm really glad you got here on time today, but we still can't get started until you do your card. Fill this out and I'll sit at my desk doing some paperwork." Five minutes later Joan gives Barbara her diary card and the two review the card and set the agenda. Joan says she needs to talk about a fight with her parents.

Barbara looks over the diary card, noting that on two days Joan had self-harm urges but no actions. Barbara says, "Wow, how did you manage not to cut?" "I thought about the drinking sea water thing," Joan says, "and I didn't want to do it." Barbara acknowledges this as very skillful and asks how long the urges lasted. "Until I went to bed," Joan says. Barbara notes, "Those were the nights you drank this week." "Yes," Joan says. "Instead of cutting, I drank to relieve the pressure." Barbara then conducts two behavioral analyses of the self-harm urges. She discovers that in one incident the prompting event was encountering an acquaintance at her retail job and feeling shame, and the other was having a fight with her father about a car repair bill, where she felt anger, then shame. Barbara points out how Joan has been quite skillful in not cutting but then has to turn to alcohol to soothe herself. Joan says that alcohol doesn't soothe as quickly as cutting, and that it also costs money and gives her a headache. Barbara acknowledges that alcohol is not a good alternative to cutting, but that not cutting was still skillful. "But you managed not to drink the other five nights, is that true?" "I just smoked weed." Joan said. Barbara refers again to how skills class will help Joan by teaching her ways to cope with her emotions that don't have side effects. "Yeah," Joan says, "I'm just about ready to do anything at this point. Even go to a group."

Barbara then conducts another behavior analysis of Joan not bringing her diary card. "Actually, I didn't really do it," Joan admits. "I had every intention of doing it, but I left it in my car and never got it out. But I'll do better this week. I don't want to have to use my time in here to fill it out and besides, I can't really remember what happened that well." Barbara takes note that sometimes Joan lies to cover up behavior and muses that she also might lie about substance use. She will bring this up in the next session. Now she wants to focus with Joan on a plan to help her complete her card for next week.

Finally, Joan asks Barbara for her help with a problem with her father. Joan says that since she started DBT her father now expects her "to be cured" and has decided to cut down on her support. "He doesn't want to pay for the repairs on my car and I have no money, whatsoever." The rest of the session focuses on problem solving around this crisis and Barbara decides it is time to bring the parents back for a family session. She knows these parents have been very supportive but are exhausted and overwhelmed with their daughter's needs. Barbara wants to give them information about DBT and wants Joan to talk with them herself in the session about her goals and commitments. The goal of the family session will be to come to agreement about how to manage their support for Joan over the year of treatment and how to encourage them to get into therapy also. Joan says she will invite them to the next session.

At the end of session four, Barbara asks Joan if she will be ready to start group in two weeks. Joan says she "as ready as she's going to be" and then says she feels less worried about it because things are going well with Barbara. Barbara reflects that she feels they are off to a good start. Many problems still remain to be addressed and new problems will arise, but treatment is well begun. Next week in the team meeting, she will announce that Joan will be starting group and let the team know about her target behaviors and concerns about group. Barbara will receive support and consultation from her team throughout the course of this treatment, especially from Joan's skills trainers, and from the teammate who begins seeing the parents.

CONCLUSION

DBT is a very promising treatment for individuals with BPD in that it has been shown to reduce the incidence and medical severity of self-harm behavior, the number of hospitalizations and length of stay, and client anger while increasing treatment compliance (Linehan et al., 1991). Some studies have shown reductions in depression and hopelessness in women veterans (Koons et al., 2001), suicidal behavior in adolescents (Rathus & Miller, 2002), and depression in the elderly (Lynch et al., 2003). For more discussion of the current research on DBT, see Robins and Chapman (2004).

Adaptations of DBT: Standard DBT has been adapted for other treatment delivery settings including inpatient, day treatment, vocational rehabilitation, and juvenile and adult forensic settings. In those settings, providing the four primary modes of treatment may not be feasible because of the structure of treatment delivery. For example, many inpatient units do not offer individual therapy and the length of stay is short.

However, the functions of comprehensive treatment have been adapted to these differing settings with some success. In some settings, e.g., in emergency departments, it is not possible to provide comprehensive DBT. In those cases, some clinicians have elected to offer "DBT-informed" treatment, such as awareness of the biosocial theory, behavior analysis or skills coaching only, even though there is no evidence that these component parts offered alone are effective treatment. Standard DBT also has been adapted to serve populations other than persons with BPD, including those with substance use disorders, suicidal adolescents, and persons with binge eating disorder, among others.

DBT is also a complex, time-consuming, difficult to learn and challenging treatment to implement in many settings. Training and sustaining a team of therapists is necessary, expensive, and time-consuming, a reality some clinic administrators may not want to face. And, while some third party payers appreciate the efficacy of DBT, others are unwilling to commit to the costs over time. Nevertheless, for clinicians treating severely disordered individuals with BPD, the lasting change that can be achieved is well worth the effort required to learn and implement this evolving, sophisticated, and exciting treatment.

REFERENCES

Ben-Porath, D. D., & Koons, C. R. (2005). Telephone coaching in dialectical behavior therapy: A decision-tree model for managing inter-session contact with clients. *Cognitive and Behavioral Practice*, 12, 448-460.

Koons, C. R., Robins, C. J., Tweed, J. L., Lynch, T. R., Gonzalez, A. M., Morse, J. Q. et al. (2001). Efficacy of dialectical behavior therapy in women veterans with borderline personality disorder. *Behavior Therapy*, 32, 371-390.

Linehan, M. M., Armstrong, H. H., & Suarez, A. et al. (1991). Cognitive-behavioral treatment of chronically parasuicidal borderline patients. *Archives of General Psychiatry*, 48, 1060-1064.

Linehan, M. M. (1993a). *Cognitive-behavioral treatment of borderline personality disorder*. New York: Guilford Press.

Linehan, M. M. (1993b). *Skills training manual for treating borderline personality disorder*. New York: Guilford Press.

Lynch, T. R., Morse, J. Q., Mendelson, T., & Robins, C. J. (2003). Dialectical behavior therapy for depressed older adults: A randomized pilot study. *American Journal of Geriatric Psychiatry*, 11, 33-45.

Rathus, J. H., & Miller, A. L. (2002). Dialectical behavior therapy adapted for suicidal adolescents. *Suicide and Life Threatening Behavior*, 32, 146-157.

Robins, C. J., & Chapman, A. L. (2004). Dialectical behavior therapy: Current status, recent developments, and future directions. *Journal of Personality Disorders*, 18, 73-89.

Safer, D. L., Telch, C. F., & Agras, W. S. (2001). Dialectical behavior therapy for bulimia nervosa. *American Journal of Psychiatry*, 158, 632-634.

Telch, C. F., Agras, W. S., & Linehan, M. M. (2001). Dialectical behavior therapy for binge eating disorder. *Journal of Consulting and Clinical Psychology*, 69, 1061-1065.

doi:10.1300/J200v06n01_10

APPENDIX

DIALECTICAL BEHAVIOR
THERAPY DIARY CARD

Name _____

Date Started _____

Date	Alcohol (How Much?)		Cannibis (How Much?)		Suicide Ideation (0-5)		Inter-Personal Conflicts		Anger (0-5)	Joy (0-5)	Self-Loathing		Self-Harm				*Used Skills (0-7)
	#	Specify	#	Specify	#	Specify	#	Specify			(0-5)	What	Urges (0-5)	Prompting Event	Actions	
Mon																
Tues																
Wed																
Thurs																
Fri																
Sat																
Sun																

GOALS WORKED ON: 1) Independence from Parents
                 2) Learning Skills

Mon	
Tues	
Wed	
Thu	
Fri	
Sat	
Sun	

0= Not thought about or used
1= Thought about, not used, didn't want to
2= Thought about, not used, wanted to
3= Tried, but couldn't use them
4= Tried, could do them, but they didn't help
5= Tried, could use them, helped
6= Didn't try, used them, they didn't help
7= Didn't try, used them, helped

Combined Medication and Dialectical Behavior Therapy for Borderline Personality Disorder

S. Charles Schulz
Michael P. Rafferty

SUMMARY. Medication treatment for BPD has developed in recent years as interest in pharmacotherapy of BPD has increased and as new medications have become available. With these developments has come the need for those clinicians working with BPD patients to learn and practice working together. This chapter reviews the pharmacotherapy options for patients with BPD so that all clinicians on a treatment team may be acquainted with the data supporting medication intervention. Following the section on medication, there is a discussion of DBT, an empirically supported psychotherapy now commonly used for the treatment of BPD. A description of how the treatment team can work together is offered. Because some BPD patients may provide challenges due to a tendency toward splitting, this integrated approach may lead to better treatment outcomes. doi:10.1300/J200v06n01_11 *[Article copies available for a fee from The Haworth Document Delivery Service: 1-800-HAWORTH. E-mail address: <docdelivery@haworthpress.com> Website: <http://www.HaworthPress.com> © 2008 by The Haworth Press. All rights reserved.]*

[Haworth co-indexing entry note]: "Combined Medication and Dialectical Behavior Therapy for Borderline Personality Disorder." Schulz, S. Charles, and Michael P. Rafferty. Co-published simultaneously in *Social Work in Mental Health* (The Haworth Press) Vol. 6, No. 1/2, 2008, pp. 133-144; and: *Borderline Personality Disorder: Meeting the Challenges to Successful Treatment* (ed: Perry D. Hoffman, and Penny Steiner-Grossman) The Haworth Press, 2008, pp. 133-144. Single or multiple copies of this article are available for a fee from The Haworth Document Delivery Service [1-800-HAWORTH, 9:00 a.m. - 5:00 p.m. (EST). E-mail address: docdelivery@haworthpress.com].

KEYWORDS. Borderline personality disorder, psychotropic medications, dialectical behavioral therapy, treatment team

MEDICATION TREATMENT FOR BPD

Over the years, different types of medication have been evaluated for conditions thought to be related to borderline personality disorder, such as emotionally unstable character disorder (Rifkin et al., 1972). The development of descriptive criteria for BPD (APA, 1980; Gunderson & Singer, 1975) led to a further examination of medications for BPD. At this time, a variety of classes of psychotropic medications have been tested in BPD patients and a brief overview of each class follows below. A summary of medications used to treat BPD appears as Appendix.

Lithium

Lithium was first tested in patients diagnosed as having emotionally unstable character disorder (EUCD) shortly after this medication was first approved for bipolar disorder. Rifkin and colleagues (1972) found lithium to be better than placebo for mood variability in EUCD patients. Unlike sedating medications used in that era, few side effects were reported. This led to significant use of lithium for BPD through the 1970s and early 1980s. During the 1980s, trials of lithium were reported showing some positive effect (for a review, see Goldberg, 1989), but this medication began to be used less frequently. At the time of this writing, lithium is used in some BPD patients, perhaps those who are co-morbid for bipolar I or II.

When used for BPD, lithium is prescribed in doses similar to those used for bipolar disorder, and monitoring of lithium blood level is necessary. Side effects in BPD patients are similar to those seen in mood disorders: fine tremor, thirst, and increased urination. Other side effects are more infrequent and anyone prescribing lithium should be familiar with the package insert.

Antipsychotic Medication

There are two general classes of antipsychotic medication: traditional or first-generation antipsychotics and atypical or second-generation antipsychotics. Traditional antipsychotics have been used to treat personality disorders since the 1950s, but it was not until 1979 that an approach termed "low-dose neuroleptic therapy" gained recognition (Brinkley et al., 1979). Double-blind and placebo-controlled trials in the mid-1980s demonstrated the efficacy of this approach in reducing a number of BPD symptoms (Goldberg et al., 1986; Soloff et al., 1986). However, even with low doses, many patients experienced feeling physically slowed or had other side effects that reduced effectiveness (Cowdry & Gardner 1988; Soloff et al., 1993). Since the introduction of the atypical antipsychotic medications, the use of traditional antipsychotic medications has receded significantly.

The atypical antipsychotic medications were introduced to treat schizophrenia and subsequently for bipolar disorder during the 1990s and early 2000s. The first case series of an atypical antipsychotic described the positive effects of olanzapine (Zyprexa) in BPD patients (Schulz et al., 1999). Subsequent studies have shown olanzapine to be efficacious in BPD patients compared to placebo (Bogenschutz & Nurnberg, 2004; Zanarini & Frankenburg, 2001). In another trial, Zanarini et al. (2004) showed olanzapine and olanzapine/fluoxetine combination to be superior to fluoxetine (Prozac) alone. Recently, a double-blind, placebo controlled study showed aripiprazole (Abilify) to be significantly better than placebo (Nickel et al., 2006). Other atypical antipsychotics have been tested and have shown symptom reduction in case series. Both risperidone (Risperdal) (Rocca et al., 2002) and quetiapine (Seroquel) (Adityanjee & Schulz, 2002; Villeneuve & Lemelin, 2005) have shown promise.

One study examined olanzapine when used in patients receiving Dialectical Behavior Therapy. In this trial, olanzapine combined with DBT treatment was significantly better than placebo and DBT (Soler et al., 2005). As DBT is a cognitive behavioral treatment that has been empirically demonstrated to decrease symptoms of BPD (Linehan et al., 1991), to be discussed later in this chapter, studies assessing the effects of both types of intervention are the focus of future trials.

Although exact figures are hard to come by, the atypical antipsychotic medications appear to be relatively widely used in BPD. Trials to date are pointing to a dosing pattern that is one-half that used for schizophrenia. It is important to note, however, that there are no longer-term studies to guide the possible use of maintenance treatment. Side effects for second generation antipsychotic medications vary between medications, but may include sedation, weight gain, and rarely, tremor (EPS). As noted earlier, the prescriber should be familiar with the side-effect profile of the medication prescribed.

Antidepressants

Interestingly, even though BPD patients frequently describe experiencing low mood, two early studies showed a significant number of patients whose depressive symptoms worsened with tricyclic antidepressants (Klein, 1968; Soloff et al., 1986). However, when the new SSRIs (Selective Serotonin Reuptake Inhibitors) were introduced, it was of interest that symptom reduction was seen in case series (Markovitz et al., 1991) and subsequently in controlled trials of fluoxetine (Coccaro & Kavoussi, 1997), venlafaxine (Effexor) (Markovitz & Wagner, 1995), and fluovoxamine (Luvox) (Rinne et al., 2002). Of note was the effect of fluoxetine on impulsive behavior that Coccarro and Kavoussi (1997) tied to their research on the relationship of low serotonin to impulsivity. Nevertheless, one recent study of fluoxetine along with DBT did not show an advantage this combined treatment, compared to DBT and placebo (Simpson et al., 2004). This illustrates the need for future psychosocial and medication studies.

It appears that SSRIs and SNRIs are commonly prescribed for BPD and are a useful part of the armamentarium for treating BPD. Another advantage of these medications, compared to the older tricyclic antidepressants, is there relative safety following an overdose. Whether their effect on anxiety plays a role has yet to be determined. When using SSRIs, it is important to remember that they may be associated with headache and nausea as well as sexual side effects.

Anticonvulsant Mood Stabilizers

This group of medications has emerged as a major treatment for bipolar disorder, specifically elevated mood in the case of divalproex (Depakote) (Bowden et al., 1994). Another mood stabilizer, lamotrigine (Lamictal), has emerged as an intervention for bipolar depression, a difficult phase of the illness to treat (Calabrese et al., 1999). Some early studies of divalproex have shown promise in the treatment of BPD (Hollander et al., 2003) with perhaps the greatest effects seen in treating impulsivity and aggression (Hollander et al., 2005). Since these early studies were reported, Frankenburg and Zanarini (2002) have demonstrated the efficacy of divalproex in BPD in a placebo controlled trial. One case series of lamotrigine has been reported pointing to some utility of this agent (Pinto & Akiskal, 1998). The authors note that the results point to the relationship of bipolar disorder to BPD.

Currently, our research group has just completed a study examining valproic acid and DBT and expect the results to be published shortly (Schulz, research in progress). As with other medications described in this chapter, valproic acid is frequently used for BPD. Frequency of use of lamotrigine is less clear. Both medications appear to be relatively well tolerated. Prescribers should be aware of side effects and in the case of valproic acid, blood levels and metabolic chemistries need to be monitored regularly. The dermatologic side effects of lamotrigine are well known and can be minimized by a slow titration.

Benzodiazepines

Although Hoch and Polatin (1949) described patients who had pseudo-neurotic schizophrenia as having "pan-anxiety," the use of benzodiazepines in treating BPD has not been well studied. This may be the result of a report by Cowdry and Gardner (1988) illustrating "disinhibition" in BPD patients when participating in part of the treatment trial of alprazolam (Xanax) alone. It is difficult to determine whether or not benzodiazepines are commonly used, but clearly they are not the object of current studies. Some clinicians may use benzodiazepines in conjunction with medications such as SSRIs.

DIALECTICAL BEHAVIOR THERAPY AS AN ADJUNCT TO MEDICAL TREATMENT

As currently conceptualized in DBT, the biosocial theory of BPD is the result of dysfunction in the emotion regulation system that arises from transactions of a vulnerable biology with environmental invalidation over time (Linehan et al., 1991). This vulnerability is expressed as high emotional sensitivity, high reactivity, and a slow return to baseline, contributing to heightened sensitivity to the next emotional stimulus. Such immediate sensitivity derives from a low emotion threshold that sparks extreme reactions leading to high physiological arousal, all of which foster profound dysregulation of cognitive processing. Interestingly, clinical neuroscience studies are appearing that support the psychological theories of vulnerability. For example, individuals with BPD have been shown to have a significantly greater metabolic activation of the amygdala, part of the limbic or "emotional" system of the brain (Donegan et al., 2003).

Tasks for the treatment team include modulating physiological arousal, re-orientating attention, inhibiting mood-dependent activity, and organizing behavior to increase the likelihood of external, non-mood dependent goals. These goals are typically subsumed under the general goal of having a "life worth living."

Other symptoms thought to result from emotional dysregulation include cognitive, interpersonal, self and behavioral dysregulation. Cognitive dysregulation takes the form of brief paranoid ideation, dissociative responses and stress-related errors of thought. Interpersonal dysregulation is typified by chaotic relationships and fears of abandonment. Dysregulation of self results in a sense of emptiness, difficulty with sense of self and identity disturbances. Behavioral dysregulation is exemplified by impulsive and life-threatening behaviors.

HIERARCHY OF TARGETS
DURING PHARMACOTHERAPY SESSIONS

From a multidisciplinary perspective, psychotherapeutic treatment sessions progress from targets of greater concern to those of lesser concern. Specifically, treating life-threatening behavior takes precedence over treatment-destroying behavior, which precedes quality-of-life issues, etc. Similarly, the psychopharmacotherapeutic sessions target a hierarchy as follows:

- Decreasing life-threatening behavior
- Decreasing treatment-destroying behavior
- Decreasing specific symptoms, demonstrated to be reduced by medication
- Increasing self-management of health-related behavior
- Decreasing pharmacotherapy interfering behavior

Although life-threatening behavior is beyond the scope of this chapter, it is generally understood that in DBT, the individual therapist is primarily responsive to life-threatening behavior, unless this presents in-session during medication management. Treatment-destroying behavior can manifest as missed appointments, failure to schedule visits to the clinic and behavior on the part of the patient or psychiatrist that results in the decreased motivation of either to continue treatment. Increasing motivation for self-management of health-related behavior is encapsulated in the PLEASE skill taught in the DBT Emotion Regulation module. Reducing emotional vulnerability with

PLEASE is a skill that stresses self-management of the following: seeking treatment for PhysicaL illness, balanced Eating, avoidance of mood-Altering drugs, balanced Sleep and regular Exercise. Finally, issues that interfere with pharmacotherapy are addressed. Of particular importance is self-management of medication, whereby patients adjust dosages and frequency without consultation.

COLLABORATIVE TREATMENT

Collaborative treatment between psychiatrist and psychotherapist is increasingly common and helpful in managing patients who are in a DBT skills group and/or individual DBT-oriented psychotherapy, while seeing a psychiatrist for medication management. It is essential that this collaboration be optimized for ongoing consultation. Such treatment makes sense in light of the biosocial theory that underpins DBT. A growing body of literature supports various forms of collaborative treatment that afford ongoing consultation, support, and greater resources for the person in treatment. Specific goals to be addressed in consultation with collaborators include providing support while acting to prevent a "split" occurring between treaters, discussing of treatment-interfering factors, and planning roles in response to crises or medication changes, without reinforcement secondary to increased attention from collaborators. Helpful topics of discussion between the treaters include an understanding of the following:

- The relationship between the therapist and prescriber
- The meaning of the medication to both therapist and prescriber
- The meaning of the medication to the patient
- The limited effectiveness of the medication may
- The way the medication fits into the overall treatment for the patient
- The potential and actual lethality of the medication
- The fact that initiation or modification of the medication cannot relieve interpersonal crises and affective storms

DIALECTICS FOR RESOLVING MEDICATION POLARITIES

Dialectics as a form of argument involves exploration of an argument (thesis), followed by analysis of its weak points, and finally synthesis of both seemingly opposing positions. As a style of thought, it differs from the common "universal formal" typified by positions suggesting absolute truth and resulting in "either/or" polarities. Distinct from this is a stance that there is no absolute truth, endorsed by a "relativist" form of thinking. Dialectics is correctly seen as a method of synthesizing polarities, and of synthesizing these styles of thought in particular. Dialectics suggests a "both/and" style where the notions that there is no absolute truth and that there is absolute truth can both be true at the same time, resulting in acknowledgement that in fact truth is constantly evolving, and that each synthesis is the starting point for a new polarity that can reach synthesis. Inherent in DBT are a variety of dialectical positions that reach synthesis in treatment. A treatment such as DBT that balances acceptance and change is exemplified in the two core treatment strategies of validation and problem solving.

Common polarities in medication management involve medications vs. psychotherapy, as many patients may believe that medication alone will provide the relief they seek, or that medications are of no benefit at all. "Medications are useless" and "Medications are the only answer" becomes a combination between the two extremes. Seen in this light, medications are more usefully thought of as helpful to biological predisposition, while therapy is emphasized for treatment of social factors such as self-invalidation, which brings about improved regulation of the neurological elements of the emotional regulation system.

When patient and physician are momentarily in polarizing positions, a patient may manifest an oppositional stance. Dialectical styles allow the physician to momentarily "unbalance" a patient from a polarized stance, in service of bringing the patient back into balance and closer to his or her ultimate goal of having a life worth living.

The patient on a sensible medication regimen who requests frequent dosage and medication changes, or who makes changes to the regimen without consulting with the physician presents a particularly difficult challenge and an equally important opportunity for use of DBT skills. Using these skills in this context, while crucial for the patient, is very helpful to the clinician as well. As such, it is suggested that psychiatrists who desire to improve their medication management of people with BPD consider learning the skills of DBT. Specific modules teach acceptance (Mindfulness and Distress Tolerance), while others encourage change (Emotion Regulation, Interpersonal Effectiveness).

Pretreatment planning for therapy necessarily includes development of and agreement upon goals between patient and clinician. Individual therapy with a DBT orientation aims specifically to decrease unsafe behaviors and those that interfere with, therapy and quality of life, as well as to increase the use of DBT skills. Similarly, pharmacotherapy appointments may be useful for decreasing pharmacotherapy-interfering behaviors such as non-compliance with medication and self-management of medication without consulting the treating psychiatrist. Other goals include referring the patient to the primary therapist for life-threatening behavior, often via direct telephone calls during appointments, and increasing the patient's self-management through the DBT skills encapsulated in the acronym PLEASE (PhysicaL illness, balanced Eating, avoidance of mood-Altering drugs, balanced Sleep, and Exercise).

A more nuanced understanding of the DBT skill set allows the treating psychiatrist to help emphasize diary card use and as such will allow the clinician access to data provided on the cards which will give a more precise understanding of mood states, med changes, use of chemicals, urges and activity related to self-harm and suicidality, and other target symptoms and behaviors. It is useful to request that patients come to appointments with a minimum of four recently completed weekly diary cards. Collaborating with the patient to make subjective data less prone to error that may be mood (or emotion) state-dependent has the added benefit of strengthening the therapeutic alliance. It also reinforces use of diary cards in skill evaluation and development, and may enhance compliance with card use for individual sessions with the collaborating therapist.

REFERENCES

Adityanjee, A. & Schulz, S. C. (2002). Clinical use of quetiapine in disease states other than schizophrenia. Journal of Clinical Psychiatry, 63 Suppl, 13:32-8.

A.P.A. (1980). Diagnostic and Statistical Manual-III. Washington, D.C.: American Psychiatric Association.

Bogenschutz, M.P. & Nurnberg, H. (2004). Olanzapine versus placebo in the treatment of borderline personality disorder. Journal of Clinical Psychiatry, 65, 104-9.

Bowden, C.L., Brugger, A.M., & Swann, A.C. et al. (1994). Efficacy of divalproex vs lithium and placebo in the treatment of mania. The Depakote Mania Study Group. Journal of the American Medical Association, 271, 918-24.

Brinkley J.R., Beitman, B.D., & Friedel, R.O. (1979). Low-dose neuroleptic regimens in the treatment of borderline patients. Archives of General Psychiatry, 36, 319-26.

Calabrese, J.R., Bowden, C.L., Sachs, G.S., Ascher, J.A., Monaghan, E., & Rudd, G.D. (1999). A double-blind placebo-controlled study of lamotrigine monotherapy in outpatients with bipolar I depression. Lamictal 602 Study Group. Journal of Clinical Psychiatry, 60, 79-88.

Coccaro, E.F., & Kavoussi, R.J. (1997). Fluoxetine and impulsive aggressive behavior in personality-disordered subjects. Archives of General Psychiatry, 54, 1081-8.

Cowdry, R.W., & Gardner, D.L. (1988). Pharmacotherapy of borderline personality disorder. Alprazolam, carbamazepine, trifluoperazine, and tranylcypromine. Archives of General Psychiatry, 45, 111-9.

Donegan, N.H., Sanislow, C.A., & Blumberg, H.P. et al. (2003). Amygdala hyperreactivity in borderline personality disorder: implications for emotional dysregulation. Biological Psychiatry, 54, 1284-93.

Frankenburg, F.R. & Zanarini, M.C. (2002). Divalproex sodium treatment of women with borderline personality disorder and bipolar II disorder: a double-blind placebo-controlled pilot study. Journal of Clinical Psychiatry, 63, 442-6.

Goldberg, S.C. (1989). Prediction of change in borderline personality disorder. Psychopharmacology Bulletin, 25, 550-5.

Goldberg, S.C., Schulz, S.C., Schulz, P,M., Resnick, R.J., Hamer, R.M., & Friedel, R.O. (1986). Borderline and schizotypal personality disorders treated with low-dose thiothixene vs. placebo. Archives of General Psychiatry, 43, 680-6.

Gunderson, J.G. & Singer, M.T. (1975). Defining borderline patients: an overview. American Journal of Psychiatry, 132, 1-10.

Hoch, P.H. & Polatin, P. (1949). Pseudoneurotic forms of schizophrenia. Comprehensive Psychiatry, 27, 248-276.

Hollander, E., Swann, A.C., Coccaro, E.F., Jiang, P., & Smith, T.B. (2005). Impact of trait impulsivity and state aggression on divalproex versus placebo response in borderline personality disorder. American Journal of Psychiatry, 162, 621-4.

Hollander, E., Tracy, K.A., Swann, A.C. et al. (2003). Divalproex in the treatment of impulsive aggression: efficacy in cluster B personality disorders. Neuropsychopharmacology, 28, 1186-97.

Klein, D.F. (1968). Psychiatric diagnosis and typology of clinical drug effects. Psychopharmacology, 13, 359-386.

Linehan, M.M., Armstrong, H.E., Suarez, A., Allmon, D., & Heard, H.L. (1991). Cognitive-behavioral treatment of chronically parasuicidal borderline patients. Archives of General Psychiatry, 48, 1060-4.

Markovitz, P.J., Calabrese, J.R., Schulz, S.C., & Meltzer, H.Y. (1991). Fluoxetine in the treatment of borderline and schizotypal personality disorders. American Journal of Psychiatry, 148, 1064-7.

Markovitz, P.J. & Wagner, S.C. (1995). Venlafaxine in the treatment of borderline personality disorder. Psychopharmacology Bulletin, 31, 773-7.

Nickel, M.K., Muehlbacher, M., & Nickel, C. et al (2006). Aripiprazole in the treatment of patients with borderline personality disorder: a double-blind, placebo-controlled study. American Journal of Psychiatry, 163, 833-8.

Pinto, O.C. & Akiskal, H.S. (1998). Lamotrigine as a promising approach to borderline personality: an open case series without concurrent DSM-IV major mood disorder. Journal of Affective Disorders, 51, 333-43.

Rifkin, A., Quitkin, F., Carrillo, C., Blumberg, A.G., & Klein, D.F. (1972). Lithium carbonate in emotionally unstable character disorder. Archives of General Psychiatry, 27, 519-23.

Rinne, T., van den Brink, W., Wouters, L., & van Dyck, R. (2002). SSRI treatment of borderline personality disorder: a randomized, placebo-controlled clinical trial for female patients with borderline personality disorder. American Journal of Psychiatry, 159, 2048-54.

Rocca, P., Marchiaro, L., Cocuzza, E., & Bogetto, F. (2002). Treatment of borderline personality disorder with risperidone. Journal of Clinical Psychiatry, 63, 241-4.

Schulz, S.C., Camlin, K.L., Berry, S.A., & Jesberger, J.A. (1999). Olanzapine safety and efficacy in patients with borderline personality disorder and comorbid dysthymia. Biological Psychiatry, 46, 1429-35.

Simpson, E.B., Yen, S., & Costello, E. et al. (2004). Combined dialectical behavior therapy and fluoxetine in the treatment of borderline personality disorder. Journal of Clinical Psychiatry, 65, 379-85.

Soler, J., Pascual, J.C., & Campins, J. et al. (2005). Double-blind, placebo-controlled study of dialectical behavior therapy plus olanzapine for borderline personality disorder. American Journal of Psychiatry, 162, 1221-4.

Soloff, P.H., Cornelius, J., George, A., Nathan, S., Perel, J.M., & Ulrich, R.F. (1993). Efficacy of phenelzine and haloperidol in borderline personality disorder. Archives of General Psychiatry, 50, 377-85.

Soloff, P.H., George, A., Nathan, R.S., Schulz, P.M., Ulrich, R.F., & Perel, J.M. (1986). Progress in pharmacotherapy of borderline disorders. A double-blind study of amitriptyline, haloperidol, and placebo. Archives of General Psychiatry, 43, 691-7.

Villeneuve, E. & Lemelin, S. (2005). Open-label study of atypical neuroleptic quetiapine for treatment of borderline personality disorder: impulsivity as main target. Journal of Clinical Psychiatry, 66, 1298-303.

Zanarini, M.C. & Frankenburg, F.R. (2001). Olanzapine treatment of female borderline personality disorder patients: a double-blind, placebo-controlled pilot study. Journal of Clinical Psychiatry, 62, 849-54.

Zanarini, M.C., Frankenburg, F.R., & Parachini, E.A. (2004). A preliminary, randomized trial of fluoxetine, olanzapine, and the olanzapine-fluoxetine combination in women with borderline personality disorder. Journal of Clinical Psychiatry, 65, 903-7.

doi:10.1300/J200v06n01_11

APPENDIX

Medication Treatment for Borderline Personality Disorder

Medication	Approved Use	Dosing for BPD	Clinical Trials Support (+ to ++++)	Current Use
Lithium	Manic episodes of bipolar disorder and maintenance of bipolar disorder	Same as Bipolar with blood concentration monitoring	+++	Not widely used, mostly with bipolar I or II
Antipsychotic Medications				
Traditional	Schizophrenia/Psychosis	One-Half that for schizophrenia	++++	Not widely used because of movement disorder side effects
Atypical	Psychosis, Bipolar Disorder (short-term)	One-Half that for schizophrenia/bipolar	++++	Widely used, concern about metabolic side effects
Anticonvulsant Mood Stabilizers	Epilepsy, Bipolar Disorder	Same as bipolar, with blood concentration monitoring when indicated	+++/++++	Widely used, especially for mood swings and impulsive aggressive symptoms
SSRI/SNRI	Depression, panic, OCD, social phobia	Same or higher than depression	+++/++++	Frequently prescribed for low mood and anger

\+ - Case Series
++ - Multiple Trials
+++ - Placebo Controlled
++++ - Multiple and Large Controlled Trials

Supportive Psychotherapy for Borderline Patients

Ann H. Appelbaum

SUMMARY. An imagined conversation between a clinician/teacher and a beginning therapist conveys the concept of a psychoanalytically informed supportive psychotherapy for borderline patients and incorporates the major hypotheses as to the origin of the disorder. Within a basically developmental point of view, the treatment recognizes the contributions of genetics, animal studies, neuroscience, early interpersonal relationships and the object relations that derive from them. The psychodynamics of a typical case are considered from all of these viewpoints, while the student-therapist is encouraged to keep in mind the basic concepts of psychoanalysis. These include: unconscious mental activity, transference, and the internalization of the therapist's attitude of respectful listening, which leads to the capacity to listen in that way to oneself and others. doi:10.1300/J200v06n01_12 *[Article copies available for a fee from The Haworth Document Delivery Service: 1-800-HAWORTH. E-mail address: <docdelivery@haworthpress.com> Website: <http://www.HaworthPress.com> © 2008 by The Haworth Press. All rights reserved.]*

KEYWORDS. Borderline personality disorder, learning state, therapeutic roles, non-interpretive, emotional safety

---

[Haworth co-indexing entry note]: "Supportive Psychotherapy for Borderline Patients." Appelbaum, Ann H. Co-published simultaneously in *Social Work in Mental Health* (The Haworth Press, Inc.) Vol. 6, No. 1/2, 2008, pp. 145-155; and: *Borderline Personality Disorder: Meeting the Challenges to Successful Treatment* (ed: Perry D. Hoffman, and Penny Steiner-Grossman) The Haworth Press, 2008, pp. 145-155. Single or multiple copies of this article are available for a fee from The Haworth Document Delivery Service [1-800-HAWORTH, 9:00 a.m. - 5:00 p.m. (EST). E-mail address: docdelivery@haworthpress.com].

INTRODUCTION: A DIALOGUE

The case of "Joan," offered as a point of departure for a discussion of the theory of supportive psychoanalytically informed psychotherapy, contains the kind of information that could be gathered in an initial interview and presented to a supervisor at a clinic. Let us imagine the discussion that might take place between a student of psychotherapy and her supervisor. The student has given the supervisor the document that represents her thinking about Joan in the light of the initial interview.

Teacher: The beginning of your write-up reveals the problem you faced, and it isn't the problem of Joan's diagnosis and what could be done about it–not yet.

Student: Is the diagnosis a problem? I thought the diagnosis of borderline personality disorder was made by the referring physician. It really does fit her symptom pattern.

Teacher: I'll explain what I mean. You begin by saying that Joan "originally presented for treatment with her parents." The implication is that the three of them are "presenting" themselves for treatment.

Student: Well, that's not exactly what I meant. It was Joan, not the parents, who had been referred to the clinic.

Teacher: True enough. And in fact you follow that initial statement with a list of Joan's symptoms, apparently provided by the referring psychiatrist: unstable relationships, drug abuse, several brief hospitalizations, incidents of self-injury, trouble with the law in the form of an arrest on the charge of assault, and "episodic employment," by which I guess is meant that she was unable to hold a job. You imply later on in your write-up that the psychiatrist had informed the parents that their daughter has a borderline personality disorder that had not responded to treatment with medications. Later on we can take up the question of whether placing her in the category of borderline personality disorder is enough to determine the treatment she needs.

For now let's see what else we know about her. You say that at age 29 she is still financially dependent on her parents, and that they urged her to come home when she proved incapable of managing her life "after college." It isn't clear whether she graduated or failed or dropped out of college.

Student: I don't know. The psychiatrist's report just said that after she came home, the situation became so difficult that the parents "helped" her find an apartment, hoping she would become more independent and take over the rental payments.

Teacher: What do you make of that?

Student: Well, when I try to read between the lines of what the parents told me, I can imagine that they got fed up with her drinking and drugging. They must have dreaded her frequent tantrums during family dinners when she would blame the whole family, and especially the father, for not understanding her, not helping her enough. There had been conflicts between the parents all along about how to manage Joan, and their disagreements must have become more acute when Joan. came home to live with them. They had to agree both on how to encourage her to leave home and how to help her accomplish that. "Hoping" that living in her own apartment would make her more independent seems completely unrealistic to me. Joan had to perceive it as being kicked out. And she apparently blamed her father for that.

THE DEVELOPMENTAL VIEWPOINT

Teacher: I agree. Now we come to a shift of focus in your write-up, from the present muddle to Joan's developmental history as it might shed some light on how the current state of affairs came about. You say that Joan, the youngest of three children, had been "a very beloved child." That must have been how the parents presented their initial response to their new daughter. They described her as "bright, charming, extremely social, and loving to perform." In retrospect, one can wonder if what they were describing were early manifestations of what later became Joan's "grandiose posturing."

THE PSYCHODYNAMIC VIEWPOINT: REPRESSION AND DENIAL

Something might have prevented the parents from looking too closely at some developing problems. This is suggested by the discrepancy between their perception of their daughter's performance in grade school and Joan's own view of how she was doing. While the parents describe her as a good student, Joan remembers school as always having been difficult. Trying to live up to an evaluation of themselves that they know to be false is stressful for these youngsters. Quite possibly, they sense that their difficulties challenge the parents' perception of themselves as competent. Troubled children could collude with the parents to protect that self-concept by keeping much of their distress to themselves.

It has been quite some time since psychiatry blamed parents for the psychological troubles of their children. We know now that there are multiple determinants of a child's failure to follow the expected path from infancy to maturity. Unconscious attitudes conveyed to the child through parental behavior may be the least significant of a number of other factors influencing the development of borderline personality disorders.

THE NEUROLOGICAL VIEWPOINT

In any case, the illusion of competence fell apart when Joan got to high school and her grades suddenly dropped. This is not an uncommon phenomenon. Children with limitations in their capacity for abstract thinking often do fairly well in school until the academic requirement for thinking in concepts proves to be beyond their limits. Failure, or the fear of it, prompts some of these children to seek solace in the numbing effect of alcohol or the excitement of promiscuity or taking risks.

Student: That fits in with how she seems to have hidden herself away from her parents once it began to be obvious that she could not live up to the standards set by the two older siblings who were doing well in life. Joan came home only when she was totally unable to keep up the pretense of being able to fend for herself.

Teacher: Exactly. And that brings us to the question of whether the category of borderline personality fully fits Joan. When we put together her early behaviors: resorting to drugs and alcohol, rather than seeking help for the trouble she was having academically; her habitual blaming of her family for her problems; her assumption about being entitled to unlimited financial support from her parents; her experience of working as a sales clerk as "humiliating"; her "grandiose posturing"; and her goal for treatment as getting help for her parents, a configuration emerges that is similar to the description of the narcissistic personality disorder. These behaviors supplement the list provided by the referring psychiatrist and, I believe, justify the diagnosis of borderline personality disorder with narcissistic features and co-morbid substance abuse.

Student: If that is the case, she will probably need group therapy along with transference-focused psychotherapy, will she not?

Teacher: Quite possibly. But we are far from being able to refer her for that or any other treatment at this point. Remember that in Joan's eyes, she is not a patient; her announced goal is to find someone who could "help her family understand her and be more supportive."

THE THERAPIST'S ROLE

Student: If Joan is not the patient, what do I do with her?

Teacher: Well, suppose you were to accept the role of the "someone" who will help the parents?

Student: I'd feel like an imposter, because I don't see myself that way. I see Joan as really ill, and I see myself as designated to help her. The parents may have their problems, but they aren't drinking and drugging and having temper tantrums.

Teacher: Don't forget that as a therapist you are playing a role, too. There really isn't any normal, authentic human relationship that matches therapy. If you try to be a therapist to a friend, a classmate, or even to your own child, you are likely to find that it doesn't work. There's a reciprocal element in such relationships: you tell me your troubles and I'll tell you mine; I love you, and you love me back, or else I have to accept being rejected. If you get mad at me and insult me, I'm entitled to get mad at you. None of that goes on in therapy. You are trained to play the therapist's role, which feels strange and unnatural at first to many beginners, (and to borderline patients, as well). You will remain calm, listening to whatever patients want to tell you, while listening as well to your own reactions and thinking about the meanings of your interchange. You will keep what they tell you confidential, and you will give advice sparingly, if at all. You will devote your entire attention to your patient during the time allotted for the therapy session, and you will usually expect to be paid. Joan doesn't sound like she's ready for that sort of relationship.

Student: I see. I'd taken the therapist role for granted. And I must admit that I feel sort of at sea without my therapist role to fall back on. But even if I accept Joan's goal, I can't treat the parents. They are no more my patients than Joan is.

Teacher: Let's say you have already made an appointment with Joan, to see her privately.

Student: Well, I have, actually.

THE INTERPERSONAL VIEW OF PSYCHOTHERAPY

Teacher: So, assuming that Joan shows up for her appointment, you might tell her that you've been thinking about how to accomplish the task of helping her parents understand her better. And you are almost certain that it can be done if Joan will be your partner in this endeavor.

And then you explain that you will continue meeting with the three of them for a while, to develop a plan for helping Joan. She will need to be off drugs and alcohol during this process; she must have her wits about her if her parents are to take her ideas seriously.

Student: She'll probably say she can't do it, that she needs something to keep her from being too anxious to function.

Teacher: You can refer her to an expert pharmacologist if need be, but it would be better if she could go through this experience without medication. You could tell her that no one knows what is making her so anxious that she needs alcohol or drugs to calm down, and you may need her to take some tests that would shed some light on this problem. Then, if all goes well, you meet with Joan and her parents, perhaps for several sessions. You can explain to them that Joan may have some developmental problem that, if unrecognized, could contribute to some of the troubles they have had as a family. You also would explain the neuropsychological testing procedure and why it is important for Joan to remain free of drugs and alcohol during this diagnostic period.

Let us suppose that the care you are taking to understand the nature of Joan's unhappiness and her parents' inability to help her will convince all three of them to play their parts in sorting out the issues. The parents can be referred to a social worker skilled in family therapy who can help them revisit the early months and years of Joan's life. Perhaps they can take a fresh look at the friction that apparently developed between them about Joan's upbringing, and reflect on whether similar disagreements arose in the course of raising the two older children. If no such disagreements arose, how might they understand that disparity now? Meanwhile Joan may be willing to continue meeting with you for support in achieving and maintaining abstinence from drugs and alcohol.

Student: So for the time being, during this diagnostic phase, I'll just be doing supportive therapy—you know, just keeping her on task by reassuring her and listening sympathetically until real treatment can begin.

Teacher: "Just?" You will see that providing the kind of support Joan needs now is the most challenging and difficult of all psychoanalytic psychotherapies. That is the main reason we don't have a manual that adequately describes it. Another reason is that everyone needs "support" of one sort or another. So the clientele for supportive treatment ranges all the way from healthy people who need a bit of help in getting over a bumpy place, to desperately embattled people who require the therapist to have a mixture of knowledge, tact, insight, flexibility and patience even to get to first base.

Some manuals present supportive psychotherapy as defined by its techniques and provide step-by-step procedures for the therapist to take. Seasoned therapists tend to see these manuals as somewhat simplistic. Others define the treatment in terms of its goals, for example, "strengthening healthy defenses and undermining non-adaptive ones." On closer inspection, one realizes that "defenses" are hypothesized unconscious processes and can only be inferred from behaviors that mitigate anxiety. So the description boils down to encouraging certain behaviors and discouraging others. We know very well, however, that a person is unlikely to respond to a therapist's encouragement or advice unless a very trusting relationship has been formed. Again, healthy people tend to trust therapists naturally, as they assume that a highly trained and well-qualified therapist is worthy of their trust. But people who are struggling, as Joan is, with feelings of shame about needing help, and feeling swamped by resentment over being unable to handle everyday living, have great difficulty in trusting anyone they see as standing in the place of their parents.

In short, the best prescription that can be made for a therapist starting out with a new patient in serious emotional trouble is to avoid interventions that increase anxiety until you are reasonably sure of the patient's strengths and vulnerabilities, and until the environment, whether home or hospital, includes people who can shore up the patient's resolve to persist in the treatment. We'll talk later about the interventions that arouse anxiety.

PSYCHOTHERAPY AS FOSTERING NEW LEARNING

Here is where both the neurological and the developmental viewpoint bear upon a theory of supportive psychotherapy. If we assume that successful psychotherapy represents the learning of new ways of coping with psychological pain, then we will look for ways of promoting that learning. We know that infancy is the period of life in which the most rapid learning occurs, and that from the very beginning babies pay attention to the world around them. Close observation of newborns has found that they have only six recognizable states, ranging from deep sleep to a state of quiet alertness. That quiet, alert state, fleeting at first, lasts longer as the infant matures (Wolff, 1966). Parents try to prolong this state because they feel they make contact with their baby during this "learning" state. Parents learn that certain actions on their part, such as making the baby comfortable, excluding disrupting sounds, and staying in tune with the baby's rhythms serve to extend the periods of quiet alertness when they can play with their baby. In healthy development, babies learn to recognize and trust the parents, and the quiet alert state of infancy merges into the calm, educable state of school children (Sarnoff, 1966). As this process goes on, parents begin to notice the many ways their child tries to imitate them, seems to take in their tastes and preferences, and later their values and beliefs. The process of identification with the parents begins with the "learning" state.

Parents, and later teachers, find that providing conditions of comfort, serenity and appropriate stimulation fosters play and learning. Aversive stimulation, whether from outside or within the individual, disrupts the "learning state." Application of these ideas to supportive therapy leads to the basic therapeutic strategy of seeing to the emotional safety of the therapy situation (Havens, 1989) and introducing measures designed to foster change as trust develops between therapist and patient.

The essential difference between supportive and exploratory therapy is that in supportive psychotherapy the basic elements of exploratory work are not applied until patient and therapist have established a solid working relationship. Especially important among those elements are: clarifying (asking questions); confronting (pointing out discrepancies between patients' stated intentions and what they say and do in the sessions); and interpreting (explaining the unconscious meanings of a given behavior). These are the interventions that would-be psychoanalysts take pains to master through years of training. These measures are designed to keep an active process of self-exploration moving along. The assumption is that the neurotic symptom represents an unconscious fantasy that serves to diminish anxiety and is thus "frozen," safeguarded by layers of defensive mental activity. Asking patients questions, confronting them with the contradictions in their communication, and interpreting the unconscious meanings of their behavior stir up anxiety and "shake up" the neurotic structure, so that new understandings can arise and be assimilated (Schlesinger, 2005). As borderline patients begin therapy, they react very negatively to interventions that stimulate anxiety. It is only when these patients feel safe with the therapist and have begun to identify themselves with the therapist's interest in their inner lives that exploratory interventions become useful.

Teacher: This brings me to several other matters that I want to discuss with you. First there is the widespread misconception among therapists, patients and the general public that supportive psychotherapy is a kind of "babying" of patients. This disparaging and inaccurate stance toward supportive therapy is difficult for many psychoanalytically trained therapists and researchers to renounce. All patients need kindness. They also need respect for their sensitivities and limitations, but this is not the same as infantilizing them. Some patients need the bolstering of their resolve to resist the temptation to dull inner pain with drugs and alcohol, as is the case with Joan. Such support is skillfully provided in various 12-step programs, but she has already rejected this avenue of self-help.

Joan seeks relief of pain, and blames others for causing it. In a way she may have a point. It is not hard to imagine her parents noticing that their third and last child was in some ways slower developmentally than their first two children. And we can see how they might have coped with their uneasiness about her by assuring themselves, and Joan herself, that she was "a very beloved child." They may have misunderstood her childish charm and love of performing as valuable attributes, without also recognizing in them a desperate effort to compensate for what she perceived as their rejection, however subtle and unintentional it may have been. When she reached school age and told her parents about her difficulties in school, they may have turned a deaf ear to her complaints and insisted upon seeing her as "a good student." As her grades dropped "precipitously" in high school, Joan may have felt unable to face her parents' disappointment, and turned to drugs and alcohol in a futile attempt to hide from herself her increasing sense of failure. This scenario is described by Linehan (1993) as the common experience of people with borderline personality disorder, the plight of the "supposedly competent person." Joan's enactment of a wish for family therapy by bringing her parents to the initial interview may have expressed a valid suspicion that the parents were somehow implicated in the way her life went wrong in adolescence. Nevertheless, an honest review of those earliest years of Joan's life may be too taxing for the parents, who have been suffering now for years under the lash of Joan's recriminations. They may need the support of a skilled family therapist in order to provide the cooperation that Joan's therapist will need from them if her therapy is to be effective.

Student: So what are we supporting in this therapy? It's clear to me that we are supporting the people involved in Joan's care–the parents and the hospital staff if she needs to be hospitalized. We are also supporting the patient's motivation to stay in treatment. I understand the idea of promoting the patient's ability to stay in the "learning" state that you described. It's clear to me now that there is an analogy for supportive therapy in the way parents influence their children by modeling civil behavior, praising their achievements, and rewarding signs of progress toward maturity. But parents also punish their kids for behaving badly.

Teacher: Punishment plays no role in psychotherapy. We can rely upon the environment to punish patients for obnoxious behaviors. The therapist's role is to help the patient find the motives and meanings of unacceptable behavior. Much is said about the therapist's need to "set limits" as a way of preventing actions that harm the patient or that jeopardize the treatment. Linehan (1993) has rightly pointed out that one cannot control another's behavior. In the long run, control can be exercised only by the individual. The therapist can and must make clear to the patient the limits of the *therapist's* tolerance, that is, by announcing his/her limits. An example is the therapist who says, "I can accept telephone calls only between 5:00 and 9:00 p.m.," or one who says, "I need to be paid promptly every month." Such statements pave the way for open discussion, as the simple statement of a need or a limitation does not imply an ultimatum or a threat.

SUPPORT FOR THE THERAPIST

You mentioned supporting the family, an important task but not one the therapist typically carries out. And how about the therapist's need for support? Practicing the psychotherapy of personality disorders, however, is fraught with high levels of anxiety and frustration, and often arouses feelings of inadequacy and guilt in excellent therapists. Facing impasses and seemingly insuperable obstacles, therapists may feel ashamed of their inability to help and so postpone seeking supervision until matters get out of hand. It is far better to have ongoing supervision so that impasses and misunderstandings can be dealt with early; sometimes, if these situations are foreseen, they may even be prevented. We have found that using a small group of six to eight professionals with a mixture of experience is an invaluable way to provide supervision for these cases. In such a group, the therapists tend to form bonds of mutual respect and trust, becoming able to present their cases candidly to each other and learn from the accumulated wisdom of the entire group. As each member of the group will experience a patient in an individual way, the group has the potential to mirror the diversity of the patients' sense of themselves. Articulating these various versions of the patients' representations of themselves and others leads to the development of an integrated understanding. In the course of this integration, therapists gain a deeper understanding of their own reactions to their patients. Of course, these groups must protect the confidentiality of each patient's treatment. Patients know of the work of the supervision group, and they often feeling protected in knowing that their therapists have the support of the group of peers.

SOME FINAL THOUGHTS

Being informed by psychoanalysis, the therapist is sensitized to manifestations of the patient's unconscious wishes and fears and uses this sensitivity to assist patients in making their own interpretations when they become secure enough to do so. This avoidance of explicit verbal interpretation distinguishes supportive from exploratory psychotherapy and serves to forestall regression, which is neither necessary nor helpful in the early stages of treatment of severe borderline pathology. Indeed, there is ongoing controversy in psychoanalysis as to whether insight and interpretation account for change for the better in psychoanalytic therapy, or whether such changes are the result of favorable conditions of therapy that promote identification with the analyst's benign interest in the patient's mind. Adequate research on this issue is still pending (Fonagy & Target, 2003; Holinger, 1999).

REFERENCES

Fonagy, P. & Target, M. (2003). *Psychoanalytic theories: Perspectives from developmental psychopathology.* Philadelphia: Whurr.

Havens, L. (1989). *A safe place.* Cambridge, Mass.: Harvard University Press.

Holinger, P. C. (1999). Noninterpretive interventions in psychoanalysis and psychotherapy: A developmental perspective. *Psychoanalytic Psychology,* 16, 233-253.

Linehan, M. M. (1993). *Cognitive-behavioral treatment of borderline personality disorders* (pp. 80-84). New York: Guilford Press,

Sarnoff, C. (1966). *Latency.* New York: Jason Aronson.

Schlesinger, H. J. (2003). *The texture of treatment.* Hillsdale, N.J.: Analytic Press.

Wolff, P. (1966). *The causes, controls, and organization of behavior in the neonate.* Madison, Conn.: International Universities Press.

doi:10.1300/J200v06n01_12

Transference-Focused Psychotherapy for BPD

Frank Yeomans
Jill Delaney

SUMMARY. Transference-Focused Psychotherapy (TFP) is a modified psychodynamic psychotherapy, based on object relations theory of personality and psychoanalytic principles of the dynamic unconscious, the importance of transference and counter-transference, and the reliance upon interpretation of the transference as the dominant therapeutic intervention. TFP has been shown to be effective in reducing symptoms and improving reflective function in a randomized clinical trial with borderline patients. Beyond initial symptom reduction, TFP has as a goal the integration of identity through interpretative elaboration of split off internalized representations of self and others that underlie the DSM IV-TR descriptive phenomena of borderline personality disorder. doi:10.1300/J200v06n01_13 *[Article copies available for a fee from The Haworth Document Delivery Service: 1-800-HAWORTH. E-mail address: <docdelivery@haworthpress.com> Website: <http://www.HaworthPress.com> © 2008 by The Haworth Press. All rights reserved.]*

KEYWORDS. Borderline personality disorder, psychodynamic psychotherapy, transference-focused psychotherapy, object relations theory, identity, identity diffusion, identity integration, personality structure

[Haworth co-indexing entry note]: "Transference-Focused Psychotherapy for BPD." Yeomans, Frank, and Jill Delaney. Co-published simultaneously in *Social Work in Mental Health* (The Haworth Press) Vol. 6, No. 1/2, 2008, pp. 157-170; and: *Borderline Personality Disorder: Meeting the Challenges to Successful Treatment* (ed: Perry D. Hoffman, and Penny Steiner-Grossman) The Haworth Press, 2008, pp. 157-170. Single or multiple copies of this article are available for a fee from The Haworth Document Delivery Service [1-800-HAWORTH, 9:00 a.m. - 5:00 p.m. (EST). E-mail address: docdelivery@haworthpress.com].

INTRODUCTION

Psychoanalytic theory, once the central conceptual model in understanding psychiatric conditions, now sometimes seems relegated to the status of historic artifact. The psychoanalytic community is partly to blame for this, having at times expressed excessive confidence in its ability to address all types of mental illness equally well. However, analytic concepts and techniques can be very effective in addressing problems of the mind if used in focused and specific ways. The term "psychodynamic" may be more appropriate than "psychoanalytic." Psychodynamic refers to the interaction of competing forces or motivations in the mind–in particular, forces that favor acting on a feeling or impulse, forces that prohibit such action, and forces that monitor and respect the constraints of external reality. Conflicts among these forces can give rise to specific symptoms, such as depression, anxiety, intense emotions, and acting out.

BPD AND OBJECT RELATIONS THEORY

In the DSM-IV (4th Ed., 2000), borderline personality disorder is defined by a set of symptom criteria. In a psychodynamic diagnostic system (Kernberg & Caligor, 2005), borderline pathology is understood as based on a particular way the mind is structured. A brief description of this structure involves examining a theory of how the mind develops. A hypothesis of object relations theory (Klein, 1957; Jacobson, 1964; Kernberg, 1975, 1980, 1984), is that the development of the infant's mind is intimately linked with interactions and relations with care giving figures. Infant development includes normal cognitive development (learning) during periods of relatively low emotional intensity and a different kind of learning during periods of high emotional intensity. In these latter periods, the infant experiences a felt need–to satisfy hunger, to relieve pain or discomfort–as well as a response from the caregiver that can either satisfy the need/resolve the pain and discomfort, or not. In the former case, when needs are well met, the infant feels, and internalizes, an experience of a contented and satisfied self in a feeling of love and warmth toward the other, who is perceived as nurturing and caring. In the latter case, when needs are inadequately met or not met at all, the infant internalizes an experience of a suffering, frightened, possibly angry self in relation to a neglectful, abandoning, and possibly sadistic other. The theory is that these two experiences, repeated again and again, are internalized in very early development as *separate*: the satisfied, loved self linked with the nurturing, caring provider is internalized separately from the suffering, frightened, or angry self in relation to the neglectful or persecutory other. Each of these paradigms becomes an internal model of the experience of self and other in the world. These self and objects pairs, linked by an intense affect, are referred to as "object relations dyads" (see Figure 1).

The affective link between these internalized self and other representations will be an important factor in subsequent development and experience. As development progresses, these internal dyads become templates that shape the individual's perception of experiences in the world: a satisfying experience will activate the internal paradigm of the totally cared-for self in relation to the perfectly nurturing other; and a frustrating experience will activate the paradigm, and thus the perception, of the totally abandoned, uncared-for self in relation to the bad other. This state of affairs, a normal phase for all infants, would be quite disastrous if it did not develop further. Indeed, in normal human development the internal paradigms do not remain so extreme and rigidly divided. Normal cognitive learning and, in the case of most individuals, a predominance of positive experience over negative, lead to the bringing together or integration of the extreme representations of self and other that have been internalized. What results is the development of a more nuanced, full-bodied, and realistic internal representation of who one is and what others are like (see Figure 2).

However, in some individuals this integration and fleshing out of the representations of self and other does not take place, leaving the individual with internal images that are more extreme, simplistic and rigid than they actually are. We believe that this is the case for individuals with BPD, and that this internal state of extreme and opposite (polarized) images coloring the individual's perceptions of self, people, and events leads to the specific symptoms of BPD (see Figure 3).

For example, chaotic interpersonal relations make sense and logically follow if others are seen as *only* all good or all bad. It then becomes understandable that the mildest frustrations, experienced by the patient as absolute and total abandonment, can cast a loved one into the darkest place, only to be restored to perfect good graces if adequate amends and reassurances are perceived. Borderline patients experience anxiety and frustration as painful self-states caused by others who fail to adequately love or protect them. The well known maladaptive coping strategies so common to borderline patients–cutting, burning, substance abuse, eating disorders, rage attacks, tantrums, etc.–are attempts to control or rid

FIGURE 1

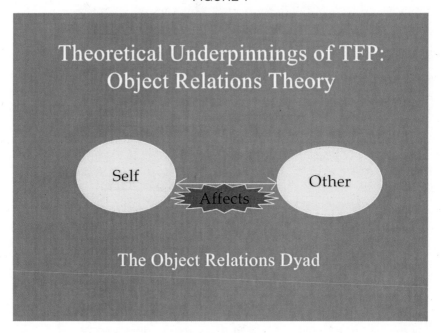

oneself of these painful states. In this object relations model of an unintegrated sense of self and other, the absence of a stable sense of identity often prevents successful investment in school, work and relationships. At the core of the borderline disorder is the emotional lability, the clinging dependency alternating with intense rage that arises when one's sense of well-being is so totally dependent upon the validation and gratification of one's needs by others. Individuals with BPD have not developed the ability to be "OK" within themselves unless the world without is attuned to their needs. A powerful sense of helplessness and rage results from their experience of help that they perceive as being cruelly withheld by others.

What would prevent the desired integration and leave an individual in the "split" state? Theory and clinical experience, and a growing body of data (Paris, 1994) suggest two influences: (1) the individual's temperament: a fiery, "choleric" temperament that predisposes the individual to strong angry reactions might intensify the negative side of the split structure to the point that it is hard to blend it with the more benevolent and benign positive side; and (2) a developmental experience

FIGURE 2

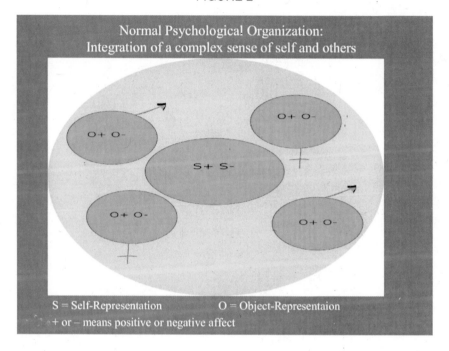

Normal Psychological Organization:
Integration of a complex sense of self and others

S = Self-Representation   O = Object-Representaion
+ or – means positive or negative affect

characterized by physical, sexual or psychological abuse and/or by trauma.

TRANSFERENCE-FOCUSED THERAPY AND BPD

Although concerned with the etiological roots of borderline personality, TFP focuses on shedding light on the internal structure and working of the patient's mind as they play out in immediate experience when feelings and thoughts are simultaneously present, especially in the relation between patient and therapist. We call the therapy "transference-focused" because of the concept that elements of the patient's internal world are transferred from within the mind and played out/experienced as the reality of the current moment. In other words, the person's experience of a given moment is a combination of perception of external stimuli and of internal images that are not fully conscious but which the patient "reads into" the current experience (see Figure 4).

FIGURE 3

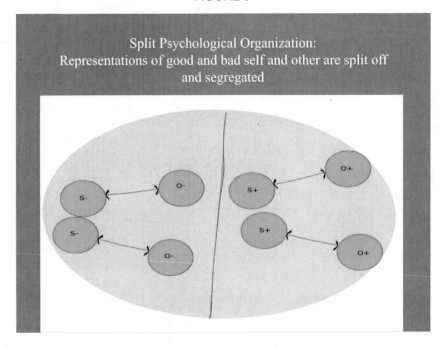

Split Psychological Organization:
Representations of good and bad self and other are split off
and segregated

An overview of the treatment is as follows: an initial assessment establishes the diagnosis and the specific problem areas that are relevant
to the individual patient. The therapist then proceeds to the discussion
of the treatment contract (Yeomans et al., 1992). The contract-setting
phase is considered to be "pre-treatment" because it establishes, in collaboration with the patient, the conditions necessary for the treatment to
be successful. In this phase, previous barriers to successful treatment
will be identified and parameters to deal with them will be agreed upon.
Typical issues included in the contract would be how to address substance abuse, self-injury, suicidality, precipitous drop out, and withholding of important information. TFP makes use of adjunct resources,
such as attending 12-step programs, managing eating disorders by monitoring weight and electrolyte balances at doctor's office or clinic, and
establishing a plan for the patient to follow in the event he or she feels
unable to control suicidal or self-harming impulses. The responsibility
and expectations of both patient and therapist will be elaborated and
agreed upon. This discussion requires at least two sessions and may include a meeting with close family members so that those involved share

FIGURE 4

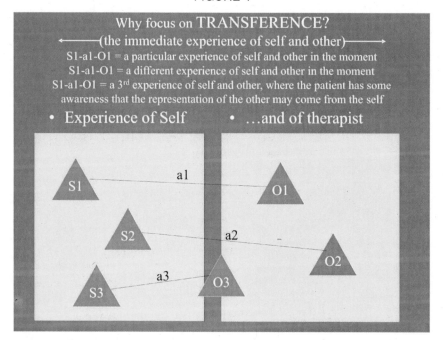

a common understanding of the nature of the patient's problems and the approach to be used to address them. These meetings involve an element of psychoeducation and an opportunity to answer patient and family member questions and address their concerns. It should be stressed that the contract phase of TFP is important because it will serve as the "frame" of treatment for both patient and therapist. It will help the patient remain vigilant to patterns of behavior which have led to a precipitous and unsuccessful ending of previous treatments, and it will help the therapist monitor his or her own counter-transference acting out in the face of the powerful pulls and demands common to the treatment of borderline patients.

If and when the therapist and patient agree to the conditions of treatment, the therapy begins. The core of the therapy is to engage the patient in observing and becoming aware of the different representations of self and other that are activated in the relation between the patient and therapist. Until these representations are observed and discussed, many of them are not in the patient's conscious awareness, but are acted out without awareness of their meaning and the possible distortion that they represent. For example, a patient asked if her therapist could change the time of a session. After checking in his appointment book, he replied that he was not able to do so. The patient became enraged and started to yell at him that this was proof that he did not like her, did not want to treat her, and that he even enjoyed treating her badly and watching her suffer. This example illustrates the activation of the deprived/rejected self in relation to the uncaring, neglectful and perhaps even sadistic other. As the patient's anger increased, she began pacing back and forth in front of the therapist and began to shake her fist at him in a menacing way. The therapist asked if the patient might join him in observing and reflecting on the situation. He suggested that an observer might see her as treating him badly in much the same way she accused him of treating her. He added that such feelings were part of the human repertoire and could be mastered and controlled. These feelings pose a special problem if they are denied, since it is not possible to master something that one has no awareness of.

As patient gain awareness of the different images they have of self and others, they are able both to compare these images to the lived reality and to reflect upon the experience and intentions of the other. For example, the patient described above was able to recall occasions when her therapist did change the session time for her. As patients develop greater awareness of their shifting and contradictory mental states (all good/all bad self and other), they can begin to integrate these images into a more full-bodied, nuanced and realistic sense of themselves and others. The primary techniques used in TFP are (1) *clarification*–seeking a better understanding of what the patient is thinking and understanding in the moment; (2) *confrontation*–encouraging reflection on contradictory mental states within the patient; and (3) *interpretation*–attempts to clarify conflicts within the patient that might make it difficult to bring contradictory states together into an integrated whole. As the patient can begin to think with the therapist about him or herself and others in less rigid and dichotomous ways, there is less need to keep good and bad aspects of the self and others separate. In our experience, these techniques help the patient achieve a sense of a more cohesive, intact self; this greatly reduces both the need to act out painful emotions and the severe symptoms of borderline personality disorder.

THE CASE OF JOAN

Joan displays many typical characteristics of BPD: self-injury, unstable relationships, drug and alcohol use, and unstable work history. Her history reveals that her problems started with feelings of depression and a sense of failure and led to her attempts to self-medicate with drugs. This suggests that Joan's condition may have narcissistic features, the type of self-berating that can afflict an individual who has developed impossibly high standards by which she judges herself. This impression is reinforced by the mention of "grandiose posturing" and by her fear of humiliation should she encounter more successful friends in her position as a sales clerk. As with most BPD patients, and perhaps most individuals, Joan has difficulty in assessing accurately the source of her critique of herself, i.e., difficulty separating the internal from the external source of some of her thoughts and feelings. The mention of her father's "critical and judgmental" attitude adds to this confusion about the source of her sense of being criticized. She focuses on the hope that if *he* changes, she will feel better. She complains that her entire family judges her as a failure. However, it is likely that she has internalized a critical voice that has become part of her own mental functioning - a voice that she projects onto and then perceives as coming from others, probably contributing to the stormy relations with others. This is an attempt to free herself from a part of her own thinking that is relentlessly embedded and that needs to be dealt with in therapy. A goal of TFP therapy would be to help Joan come to *accept* (not have to project) those aspects of herself that she has difficulty tolerating, e.g., her own aggression and need to criticize. Borderline patients tend to think in absolute, "all-or-nothing" terms, so the idea that they might have "bad" within them tends to overwhelm and eliminate any "good" within them. If Joan could better tolerate all aspects of her internal world, she would be less dependent on needing others to change in order to feel better about herself. As patients come to have a more accepting and nuanced understanding of themselves, they begin to understand the complexity of others, leading to more flexible, realistic, and therefore more satisfying interpersonal interactions.

Joan was frequently "hurt or rejected by some small slight." The principle here is that a small element of external reality (a small slight) will activate a more intense element of her internal world of self and object representations (the experience of a harsh judgmental father that she has identified with and that has now become part of herself). Incidental hurts and injuries are more easily absorbed when an individual can draw upon an integrated "good/ bad" sense of self to mediate experience. For patients with borderline structure, the "small slight" activates the split off "all bad" self, leaving the patient at the mercy of only the bad self-other object relation experience. This is all they are able to access or draw upon in such moments, resulting in a greatly exaggerated sense of hurt or injury.

Joan's vehement attacks on her family would often "precipitate retaliation from her father." This represents another feature of BPD. An individual who experiences life through the lens of particular internal representations often elicits the feared response from an individual in the outside world. This principle would be clearer in this case if the example given described Joan eliciting retaliation from an individual in the outside world, e.g., a friend or boyfriend; such an individual would be more neutral than the father who may have had a role in the establishment of her internal critical voice. Nevertheless, borderline individuals often provoke from others the negative response that they say they fear. This may seem paradoxical, but it serves the dual purpose of allowing the individual a bit of distance between him/herself and the criticizing voice ("better that it come from outside than constantly be within me") and of putting an end to the anxious anticipation that the negative response will eventually come anyway. This explains the frequent borderline dynamic of constantly testing those who love her until there is the inevitable frustrated response, at which point the individual who, for various reasons does not believe that anyone truly loves her, can say: "See, I knew no one really cared for me." In short, believing in loving and caring is risky business for a borderline individual. This may relate to Joan's history of driving her boyfriends away.

Joan's treatment goals–for her family to understand her better and be more supportive–are reasonable, but limited. They make sense for someone who externalizes parts of herself that are in conflict with other parts; Joan externalizes the harshly critical part that is attacking the part that is trying to function and have a decent life. Unfortunately, no matter how much the family tries to accommodate and support Joan, she will never be able to find peace and a satisfying life until she integrates the harsh voice into her broader sense of self and gains mastery over it. A tenet of TFP is that all individuals have by nature a mix of both libidinal (loving) and aggressive affects. It is not assumed that aggressive affects must be expunged from the individual, since they can be the basis of healthy adaptations in the world, such as competitiveness, ambition, self-defense, and creativity. TFP's position is rather that if aggression is split off and not integrated into the rest of an individual's psyche, it remains a destructive force that can at times exert control over the individual and inhibit libidinal expression, instead of being put to effective use within a cohesive sense of self.

The treatment contract with Joan would involve enlisting her agreement that her continued substance abuse would make effective treatment untenable. Her use of drugs and alcohol is undoubtedly contributing to her assaultive behavior, self-injury, stormy relationships, and episodic employment. Sobriety and active participation in a 12-step program would be important and necessary adjuncts to the therapy. In addition, before beginning the treatment, we would have Joan and her parents come in together to discuss reasonable parameters within which her parents would feel less emotionally blackmailed and controlled by Joan's volatility. Joan, in turn, would be helped to understand what her parents realistically could and could not do to help her. Needless to say, a goal of TFP would be to foster increasing responsibility for herself.

In TFP, the challenge of integrating this split-off part would be addressed, as described above, by observing the patient's interaction with and experience of the therapist. As she does with probably many other people in her life, Joan will inevitably have moments when she experiences her therapist as harshly critical of her–moments of which she will be highly aware–and moments when she will be harshly critical toward her therapist–moments of which she may be less aware.

THE WORK OF THE TFP THERAPIST

The TFP therapist's work will focus on maintaining the frame of treatment (e.g., monitoring Joan's continued sobriety and participation in a 12-step program), monitoring her functioning in the activities of her life, and helping her observe and evaluate the experiences that she brings to the sessions, with a focus on what goes on between Joan and her therapist in the sessions. TFP actively fosters reflective function by making the patient aware of contradictory states that emerge in the sessions. The patient is helped to see that although she may be seeing you, the therapist, in a certain way in the moment, she may have a very different experience of you in another moment, often within the same session. We encourage the patient to be interested in these contradictory experiences, while remaining non-defensive and technically neutral. For the therapist, technical neutrality, i.e., not identifying with either side of the patient's conflict is very important, although not always easy to maintain with borderline patients. From a position of neutrality, which in no way implies that the therapist is aloof or silent, the therapist would ask the patient to consider whether the therapist is indeed as critical as she perceives? Might there be another way of looking at things?

And what about her judgments of him? Is she aware that *her* words are extreme and harshly critical? While she may be saying these things to defend herself from a perceived attack, was the attack real, and was her defense an attack in disguise? Is it difficult for the patient to acknowledge her own critical aggressive side? Does it suggest an identification with others, possibly her father, and would she deny this because it suggests unwanted aspects of herself?

Joan's experience of her family as needing to understand her better and be more supportive is a fairly typical position for borderline patients. In our experience, we have yet to encounter a patient who reported that her family was wonderfully supportive and that if only *she* could get better, all would be well.

Indeed, while families of borderline patients can be moderately to severely dysfunctional, the challenge in working with these patients is to help them see that despite very legitimate complaints and grievances, their difficulties are made worse and perpetuated by the dysfunction within themselves. This is an extremely difficult and foreign concept to many patients. Defending against the internal experience of "badness" is central to the borderline structure and accounts for their predominant reliance upon projective mechanisms of defense.

WHAT KIND OF CHANGE CAN BE EXPECTED FROM TFP?

Like most treatments for BPD, TFP is a long-term treatment (Perry et al., 1999). Unlike more behaviorally oriented treatments, TFP aims at *changing underlying personality structure* as well as reducing symptoms and changing behaviors. An empirical study comparing one year of TFP to "treatment as usual" (TAU), has shown that TFP is effective in reducing suicidal and parasuicidal behaviors, ER visits and hospitalizations, and symptoms of depression and anxiety, as well as improving GAF scores (Clarkin et al., 2001). However, beyond these behavioral changes, TFP targets change in psychological structure and functioning. Change at this level is more difficult to operationalize for empirical studies than behavioral change. The scale developed for reflective function (Fonagy et al., 1998) provides a measure of mentalization, the capacity to conceptualize the mental processes that occur in both self and others, such as feelings, beliefs, intentions, conflicts and motivations. This reflective capacity may serve as a mediating variable between current adjustment and the impact of an early abusive environment (Fonagy et al., 1995, 1996). In our view, identity diffusion is the central pathology in borderline patients, and therefore successful treatment would enhance the patient's ability to conceptualize self and others. Thus, one would expect that successful TFP treatment would result in an increase in reflective functioning as measured from patient verbalizations on the Adult Attachment Interview (AAI) (George et al., 1996). We have examined changes in reflective functioning in patients who received one year of outpatient treatment in supportive therapy, TFP and DBT. At the end of one year, significant improvement in reflective function was specific only to TFP (Levy, Clarkin et al., 2006). If treatment succeeds in integrating BPD patients' split and fragmented internal structures, these patients can experience significant changes in the way they experience themselves and their relationships with others, leading to a more rewarding and satisfying life experience. With changes in mental processes themselves, we believe that patients will be more able to maintain the behavioral gains they make in therapy.

REFERENCES

Clarkin, J. F., Foelsch, P, A., Levy, K. N., & Delaney, J. C. et al. (2004). The development of a psychodynamic treatment for patients with borderline personality disorder: a preliminary study of behavioral change. *Journal of Personality Disorders,* 18, 52-72.

Diagnostic and statistical manual of mental disorders (4th Ed.) (DSM-IV). (2000). Washington, DC: American Psychiatric Association.

Fonagy, P., Leigh, T., & Steele, M. et al. (1996). The relation of attachment status, psychiatric classification and response to psychotherapy. *Journal of Consulting and Clinical Psychology,* 64, 22-31.

Fonagy, P., Steele, M., & Steele, H. et al. (1995). The predictive validity of Mary Main's Adult Attachment Interview: A psychoanalytic and developmental perspective on the transgeneration transmission of attachment and borderline states. In S. Goldberg, R. Muir, & J. Kerr (Eds.), *Attachment theory: Social, developmental and clinical* perspectives (pp. 233-278). Hillsdale, NJ: Analytic Press.

Fonagy, P., Target, M., Steele, H., & Steele, M. (1998). *Reflective-functioning manual, version 5.0, for application to adult attachment interviews.* London: University College London.

George, C., Kaplan, N., & Main, M. (1996). *Adult attachment interview protocol, 3rd edition.* Berkeley, CA: University of California.

Jacobson, E. (1964). *The self and the object world.* New York: International Universities Press.

Kernberg, O. F. & Caligor, E. (2005). A psychoanalytic theory of personality disorders. In M. F. Lenzenweger & J. F. Clarkin (Eds.), *Major theories of personality disorder, 2nd Edition* (pp. 114-156). New York, Guilford.

Kernberg, O. F. (1975). *Borderline conditions and pathological narcissism.* New York: Jason Aronson.

Kernberg, O. F. (1980). *Internal world and external reality: Object relations theory applied.* New York: Jason Aronson.

Kernberg, O. F. (1984). Severe personality disorders: Psychotherapeutic strategies. New Haven: Yale University Press.

Klein, M. (1957). Envy and gratitude: A study of unconscious sources. New York: Basic Books.

Levy, K., & Clarkin, J. F. et al. (2006). Change in attachment patterns and reflective function in a randomized control trial of transference-focused psychotherapy for borderline personality disorder. *Journal of Consulting and Clinical Psychology,* 74 (6), 1027-1040.

Paris, J. (1994). *Borderline personality disorder: A multidimensional approach.* Washington DC, American Psychiatric Press.

Perry, J. C., Banon, E., & Ianni, F. (1999). Effectiveness of psychotherapy for personality disorders. *American Journal of Psychiatry,* 156, 1312-1321

Yeomans, F. E., Selzer, M. A., & Clarkin, J. F. (1992). Treating the borderline patient: A contract-based approach. New York: Basic Books.

doi:10.1300/J200v06n01_13

Systems Training for Emotional Predictability and Problem Solving (STEPPS) for the Treatment of BPD

Nancee Blum
Donald W. Black

SUMMARY. Systems Training for Emotional Predictability and Problem Solving, or **STEPPS**, a group treatment for outpatients with borderline personality disorder (BPD), is described. The 20-week program was developed to address the cognitive distortions and behavioral dyscontrol that occurs in borderline patients. STEPPS combines psychoeducation and skills training with a systems component, the latter involving significant others, health care professionals, and others with whom the patient regularly interacts. Data from the U.S. and The Netherlands have shown that the model is well accepted by patients and therapists, and is effective in relieving depression and other symptoms associated with the disorder. doi:10.1300/J200v06n01_14 *[Article copies available for a fee from The Haworth Document Delivery Service: 1-800-HAWORTH. E-mail address: <docdelivery@haworthpress.com> Website: <http://www.HaworthPress.com> © 2008 by The Haworth Press. All rights reserved.]*

KEYWORDS. STEPPS, cognitive-behavioral therapy, group therapy, borderline personality disorder, VERS

[Haworth co-indexing entry note]: "Systems Training for Emotional Predictability and Problem Solving (STEPPS) for the Treatment of BPD." Blum, Nancee, and Donald W. Black. Co-published simultaneously in *Social Work in Mental Health* (The Haworth Press) Vol. 6, No. 1/2, 2008, pp. 171-186; and: *Borderline Personality Disorder: Meeting the Challenges to Successful Treatment* (ed: Perry D. Hoffman, and Penny Steiner-Grossman) The Haworth Press, 2008, pp. 171-186. Single or multiple copies of this article are available for a fee from The Haworth Document Delivery Service [1-800-HAWORTH, 9:00 a.m. - 5:00 p.m. (EST). E-mail address: docdelivery@haworthpress.com].

Available online at http://swmh.haworthpress.com
© 2008 by The Haworth Press. All rights reserved.
doi:10.1300/J200v06n01_14

HISTORY OF STEPPS

Systems Training for Emotional Predictability and Problem Solving, or STEPPS, was developed in 1995 in response to various pressures that beset the treatment of patients with borderline personality disorder (BPD) in Iowa. Managed care programs had spread throughout the state, placing pressure on mental health programs to reduce length of stay, rehospitalization rates, and to provide lower cost outpatient alternatives. Merit Behavioral Care (MBC) had contracted with Iowa to manage the mental health benefits of Medicaid recipients. Because the University of Iowa Hospitals and Clinics (UIHC) has traditionally cared for indigent, underinsured, and publicly insured patients, a significant number of patients with BPD came under the management of MBC. In responding to these concerns, we set out to create a new program for outpatients with BPD. We had observed that traditional modes of therapy were not helpful in reducing the frequency of deliberate self-harm and acting out behaviors, or in reducing hospitalization rates in these patients. In addition to establishing a Partial Hospital program, and an Assertive Community Treatment (ACT) program specifically for patients with severe personality disorders, we were motivated to create a treatment program for ambulatory outpatients with BPD that could be delivered conveniently and cost-effectively in a group therapy setting.

We reviewed the available models, including Dialectical Behavior Therapy (Linehan, 1993) and selected one developed by Norman Bartels and Theresa Crotty (1992), as described in their treatment manual, *A Systems Approach to Treatment: Borderline Personality Disorder Skill Training Manual*. The psychoeducational approach and the systems component employed by Bartels and Crotty, as well as its use of cognitive-behavioral principles, suited our training and interests. With their permission, we modified the program by increasing its length from 12 weeks to 20 weeks, and by creating specific lesson plans with accompanying homework assignments (Blum et al., 2002a). We also renamed the program, creating the acronym STEPPS, which was a tacit acknowledgement that patient improvement typically occurs in small increments, or steps. Other changes included the increased use of algorithmic worksheets for specific situations that the patient might encounter, specific facilitator guidelines for each session, and the addition of a new section on goal setting.

Our primary goal was to develop a detailed treatment manual that would specify the contents presented and methods used for each session. We intended the manual to be analogous to a well-developed and detailed school curriculum with its combination of handouts, worksheets, and other ready-to-use media. We specifically provided a high level of structure and a detailed agenda for patients and facilitators in order to minimize any confusion or ambiguity about what would be happening during the session, what topics would be covered, and how they would be covered during each of the 20 weekly two-hour group sessions. This detail simplifies the training of group leaders and insures fidelity to the model in a variety of treatment settings. The manual has been refined over the years as we learned more about our patients' needs and gauged their response to the material presented. In addition to increasing the program length to 20 weeks, we created the BEST, a self-report questionnaire to assess change (as described below), and continued to modify the course content. The STEPPS manual (Blum et al., 2002a) is now available on CD-ROM through one of the authors (NB).

A unique and appealing aspect of the Bartels and Crotty program was its inclusion of a "systems" component that integrates the social and professional support system already available to the patient. In the emerging language of STEPPS, support system members (i.e., friends, spouses, family members, therapists) become the patient's "reinforcement team." This component, as revamped for STEPPS, includes a workbook, outline cards, and other materials that can function as learning aids for both the patient and other people in their support system. Our goal with STEPPS is to train patients to use their existing support system more effectively, and to offer specific responses for support system members when interacting with the STEPPS participant.

In developing STEPPS, the needs of our patient population and the demands placed on us by our rural setting were paramount concerns. Because many patients must drive long distances to Iowa City, attendance is particularly difficult in winter months. For that reason, we concluded that the program should be brief, and not require an extended commitment. Next, we wanted to create a model that would be easier to implement in small clinics and in rural settings, and would not be labor intensive. In our opinion, the program could not require the lengthy training of mental health professionals already strapped for time, nor could the training be costly. We were satisfied that the STEPPS program employed general principles and techniques common to most psychotherapy education programs, so that it could be used by therapists with both widely varying professional backgrounds and theoretical orientations. Lastly, we sought to create a program that would not disrupt the patient's ongoing treatment regimen, but would potentially boost its effectiveness. With DBT, for example, emotionally fragile borderline patients may be separated from their current treatment team so that they can be connected with a "DBT" therapist. Because patients with BPD often fear abandonment by those important to them, we felt that including such an element in our program would be counterproductive.

DATA SUPPORTIVE OF STEPPS

Two uncontrolled studies are supportive of STEPPS: our own (Blum et al., 2002b), and one from colleagues in The Netherlands (Freije, Dietz, & Appelo, 2002). The results of both are remarkably consistent in showing overall improvement, with specific improvement in multiple BPD symptom domains. Our study was retrospective and showed a significant decrease in symptoms associated with BPD as measured by the Borderline Evaluation of Severity Over Time (BEST), as well as a significant drop in the Beck Depression Inventory (BDI) score (Beck, 1978), and in the negative affect scale of the Positive and Negative Affectivity Scale (PANAS) (Watson & Clark, 1994). In the study reported from The Netherlands by Freije et al., 85 patients were enrolled in VERS groups and were assessed pre- and post-treatment using the Symptom Checklist-90 (SCL-90) (Derogatis, 1983), a scale used to rate important psychiatric symptoms, as well as a Dutch version of the BEST. Significant improvement was seen on all SCL-90 subscales, especially those rating anxiety, depression, and interpersonal sensitivity; BEST scores were also significantly improved. Both studies were consistent in showing that patients and therapists were enthusiastic about the program and reported high levels of acceptance for the treatment.

The BEST scale was developed in the course of our work to rate severity and change in patients with BPD. The self-rated scale has 15 items in which patients rate themselves on a five-point scale; scores can range from 12 to 72. The BEST shows evidence for good internal consistency and for both face and content validity, because the items were constructed to assess behaviors relevant to BPD (Blum et al., 2002b).

Randomized controlled trials of the STEPPS program are now underway at both at The University of Iowa and in The Netherlands (van Wel et al., 2005). In both studies, the comparator arm is "treatment as usual" (TAU). Also, in each study the subjects have been required to be at least 18 years old and to meet DSM-IV criteria for BPD. In the Dutch study, subjects have been assessed with a Dutch version of the Structured Clinical Interview or DSM-IV Personality Disorders (SCID-II; Weertman et al., 2003), and rated using the SCL-90 and the BPD Severity Index (Arntz et al., 2003), along with measures of health care utilization. At Iowa, we randomized 163 subjects who had been assessed with the SCID (Spitzer, Williams & Gibbon, 1994) and the SIDP-IV (Pfohl et al., 1997), and were rated using the BEST, the BDI, the PANAS, the Diagnostic Interview for DSM-IV Personality Disorders (Zanarini & Shea, 1996), and other instruments. We have also rated social and interpersonal functioning, monitored adjunctive medication usage, suicidal behaviors and deliberate self-harm, and collected health care utilization data. A preliminary analysis shows that in comparison to TAU, the STEPPS program produces significantly better global improvement, as well as improvement in specific BPD symptoms, including the mood, cognitive, and impulsive domains. STEPPS also produced reductions in health care utilization (Black et al., 2006).

THE STEPPS MODEL

The STEPPS format involves 20 two-hour weekly sessions with two facilitators who are provided with specific lesson plans for each session (Black et al., 2002; Blum et al., 2002b). Each group typically consists of 6-10 patients. Patients are given a detailed agenda to explain what each lesson provides, as well as specific homework assignments. Additional exercises and assignments are included to make abstract concepts about BPD easily understood. The lessons are contained in a red notebook containing the training materials. Patients are urged to share their notebooks and lesson materials with others in their system. By the end of the training, most patients view the notebook as a resource they can turn to in difficult times. Patients are given training to:

1. improve their understanding of BPD;
2. utilize specific skills to help them regulate their emotional intensity; and
3. provide techniques to behaviorally manage their disorder.

Rather than following a traditional group therapy model, sessions have the look and feel of a seminar. Patients sit at a conference table facing a board. There is a short break between the first and second hours. Each week is organized around a skill that is the focus of the session. Some skills require more than one weekly session to teach. The emotion management skills include: distancing, communicating, challenging, distracting, and managing problems. Behavioral skill areas include goal setting, eating/sleep behaviors, exercise and physical health, relaxation and leisure behaviors, interpersonal relationships, avoiding abusive behaviors, and a review and wrap-up session. An optional unit on managing holiday stress is included for those groups meeting through a major holiday season. Besides the use of a board and the printed materials, the training is facilitated by poetry, audio recordings of songs, art activities, and relaxation exercises. Patients are strongly encouraged to bring in materials or artwork they have created to help reinforce the skills and themes of the meetings.

Patients are asked to monitor their thoughts, feelings, and behaviors over the course of the program; this enables them to self-monitor their improvement, for example, seeing the decrease in the intensity and frequency of their emotional episodes. Most patients see a noticeable decrease in their BEST scores as the weeks progress. STEPPS patients are permitted to continue with their other treatment (e.g., individual therapy, medication management) and most have been followed by UIHC or community psychiatrists. Those who have an individual therapist are asked to familiarize the therapist with the program so that the members of the patient's treatment team employ a consistent approach and terminology. Patients are encouraged to take an extra copy of the handouts to their therapist, and to review their homework assignments during their individual therapy sessions.

STEPPS emphasizes cognitive behavioral-treatment (CBT) and skills training. Patients learn specific emotion and behavior management skills. Underlying this approach is the assumption that the core of BPD is a defect in the person's internal ability to regulate emotional intensity. As a result, the patient is periodically overwhelmed by abnormally intense emotional upheavals that drive him or her to seek relief. Identifying someone to "blame" is viewed as counterproductive. Patients tend to view the term *borderline personality disorder* as pejorative, and often resist the diagnosis, although they may readily acknowledge having the behaviors. For this reason, Bartels and Crotty (1992) originally suggested the name *emotional intensity disorder* as a more accurate term, and one which patients find easier to understand and accept. Patients learn to see themselves as driven by BPD to seek relief from emotional pain through desperate behaviors, which are reinforced by cognitive distortions.

With STEPPS, patients are educated about the disorder, including the DSM-IV criteria, and are introduced to the concept of an "emotional intensity continuum," so they can learn to recognize the early warning signs of an impending emotional outburst. We often use metaphors with patients to describe these emotionally intense episodes. For example, extreme emotional intensity is compared to having a very high flame under a pot on a burner that is boiling over. The skills they are learning become the tools to prevent the heat from getting too high, thereby reducing the chance that the pot will "boil over." With this and other metaphors, we make abstract concepts more concrete and understandable and help patients to identify their own emotional intensity continuum. As patients progress, they are asked to assess the skills they have employed to manage their emotional intensity and to identify various cognitive distortions. Patients gradually become more aware of their emotional triggers, as well as early warning signs of emotionally intense outbursts.

INVOLVING THE SUPPORT SYSTEM

A unique aspect of STEPPS is the *systems* component, which refers to the fact that both patients and those within their system are included in the training. The patient's system can include family members, significant others, health care professionals, or anyone with whom they regularly interact, and with whom they are willing to share information about their disorder. The goal is to provide the patient and those in his or her system with a common language to communicate clearly about the disorder and the skills used to manage it. This aspect allows others within the system to give patients a consistent response using a common language. "Reinforcement team" members learn to reinforce and support newly learned skills. This helps the patient to avoid the phenomenon of "splitting," a process in which he or she may externalize internal conflicts by drawing others into taking sides against one another. Like other behaviors common to BPD, splitting is conceptualized not as an intentional act of aggression but as an automatic response to the emotional dysregulation, which the patient can learn to anticipate and replace with more effective behaviors.

The training has three distinct steps:

> *Step 1–Awareness of the Disorder.* The first step for the patient is to replace misconceptions about BPD with an awareness of the behaviors and feelings that define the disorder. Patients learn that behaviors can be changed and feelings can be managed. They are provided with a printed handout listing the DSM-IV criteria for BPD and time is provided for them to acknowledge examples of

the criteria in their own behavior. This is called "owning" the illness. The second component is the introduction of the concept of schemas, which we refer to as cognitive filters. With the author's permission, we have extracted 64 items from the Schema Questionnaire from *Cognitive Therapy for Personality Disorders: A Schema-Focused Approach* (Young, 1999). We use Young's Schema Questionnaire to help patients identify their early maladaptive schemas, or cognitive filters. We encourage patients to understand the relationship between these filters, the DSM-IV criteria, and their subsequent pattern of feelings, thoughts, and behaviors.

Step 2–Emotion Management Training. We describe the five basic skills that help the patient to manage the cognitive and emotional effects of the illness (Table 1). In helping him or her to understand how the illness works and recognize the cognitive filters that have been triggered in a given situation, these skills assist the individual in predicting the course of an episode, anticipating stressful situations in which the illness is aggravated, and building confidence in his or her ability to manage the illness.

Step 3–Behavior Management Training. There are eight behavioral skill areas that patients are encouraged to master (Table 2). As the BPD syndrome progresses between the disruptive interplay of the emotionally intense episodes and a social environment that becomes increasingly unempathic and unresponsive, many functional areas begin to break down. Learning or relearning patterns of managing these functional areas helps patients to keep their intense emotions under control during such episodes.

Each weekly session begins with patients completing the BEST, which allows them to rate the intensity of their thoughts, feelings, and behaviors over the past week. They keep track of their weekly score on a graph. This helps them to see the variability typical of BPD and to note over time the decrease in the intensity and number of their emotional episodes and the increased use of the positive behaviors and skills being taught. This is followed by a brief relaxation/observation exercise–a different one each week, so that patients can practice and discover which ones are most effective for them.

The first half of each session is spent reviewing the Emotional Intensity Continuum (EIC), allowing patients to operationalize the concept

TABLE 1. Emotional Management Skill Areas

Skill	Action
Distancing	Learning to "step-back", to decrease physical/ emotionally intense thoughts or behaviors
Communicating	Learning to describe one's emotions
Challenging	Replacing one's distorted/negative thoughts with more rational/positive ones
Distracting	Creating a list of pleasant activities to distract oneself during times of emotional intensity
Managing problems	Generating alternative responses to problems and understanding their consequences

of varying degrees of emotional intensity on a 1-5 point scale: 1 is feeling calm and relaxed, and 5 is feeling out of control, engaging in self-destructive impulses, or angry outbursts. Patients are expected to complete the EIC daily and to summarize the percent of time spent at each level during the previous week. Through self-rating, patients often achieve a more balanced view of themselves; they often are surprised to learn that they have significant periods of time when they are not at the extremes of the scale.

A skills monitoring card lists the skills being taught and allows trainees to indicate those they have used in the previous week. A version of this card is given to the members of the individual's reinforcement team as part of the family/caregiver education component; these cards help guide the reinforcement team members in responding to the patient. The previous week's homework assignments are reviewed and the remainder of the session is devoted to introducing the material for the current lesson.

During the session, the patient may try to reframe his or her emotional experience in the context of, or as the result of, some personal or interpersonal problem. While there is an opportunity for patients to respond and share experiences relevant to the skills being taught, the structure does not allow the group to spend long periods of time focusing on a given group member. One effect of the structured format is to model how to acknowledge problems and offer support while still imposing reasonable time lim-

TABLE 2. Behavior Management Skill Areas

Skill	Action
Goal setting	Identifying and ranking one's problems
Eating behaviors	Increasing awareness of appropriate eating
Sleeping	Emphasizing appropriate sleep hygiene
Exercise	Encouraging regular exercise
Leisure	Expanding one's repertoire of leisure activities
Physical health	Encourage treatment adherence
Interpersonal relationships	Increasing interpersonal effectiveness/establishing appropriate boundaries
Abuse avoidance	Avoiding self-damaging/self-destructive behaviors

its and boundaries on the scope of the interaction so that the main goal of the meeting is not lost. The group facilitators are prepared to reframe problems in the context of the disorder and cognitive filters. The rule used is "focus on the disorder, not the content."

During the 20-week program, at least one two-hour evening session is held for family members and significant others (i.e., the reinforcement team). In a community setting where patients and reinforcement team members do not have to travel a significant distance, it might be desirable to expand this component of the program. Many patients bring their therapist or other treating professionals to the education session. During these sessions, reinforcement team members are educated about BPD and the way it presents in the patient's daily behavior. We then describe the skills that patients are being taught, and give family members and others in their system a card that contains four responses to use when a STEPPS patient seeks their help:

1. Where are you on your Emotional Intensity Continuum (i.e., 1-5)?
2. Have you used your notebook?
3. What skill can you use in this situation? How will you use it?
4. If the person cannot think of what skill to use, ask about each one on the list.

Our goal is not to turn family members into therapists but to empower them to make consistent responses that are more neutral in emotional content. Hearing the same language calmly repeated by members in their system reminds patients of what they are learning and does not give them another confusing language to process during a time of emotional intensity. This information is presented to family and systems members in a non-blaming atmosphere, because families and others have often been blamed by patients with BPD for various symptoms they may be suffering. Our experience is that the family and systems members are quite interested in attending the meeting and afterwards have told us how helpful the session was to them.

SUITABILITY FOR STEPPS TRAINING

We recommend that patients be screened to ensure that they will "fit in." We have observed that to be an effective and fully participating member of the group, in addition to fulfilling DSM-IV criteria for BPD, patients need to be able to share time with the other group members and limit discussion of their own problems. A person's capacity for these attributes often can be gauged by his or her ability to allow the facilitator to direct discussion during the introductory screening. Narcissistic persons are not well suited because they have little capacity for empathy and tend to dismiss other group members' problems as inconsequential compared to their own. Antisocial persons are not well suited to the group either, particularly men who might be physically threatening or intimidating to the others. Many borderline women have been abused by men in the past, and sometimes even the presence of a male group member may be viewed as threatening. Patients must be assured that their comfort and safety is paramount. When men are present, we suggest that there be at least two enrolled in the group, so that they will find at least one other person with whom they will have sufficient common experiences. Having two men present can help minimize the problem of having a lone male seem "responsible" for representing the feelings and opinions of all men. Patients with comorbid substance misuse or eating disorders should be asked to seek an appropriate treatment program; both problems are seen as counterproductive to accomplishing the treatment goals of the STEPPS program.

Group facilitators themselves need to avoid being drawn into the issues and past traumas of a particular patient, except as they apply to the current group content. Facilitators need to focus on the goal of teaching patients new skills, not on "putting out fires." Crises that can sometimes arise in a group (e.g., suicidal threats, flashbacks) should not be managed in the group, but through another mechanism, such as referral to an emergency department. Facilitators should strive to treat all group members equally and not give particular members special attention. Patients themselves should be discouraged from contacting one another until they feel safe in the group, and should not feel coerced into sharing phone numbers or email addresses.

FUTURE DEVELOPMENTS

The STEPPS program has attracted attention and interest around the U.S. and internationally. Programs have been started in at least half the states in the U.S. Overseas, STEPPS groups have been started in Argentina, Australia, New Zealand Belgium, Canada, Spain, and The Netherlands. In the latter, the program was adopted by mental health professionals in the late 1990s following a visit by one of the authors (NB) in 1998. Once translated, the program was implemented under the acronym VERS, and is now reported to be the most widely used group treatment for BPD in The Netherlands (van Wel et al., 2006). The VERS manual has been translated into Norwegian, and the program will soon be started there.

In the U.S., STEPPS has been adapted to suit many different settings including partial hospital programs, day treatment, residential facilities, and substance abuse treatment. Programs for adolescents have been started, as has one for mentally challenged persons. Several prisons have expressed interest in STEPPS, and it is being used in prisons in California, Iowa, Minnesota, Nevada and Wisconsin.

THE CASE OF JOAN

Were Joan referred to the STEPPS program, an intake interview would involve a thorough review of her psychiatric history, including her relationship with her parents and siblings, romantic attachments, friendship patterns, educational and work history, self-harm behaviors, and use of alcohol and drugs. Treatment history, psychiatric hospitalizations, and compliance issues would also be important to review. Based on her history, the diagnosis of BPD with co-morbid major depression and substance abuse (alcohol and marijuana) would be made. While Joan is otherwise an excellent candidate for STEPPS, her misuse of substances could present an initial stumbling block, because this is strongly felt to interfere with participation in STEPPS, and violates many of the teachings regarding proper care of oneself (i.e., maintaining good nutrition, avoiding substance abuse, getting proper exercise). Although she is motivated to control her alcohol use, Joan's continued use of marijuana remains problematic. Thus, she is given the choice of first attending a substance abuse treatment program or agreeing to attend such a program concurrently with STEPPS. In fact, it is not unusual for patients in the STEPPS program to be involved in other forms of therapy, and the substance abuse treatment team would become a part of her system. Joan is encouraged to share appropriate parts of the manual with her treatment providers. As an example, one of our former STEPPS participants attended a gambling treatment program concurrently with the STEPPS program. She said, "I took my STEPPS materials to my gambling treatment program and taught them to my leader."

Joan begins the group with from 6-10 other persons, all diagnosed with BPD. At the initial session, the DSM-IV criteria are reviewed, and all attendees are encouraged to "own up" to having the symptoms. Because the diagnosis is polythetic, not all attendees will have the nine symptoms, although Joan has most of them, including mood instability, a history of self-harm, impulsive behavior, inappropriate anger, and disturbed relationships.

Joan and the other attendees fill out the BEST, our rating scale for BPD severity, and based on our experience would likely score between 40 and 50 (maximum score is 72). This establishes her baseline and over the course of the 20-week program, Joan sees that not only do symptoms vary substantially from week to week, but also that her score gradually drops. Additionally, she is introduced to the Emotional Intensity Continuum (EIC) scale, which she is asked to complete daily to rate the degree of her emotional intensity. The EIC is summarized weekly, so that she and others can achieve a more balanced view of themselves by seeing that they have substantial periods of time when their emotions are not out of control. She receives a copy of the STEPPS notebook in which to keep her weekly lessons, and a copy of a skills monitoring card listing the skills she is being taught. Joan learns that the purpose of the group is to learn skills, and not to serve as a forum to discuss her personal issues.

With STEPPS, Joan begins to understand the connection between the BPD criteria and her thoughts, emotions, and behaviors, as well as the role her cognitive filters have played in her life, for example, assuming that her family thinks she is a failure and becoming inappropriately angry in response. In the course of the program, Joan learns to recognize and challenge her many cognitive distortions and to develop a more realistic appraisal of her issues and problems. A series of strategies is taught to help Joan deal with her overwhelming feelings of anxiety, anger, depression, and self-destructive thoughts. She gradually learns to reframe problems in the context of her disorder and its many cognitive filters. She learns to "focus on the disorder, not the content."

STEPPS attendees are encouraged to comply with other treatment, including Joan's use of escitalopram (Lexapro) and clonazepam (Klonopin) to help control her depression and anxiety. Medication adherence is addressed as a behavior management skill, first by identifying regular medication use as the goal (i.e., the skill of goal-setting), and by developing an action plan to chart medication use. For Joan, both the eating and physical health skills sections are also helpful. She learns that maintaining a proper diet and getting regular exercise both contribute to better overall health, and that exercise provides a regular physical release that can help to stabilize mood and provide needed distraction from her many issues.

Joan is able to focus on her angry outbursts and impulsivity by using the emotion management skill of "distancing." This allows her to notice that her anger escalates during her emotionally intense episodes, and to "step back" by talking to a reinforcement team member or by physically distancing herself by going to another room or taking a walk. Each option gives her an opportunity to reflect and distance herself from emotions that are out of control and likely to lead to destructive behaviors. Joan gradually becomes more adept at using the skill of communication to convey her thoughts and feelings more accurately to her family members; she can then use the challenging skill to replace her distorted thoughts with more rational ones. Joan has several distracting activities, including reading, baking, and crocheting, that have been helpful in decreasing her emotional intensity. She uses the skill of problem management to increase her range of alternate responses to issues that arise in her daily life, and learns to appreciate the consequences of each alternative. Joan sees that she is not stuck in a rut as she had thought, but actually has many options available to her for each problem area.

The systems component is important to Joan. Her parents and two siblings constitute her "reinforcement team." During an evening session, Joan's family members learn about her BPD and its many symptoms, and how these symptoms have affected Joan's thinking and behavior. They are given a set of written guidelines to summarize how they might best respond to Joan when she is feeling out of control. Like other reinforcement team members, her parents and siblings show a significant capacity for change when presented with this new information and guidance. As part of the systems component, Joan also learns to develop more realistic expectations about the appropriate level of support to expect from her family members.

REFERENCES

Arntz, A., van den Horn M., & Cornelius J. et al. (2003). Reliability and validity of the Borderline Personality Severity Index. *Journal of Personality Disorders*, 17, 562-567.

Bartels, N. & Crotty, T. (1998). *A systems approach to treatment: The borderline personality disorder skill training manual*. Winfield, IL: EID Treatment Systems, Inc.

Beck A. T. (1978). *Depression inventory*. Philadelphia, PA: Philadelphia Center for Cognitive Therapy.

Black D. W., Blum, N., Pfohl, B., & St. John, D. (2004). The STEPPS group treatment for outpatients with borderline personality disorder. *Journal of Contemporary Psychotherapy*, 34, 193-210.

Black, D. W., Blum, N., St. John, D., & Pfohl, B. (2006). STEPPS versus TAU in the treatment of borderline personality disorder. Presented at the 159th annual meeting of the American Psychiatric Association, Toronto, Ontario, Canada, May 21, 2006.

Blum, N., Bartels, N., St. John, D., & Pfohl, B. (2002a). *Manual for systems training for emotional predictability and problem solving (STEPPS): Group treatment program for borderline personality disorder*. Coralville, IA: Blum's Books.

Blum, N., Pfohl, B., St. John, D., Monahan, P., & Black, D. W. (2002b). STEPPS: A cognitive-behavioral systems-based group treatment for outpatients with borderline personality disorder. *Comprehensive Psychiatry*, 43, 301-310.

Derogatis, L. R. (1983). *SCL-90-R administration, scoring, and procedures manual II*. Towson, MD: Clinical Psychometric Research.

Freije, H., Dietz, B., & Appelo, M. (2002). Behandeling van de borderline persoonlijkheidsstoornis met de VERS: de vaardigheidstraining emotionele regulatiestoornis. *Directive Therapies*, 22, 367-378.

Linehan, M. M. (1993). *Cognitive-behavioral treatment for borderline personality disorder*. New York: Guilford Press.

Pfohl, B., Blum, N., & Zimmerman, M. (1997). *Structured interview for DSM-IV personality (SIDP-IV)*. Washington, DC: American Psychiatric Press, Inc., 1997.

Spitzer, R. L., Williams, J. B. W., & Gibbon, M. (1994). *Structured clinical interview for DSM-IV*. New York: New York State Psychiatric Institute, Biometrics Research.

van Wel, B., Blum, N., Kockmann, I., Pfohl, B., Heesterman, W., & Black, D. W. (2006). STEPPS group treatment for borderline personality disorder in The Netherlands. *Annals of Clinical Psychiatry*, 18, 63-67.

Watson, D. & Clark, L. A. (1994). *The PANAS-Manual for the Positive and Negative Affect Schedule–Expanded Form*, The University of Iowa.

Weertman, A., Arnoud, A., Dreesen, van Velzen, C., & Vertommen, S. (2003). Short interval test-retest interrater reliability of the Dutch version of the Structured Clinical Interview for DSM-IV Personality Disorders (SCID-II). *Journal of Personality Disorders,* 17: 562-567.

Young, J. (1994). *Cognitive therapy for personality disorders: A schema-focused approach.* Sarasota, FL: Professional Resource Press

Zanarini, M. C. & Shea, M. T. (1996). *The diagnostic interview for DSM-IV personality Disorders (DIPD).* Belmont, MA, McLean Hospital,

doi:10.1300/J200v06n01_14

Mentalization-Based Treatment for BPD

Anthony W. Bateman
Peter Fonagy

SUMMARY. In this chapter, we will outline how the concept of mentalizing helps us understand some of the common problems associated with borderline personality disorder and how the theoretical understanding is translated into psychotherapeutic intervention. Mentalizing is the process by which we interpret the actions of ourselves and others in terms of underlying intentional states such as personal desires, needs, feelings, beliefs and reasons. This capacity develops within the context of attachment relationships during infancy and childhood. Borderline personality disorder is conceived of as being a disorder of mentalizing. Vulnerability to a loss in mentalizing particularly in interpersonal or stressful circumstances is a core feature of the disorder. If treatment is to be successful it must either have mentalization as its focus or at the very least stimulate development of mentalizing as an epiphenomenon. Treatment focusing on mentalizing itself is described. doi:10.1300/J200v06n01_15 *[Article copies available for a fee from The Haworth Document Delivery Service: 1-800-HAWORTH. E-mail address: <docdelivery@ haworthpress.com> Website: <http://www.HaworthPress.com> © 2008 by The Haworth Press. All rights reserved.]*

KEYWORDS. Mentalization, mentalizing, psychotherapy, borderline personality disorder

---

[Haworth co-indexing entry note]: "Mentalization-Based Treatment for BPD." Bateman, Anthony W., and Peter Fonagy. Co-published simultaneously in *Social Work in Mental Health* (The Haworth Press) Vol. 6, No. 1/2, 2008, pp. 187-201; and: *Borderline Personality Disorder: Meeting the Challenges to Successful Treatment* (ed: Perry D. Hoffman, and Penny Steiner-Grossman) The Haworth Press, 2008, pp. 187-201. Single or multiple copies of this article are available for a fee from The Haworth Document Delivery Service [1-800-HAWORTH, 9:00 a.m. - 5:00 p.m. (EST). E-mail address: docdelivery@haworthpress.com].

Available online at http://swmh.haworthpress.com
© 2008 by The Haworth Press. All rights reserved.
doi:10.1300/J200v06n01_15

WHAT IS MENTALIZING?

Mentalizing (Fonagy et al., 2002) simply implies a focus on mental states in oneself or in others, particularly in explanations of behavior. That mental states influence behavior is beyond question. Beliefs, wishes, feelings and thoughts, whether inside or outside our awareness, determine what we do.

Mentalization is a mainly preconscious, imaginative mental activity. It is imaginative because we have to imagine what other people might be thinking or feeling. It lacks homogeneity because each person's history and capacity to imagine may lead to different conclusions about the mental states of others. Sometimes we may need to make the same kind of imaginative leap to understand our own experiences, particularly in relation to emotionally charged issues or irrational, non-consciously driven reactions.

To adopt a mentalizing stance, to conceive of oneself and others as having a mind, requires a representational system for mental states. A focus on mental states seems self-evident for those involved in treating individuals with mental disorder. Yet even those of us engaged in daily clinical work may forget all too easily that our clients have minds. For example, many biological psychiatrists are happier to think in terms of neurotransmitter imbalance than about distorted expectations or self-representation. Parents with children who have psychological problems often prefer to understand these either in terms of genetic predispositions or direct consequences of the child's social environment. Even psychotherapists can make unwarranted assumptions about what their patients' theory about their illness and its treatment might be, and their interventions indicate that they might have lost touch with the actual subjective experience of their patients.

Allen (Allen & Fonagy, 2006) defines mentalizing as "perceiving and interpreting behavior as conjoined with intentional mental states." It is a profoundly social construct in the sense that we are attentive to the mental states of those we are with, physically or psychologically. Equally we can temporarily lose awareness of them as "minds" and even momentarily treat them as physical objects. Elsewhere we have speculated that for physical violence to be possible, we have to deliberately foreclose the possibility that the individual we violate has a mind, either by considering the person as a physical object or as a member of a large alien social group, but not as an individual with specific concerns and beliefs (Fonagy, 2003). For the purposes of therapy, mentalizing can be considered either as implicit or explicit, and it is important for the therapist who focuses on mentalizing to be aware of the differences (Bateman & Fonagy, 2006).

IMPLICIT AND EXPLICIT MENTALIZING

We mentalize implicitly within all our interactions. Yet when we try to grasp the essence of the process, it slips away into explicit mentalizing, at once destroying the quintessence of the implicit process. Implicit mentalizing is automatic, procedural, natural, and below the level of consciousness. We are not aware that we are doing it and yet, when asked, we know that we are constantly monitoring ourselves and others intuitively, without thought. We base our opinions of others on our subjective experience of them as much as on our rational deductions: "He seems very nice, but there is something about him I don't trust." There is a balance that we naturally draw as implicit and explicit mentalizing intertwined together, more like the "double helix" than a continuum in its complexity, forming a multifaceted psychological understanding of ourselves, coding our relationships, representing them and representing them as we interact.

When we mentalize others, we monitor their mental states, taking in their point of view, their emotional states, and a sense of their underlying motives. We intuitively reflect and, when things go smoothly, our mind states change in tune with theirs. We take pleasure in the interaction as it progresses, and we see that not only have we changed them a little, but we have been changed as well. We respond to their presentation of themselves and to their re-presentation of us. Yet if we tried to do all this explicitly all of the time, we would stumble and become like an automaton, emotionless and non-human. Nobody would like us or feel warmly towards us, experiencing us as hollow and without depth, and we would be unable to feel close to them. Communication of our inner selves would have been interrupted.

To reflect on our emotional states, we have to remain in them. In order to do so, we have to maintain an experience of our sense of self, otherwise our emotions will overwhelm us. We need to identify the inner experience, modulate it, understand its narrative–where has it come from, what is its meaning–and express it. Not surprisingly, it is a tall order for treatment to target this process, and this may have led some, perhaps wisely, to dismantle implicit mentalizing into smaller elements and to target them rather than the overall process in treatment. Hence there are a number of conceptual cousins–for example empathy, self-awareness, introspection, reflectiveness, mindfulness–all of which overlap. These tend to be present-centered, whereas implicit mentalizing is at once present- past- and future-centered.

We mentalize explicitly most of the time. We are continuously thinking and talking together about our emotional states and thoughts and about those of others, particularly our partners and close friends and colleagues. As clinicians we talk about our patients' beliefs, desires, wishes, feelings, and motives on a daily basis and, for the most part, ask our patients to join us in doing so. When we talk to others we tend to focus on the here and now by identifying what someone experiences at the moment, but we also mentalize ourselves and others within different time frames. We ask ourselves and others if we have experienced anything similar before (I know this feeling and it is familiar to me), and think about our mental states at the time (Why did I feel this then?). We anticipate future mental states, wondering how we will feel if we do something or how someone else will feel if we say something. Hopefully, we move seamlessly between these different time zones as we use hindsight to find foresight and to facilitate more effective ways of managing similar situations over time.

In keeping with our moves around time frames, we can mentalize within a narrower frame, and the scope of our reflection is reduced to the immediate moment or to include only recent mind states and events. Alternatively, we can hark back to distant past history and wonder about our upbringing, our parental relationships, and use this to explain our current experience. We develop a narrative–a story about our mental states–and in the end the widest context for understanding any mental state is a full autobiography.

DISRUPTION OF MENTALIZING AND BPD

Several factors can disrupt the normal deployment of mentalizing. Most important among these is psychological trauma early or late in childhood (Fonagy et al., 2003). We have found extensive evidence to suggest that childhood attachment trauma undermines the capacity to think about mental states in giving narrative accounts of one's past attachment relationships, and even in trying to identify the mental states associated with specific facial expressions. This may result from (1) the defensive inhibition of the capacity to think about others' thoughts and feelings in the face of the experience of genuine malevolent intent of others and the overwhelming vulnerability of the child; (2) a distortion of the functioning of arousal mechanisms inhibiting orbito-frontal cortical activity (mentalizing) at far lower levels of risk than would be normally the case; and (3) any trauma arousing the attachment system (seeking for protection). In seeking proximity to the traumatizing attachment figure as a consequence of trauma, the child may naturally be further traumatized. The prolonged activation of the attachment system may be an additional problem, as the arousal of attachment may have specific inhibitory consequences for mentalization in addition to that which might be expected as a consequence of increased emotional arousal.

PHENOMENOLOGY

The phenomenology of BPD is the consequence of (1) the attachment-related inhibition of mentalization; (2) the re-emergence of modes of experiencing internal reality that antedate the developmental emergence of mentalization; and (3) the constant pressure for projective identification, the re-externalisation of the self-destructive alien self. Taking these in turn, individuals with borderline personality disorder are "normal" mentalizers, except in the context of attachment relationships. They tend to misread minds–both their own and those of others–when emotionally aroused. As their relationship with another moves into the sphere of attachment the intensification of relationships, their ability to think about the mental state of another can rapidly disappear. When this happens, prementalistic modes of organizing subjectivity emerge, which have the power to disorganize these relationships and destroy the coherence of self-experience that normal mentalization generates.

In this way, mentalization gives way to psychic equivalence, which clinicians normally consider under the heading of concreteness of thought. No alternative perspectives are possible. There is a suspension of the experience of "as if," and everything appears to be "for real." This can add drama as well as risk to interpersonal experience, and the exaggerated reaction of patients is justified by the seriousness with which they suddenly experience their own and others' thoughts and feelings. Conversely, thoughts and feelings can come to be almost dissociated to the point of near meaninglessness. In these states, patients can discuss experiences without contextualizing these in any kind of physical or material reality. Attempting psychotherapy with patients who are in this mode can lead the therapist to lengthy but inconsequential discussions of internal experience that has no link to genuine experience.

Finally, early modes of conceptualizing action in terms of that which is apparent can come to dominate motivation. Within this mode there is a primacy of the physical, and experience is only felt to be valid when its consequences are apparent to all. Affection, for example, is only true when accompanied by physical expression.

The most disruptive feature of borderline cognition is the apparently unstoppable tendency to create unacceptable experience within the other. The externalization of the alien self is desirable for the child with a disorganized attachment, but it is a matter of life and death for the traumatized individual who has internalized the abuser as part of the self. The alternative to projective identification is the destruction of the self in a teleological mode, i.e., physically, by self-harm and suicide. These and other actions can also serve to create a terrified alien self in the other–therapist, friend, parent–who becomes the vehicle for what is emotionally unbearable. The need for this other can become overwhelming, and an adhesive, addictive pseudoattachment to this individual may develop.

THERAPY

A number of key points for therapy follow from our central tenet that non-mentalistic modes of function are revealed when the attachment relationship is stimulated. First, the patient in psychic equivalence mode can only experience his or her own point of view, and it is necessary for the therapist to recognize that alternative viewpoints are unacceptable; any attempt to provide one will simply lead to argument or complaints from the patient that the therapist does not understand. Second, the primacy of physical experience as the only aspect of interaction that has meaning can erode the boundaries of therapy, leading to violations of normal professional interaction. Third, the dissociated state or pretend mode can lull the therapist and patient in to a false sense that improvement has taken place. The patient appears calm and is able to talk about him/herself sensibly and coherently and listen to what the therapist has to say. Yet life does not change. This can lead to interminable therapy because the belief system of the therapist is required for stability and is lived out by the patient. This is not specific to any therapy. Borderline patients can take on the beliefs and structures that any therapy gives them, only to use them for stability rather than change. Finally, all therapies evoke an attachment relationship with patients and as a result are liable to reveal earlier forms of psychological function. To this extent, therapies are apparently iatrogenic and need to guard against over-stimulation.

Mentalization-based therapy takes into account all these dangers of therapy by addressing the structure of therapy and the therapist's attitude or stance, and by providing clear principles for intervention (Bateman & Fonagy, 2004). These aspects of therapy will be discussed briefly below.

STRUCTURE OF TREATMENT

The overall aim of MBT is to develop a therapeutic process in which the mind of the patient becomes the focus of treatment. The objective is for patients to find out more about how they think and feel about themselves and others, how that dictates their responses to others, and how "errors" in understanding themselves and others lead to actions in an attempt to retain stability and to make sense of incomprehensible feelings. The therapist has to ensure that the patient is aware of this goal, that the therapy process itself is not mysterious, and that the patient understands the underlying focus of treatment. The mentalizing process can only be developed if the structure of treatment is carefully defined.

There are three main phases to the trajectory of treatment. Each phase has a distinct aim and harnesses specific processes. The overall aims of the initial phase are assessing the patient's mentalizing capacities and personality function and engaging the patient in treatment. Specific processes during the start of treatment include: giving a diagnosis; providing psychoeducation; establishing a hierarchy of therapeutic aims; stabilizing social and behavioral problems; reviewing medications; and defining a crisis pathway. During the middle sessions, the aim of all the active therapeutic work is to stimulate an ever-increasing mentalizing ability. In the final stage, preparation is made for ending intensive treatment. This requires the therapist to focus on the feelings of loss associated with ending treatment and on how to maintain gains that have been made, as well as on developing with the patient an appropriate follow-up program tailored to his or her particular needs. In our experience, the view put forth by protagonists of particular models of therapy that patients with severe personality disorder improve adequately following 12-18 months of treatment and require no further support remains part of research mythology rather than realistic clinical practice.

THERAPIST ATTITUDE

The therapist needs to guard against over-stimulation of the attachment system. We have defined carefully a therapist stance and basic principles to follow when applying mentalizing interventions to ensure that emotional states are kept within reasonable bounds. The therapist has to steer a course between under-stimulation of emotion (which provides sanctuary and safety but leads the problems unaddressed) and over-stimulation of affect (which leads to panic and breakdown of treatment or self-destructive and impulsive behavior).

Not-Knowing Stance

The mentalizing or not-knowing stance is an attempt to capture a sense that mental states are opaque and that the therapist can have no more idea of what is in the patient's mind than the patient. The therapist attempts to demonstrate a willingness to find out about the patient, how he or she feels, and the reasons for any underlying problems. To do this the therapist has to engage in active questioning, discouraging excessive free association by the patient in favor of monitoring and understanding the interpersonal processes and how they relate to the patient's mental states. When the therapist takes a different perspective from the patient, this should be verbalized and explored in relation to the patient's alternative perspective, with no assumption being made about whose viewpoint has greater validity. The task is to determine the mental processes that have led to alternative viewpoints and to consider each perspective in relation to the other, understanding that diverse outlooks may be acceptable. Where differences are clear and cannot initially be resolved, they should be identified, stated, and accepted until resolution seems possible.

The therapist also should refrain from using certain techniques commonly used in cognitive and dynamic therapies. These include Socratic questioning and stimulation of fantasy about the therapist. In psychic equivalence, Socratic questioning is simply seen as offensive or attacking and merely implies that the therapist does not understand the underlying experience of the patient; fantasy development about the therapist is experienced as real and can excite expectation rather than illuminate underlying unconscious processes.

PRINCIPLES OF INTERVENTIONS

We have defined a number of interventions in keeping with dynamic and other therapies. These are summarised in Table 1. We have arranged the interventions in order of complexity, depth and emotional intensity with empathy and support being the simplest, the most superficial and the least intensive and mentalizing the transference being the most complex and, for the most part, the most emotionally intensive. Commonly the decision about which intervention to use when will be taken outside consciousness, but we believe that there are some general principles to follow.

The basis for our recommendations is simply that, in general, mentalizing capacity in borderline patients is inversely related to stimulation of the attachment system. As the attachment system is activated and the capacity to mentalize is inhibited, emotions become bewildering, the self fractures, and actions to restore precarious safety and a sense of balance become inevitable. Balancing stimulation of the attachment system with capacity to mentalize places the therapist in the delicate position of having to mobilize affect while controlling its flow and intensity. Without emotion, there can be no meaningful subjective experience; with excess emotion there can be no understanding of the subjective experience.

As we have argued before, one of the gravest dangers for therapists treating borderline patients is iatrogenic harm. Therapists can cause harm by using well-meaning but mistimed and misguided interventions that diminish rather than increase mentalizing capacity through excessive activation of the attachment system. When selecting interventions, it is essential for therapist to balance emotional intensity with the patient's continuing capacity to subjectively monitor his own mind and that of another.

On the surface, sensitively given support and empathy are unlikely to provoke complex mental states in borderline patients. Sensing that someone is showing interest and attempting to understand their emotional state from their point of view, borderline patients will feel safe enough to explain their feelings and give their perspective about what has happened or is happening to them. The patient's mind is not threatened. Hence these types of interventions, along with motivational interviewing, problem solving, psychoeducation, and other behavioural techniques, are useful early in therapy.

At the intermediate level of intervention, challenge creates more difficulty because it forces self-scrutiny and implies that another mind

TABLE 1

Supportive/empathic

Clarification and elaboration

Basic mentalizing

Interpretive mentalizing

Mentalizing the transference

might have a different perspective that has to be considered and integrated. If the challenge incorporates interpersonal content and current affect rather than being intellectual, it forms part of basic mentalizing; the relational world is invoked, thus raising the emotional intensity. If the intervention is then linked to "you and me" and underlying motivations are brought into play, the danger of overwhelming the patient's mentalizing capacity increases considerably, as does that of inducing action. The patient walks out of a session or cuts him/herself to restore his/her mind. This cascade of psychological disaster can be avoided if therapists move slowly down the levels of intervention, only reaching the greatest depth having worked on the earlier levels first. The therapist should only move down a level after assessing the patient's degree of anxiety. Therefore, mentalizing capacity allows the patient to consider your perspective further. If in doubt, the therapist's interventions should be tentative at first and only inject more pressure into the dialogue when the therapeutic relationship is robust.

It is not our intention to suggest that therapists must adhere rigidly to the principles outlined here. But if therapists follow our clinical pathway and sensibly implement our recommendations about timing of interventions, we believe they will be less at risk of causing harm and will have the greatest chance of stimulating a positive therapeutic relationship within which mentalizing can flourish.

THE CASE OF JOAN

There are a number of aspects of this clinical case to consider from the perspective of mentalizing. Despite considerable problems, Joan's parents have continued to be involved with her care over many years, which is a tribute to their persistence and care. Families are bewildered at the onset of any illness, often hoping that problems are short-term or a passing phase. But as time goes on and the help and support they offer is rejected or appears to be ineffective, they gradually and understandably give up, feeling hopeless. They are unable to understand what makes someone they loved and still love behave in such a way, especially if the loved one persists in self-harm and suicidal behavior. Their withdrawal is often an attempt to protect themselves from unbearable pain: watching helplessly as their daughter, son, mother or other loved one seems bent on self-destruction. At the same time, their withdrawal is a way of protecting their own mentalizing capacity. In Joan's case, her family has continued contact but finds it difficult to continue their understanding of her during close emotional interaction. At family dinners, Joan blames her entire family for thinking she is a failure, and her father retaliates, feeling unappreciated, angry, and defeated. At these times, he loses his capacity to mentalize and to understand Joan's plight. The whole family need support to maintain mentalizing even when under pressure, in order to give treatment the best chance of success. If Joan were being assessed for MBT, we would assess her along with her family. At present, we do not incorporate mentalizing family therapy in our programs for BPD, but we see families for support. In this case, we would work with Joan's parents to help them understand her behavior and emotional outbursts by helping them understand her loss of mentalizing amid emotional states and how this leaves her experiencing their motivations in a fixed way. We would provide her parents with some practical advice about what to do in situations of crisis; for example, in emotionally "hot" interactions, they should not challenge Joan. All patients engaged in MBT have a crisis plan developed during the first few sessions; in this case it would have to be done in conjunction with the family with whom she is living.

The initial phase of treatment would involve a careful assessment of Joan's mentalizing capacities and the development of a formulation. Initial sessions are occupied with giving the diagnosis, explaining the treatment, reviewing the medication, and agreeing a crisis plan. Through empathic listening and non-judgemental exploration of the problems, we emphasise the development of a therapeutic alliance. Considerable attention is paid to any problems that are likely to disrupt treatment and any factors that might support treatment. MBT has been provided to borderline patients with severe problems, which may include social disadvantage, drug misuse and housing instability. All these areas are assessed at the beginning of treatment to ensure that appropriate help is available, particularly to stabilize social circumstances. It is not possible to develop a robust crisis plan if the patient has no place to live.

Joan's mentalizing capacities show obvious vulnerability to emotional situations, and it appears that her views of others in relation to her become rigid, quickly losing flexibility. For example she states that she has always perceived her father as critical and judgmental and as favoring her siblings over herself. She accuses the whole family of thinking of her as a failure and being unwilling to support her throughout her life; she then responds to her family in ways that are predicated on these belief systems. In MBT the focus is on understanding how the patient feels as she does, accepting the reality of that experience, and moving towards alternative perspectives. Some therapies consider rigid schemas and reciprocal roles as having been learned. We prefer to see them as operating only when higher-level mentalizing functions are lost in emotional interactions and therefore being both present and absent; this leads to the confusion so often found in borderline patients and their families. We are therefore less concerned with the content of the schema than we are about stimulating a process by which continuity of the self-structure can be reinstated.

At one moment, a family can feel that their good intentions are understood and that they themselves are able to understand. At these times mentalizing can flourish. Yet things change dramatically without warning and without apparent reason, leading to confusion and puzzlement. As mentalizing fails, rigid representations appear as the patient attempts to make sense of an inner experience that is not understandable. The experience only makes sense if it can be explained by external causes: "I feel like I do because you are like this." This projective system stabilises the mind of the borderline patient but, not surprisingly, confuses the mind of the other person. In Joan's case, she is clear about her view of the father, but I suspect that he will be confused about how she can believe what she does about him. Of course, Joan's viewpoint is based on her experience, and to that extent it must be considered as valid and should not be challenged initially. The understanding of these representations will come when they are re-experienced in therapy.

We expect some aspects of Joan's commonly used dynamic interactions to occur in therapy within the relationship with the therapist. It is obvious that she is oversensitive with her friends in her apartment and in family interactions; the initial formulation would explicitly predict its development in therapy. This prediction would have been introduced in to the dialogue with Joan in the form of "transference tracers," which point the way for using the therapy relationship to understand the underlying mental states that govern Joan's actions and reactions.

As soon as a key interactional dynamic becomes evident in therapy, it is important for the therapist to act immediately using a mentalizing or "not-knowing stance." We do not know why and how Joan has developed a sense that her father is critical and judgmental, so we cannot assume that this is simply a projection of her own experience. Her experience has its own validity, which must be understood by the therapist before anything else can be questioned. The mentalizing therapist explores how Joan comes to experience her father as she does, particularly in affectively charged situations, and how she experiences the therapist in this way when this dynamic is present in the session. We do not see this as an activation of an object relationship currently active in the mind of the patient and representing earlier developmental object relationships. Instead, we see this as the activation of earlier modes of psychological functioning as a result of arousal associated with emotional interaction. First, the therapist has to be empathic and explore the antecedents of the loss of mentalizing, rather than the content of the experience.

In summary, the mentalizing therapist would concentrate on forming an initial therapeutic alliance while assessing Joan's mentalizing capacities and developing a formulation and crisis plan. The formulation is given to Joan in written form as a concrete outcome of the joint exploration to demonstrate the current understanding the therapist has of the problems–the workings of one mind about another mind explicitly modelled. The formulation can be modified according to new understandings as they occur in the sessions. As treatment progresses, the therapist is expected to challenge the assumptions Joan makes, particularly in the context of emotional states. Prior to this, the therapist must demonstrate an understanding of how Joan can reach the conclusions that she does. This validation is used to explore further the multi-faceted representation and context of the experience, rather than simply to concur with her understanding. Central to the work is exploration of events as they occur in therapy, not seeing these as repetitions of earlier relationships or activation of object relations, but by understanding the process that has led to the loss of mentalizing. In the case of Joan, this might start from a careful examination of her affective states before her outbursts with her father or episodes of self-harm before they can be detailed within the therapy relationship. If an emotional outburst occurs in therapy, the therapist should explore what happened at the point at which Joan is cooling down. In the heat of the moment, we advise the therapist to use the simpler intervention of empathy, expressing uncertainty at what has happened and questioning explicitly his role in what has occurred.

One area of the presentation that gives cause for concern is Joan's continued use of drugs. Drug misuse disrupts clinical treatment and may interfere with natural improvement of the disorder. It will be important to address Joan's drug use right from the start of treatment, but we would not enter in to a contract about her drug use in relation to continuation of treatment. We do not develop contracts that can result in termination of treatment, because this requires a patient to have a highly developed mentalizing capacity to agree such a contract. Joan would have to be able to appraise her current state and her capacity to resist her desires and impulsivity in the future. She would be unable to do this and so can only sign a contract under duress and as a way of getting treatment, rather than as an aid to control her drug use. Only later in treatment when a therapeutic alliance is established would we begin to challenge her drug misuse. Of course if she attended sessions under the influence of drugs, she would be asked to leave and only to return when her mind was clear.

In conclusion, having returned to a supportive family, developed some independence, and willingly approached services for treatment, Joan appears to have a reasonable prognosis. We would hope to join her in what might be a difficult journey, but not a journey she should make on her own.

REFERENCES

Allen, J. G. & Fonagy, P. (2006). *Handbook of mentalziation-based treatment.* Chichester: Wiley.

Bateman, A. & Fonagy, P. (2004). Mentalisation-based treatment of borderline personality disorder. *Journal of Personality Disorder*, 18, 35-50.

Bateman, A. & Fonagy, P. (2006). Mentalization based treatment: A practical guide. Oxford: Oxford University Press.

Fonagy, P. (2003). The developmental roots of violence in the failure of mentalization. In F. Pfäfflin, & G. Adshead (Eds.), *A Matter of Security: The Application of Attachment Theory to Forensic Psychiatry and Psychotherapy* (pp. 13-56). London: Jessica Kingsley.

Fonagy, P., Target, M., Gergely, G., Allen, J., & Bateman, A. (2003). The developmental roots of Borderline Personality Disorder in early attachment relationships: A theory and some evidence. *Psychoanalytic Inquiry*, 23, 412-458.

Fonagy, P., Target, M., Gergely, G., & Jurist, E. L. (2002). *Affect Regulation, Mentalization, and the Development of Self.* London: Other Press.

doi:10.1300/J200v06n01_15

In Their Own Words:
Improving Services and Hopefulness
for Families Dealing with BPD

Ellie Buteau
Kevin Dawkins
Perry Hoffman

SUMMARY. The impact of borderline personality disorder on family members of persons with BPD is articulated best by family members themselves. Despite an increase in research demonstrating more hopeful outcomes for the diagnosis, many mental health professionals remain unaware of recent advances in BPD treatments and therapies. This lack of awareness has dramatic consequences not only for patients, but for their families as well. This chapter describes the personal experiences of 12 family members with relatives with BPD. Expressed in one-hour semi-structured interviews, the family members' individual accounts centered on five key areas of their lives with their ill relative: (1) difficulty accessing current evidence-based knowledge about BPD and treatments; (2) a stigmatizing health care system; (3) prolonged hopelessness; (4) shrinking social networks; and (5) financial burdens. To improve the quality of services available to family members affected by BPD, social workers must educate themselves about the availability of professionals trained in BPD, BPD-specific treatment options, and BPD information resources. doi:10.1300/J200v06n01_16 *[Article copies available for a fee from The Haworth Document Delivery Service:*

[Haworth co-indexing entry note]: "In Their Own Words: Improving Services and Hopefulness for Families Dealing with BPD." Buteau, Ellie, Kevin Dawkins, and Perry Hoffman. Co-published simultaneously in *Social Work in Mental Health* (The Haworth Press) Vol. 6, No. 1/2, 2008, pp. 203-214; and: *Borderline Personality Disorder: Meeting the Challenges to Successful Treatment* (ed: Perry D. Hoffman, and Penny Steiner-Grossman) The Haworth Press, 2008, pp. 203-214. Single or multiple copies of this article are available for a fee from The Haworth Document Delivery Service [1-800-HAWORTH, 9:00 a.m. - 5:00 p.m. (EST). E-mail address: docdelivery@haworthpress.com].

*1-800-HAWORTH. E-mail address: <docdelivery@haworthpress.com> Website: <http://
www.HaworthPress.com> © 2008 by The Haworth Press. All rights reserved.]*

KEYWORDS. Borderline personality disorder, family members and mental illness, hopelessness, BPD knowledge, BPD treatment

INTRODUCTION

The diagnosis of borderline personality disorder is relatively new to the psychiatric community. BPD only received official recognition in the Diagnostic and Statistical Manual in 1980 (DSM-III), despite earlier writings in the literature identifying a unique set of patients experienced in clinical practice (Knight, 1938). Similarly, the struggles of patients suffering from BPD and their family members often begin many years before an official diagnosis is made. With 10% of outpatients and 20% of all psychiatric patients presenting for psychiatric treatment meeting criteria for BPD (Frances, Widiger, & Pincus, 1989), social workers often are thrust into the critical role of assisting sufferers and their families in their BPD journey. Social workers often find a lack of resources to offer when they attempt to help these families. To date, the mental health field is lacking across the spectrum with regard to BPD, from the dearth of professionals skilled in diagnosing and treating BPD to the failure of insurance companies to provide a billing code for BPD (Friedel, 2006).

The current state of the field leaves families with BPD at a loss when seeking accurate information about the disorder and useful treatment options for their ill relative. This situation prevails even decades after improvements in the mental health care system for families of persons with other major disorders, such as schizophrenia and bipolar disorder. Interestingly, this lack of services for BPD family members, runs counter to research conducted over the past decade demonstrating that: (1) a family member's emotional involvement with the ill relative may be a positive predictor of course of illness (Hooley & Hoffman, 1999; Gunderson et al., 2006); and (2) higher levels of knowledge about BPD among family members correlates with their experiencing higher levels of burden, depression, distress and hostility towards their ill relatives (Hoffman, Buteau, & Hooley et al., 2003). Thus, the importance of family members receiving both accurate information from *experts* as well as resources for treatment and support cannot be overemphasized.

In addition, despite research suggesting that a diagnosis of BPD carries more hope than many other diagnoses of mental illness (Zanarini, 2002), many mental health professionals continue to believe that persons suffering BPD remain unresponsive to treatment (Friedel, 2006). Empirical evidence of treatments shown to help those suffering from BPD has been growing but has yet to be incorporated into the everyday practice of many mental health professionals. Further, in view of the evidence, the hopelessness experienced by family members of relatives suffering with BPD (Hoffman et al., 2003) needs to be challenged. Evidence-based approaches to treatment include cognitive behavioral therapies, such as Dialectical Behavior Therapy (Linehan, 1993), psychodynamic approaches such as Mentalization-Based Treatment (Bateman & Fonagy, 1999), Transference-Focused Psychotherapy (Yeomans, Clarkin & Kernberg, 2002) and the STEPPS program (Systems Training for Emotional Predictability and Problem Solving) (Blum et al., 2002).

METHODOLOGY

In-depth semi-structured interviews were conducted with 12 family members of persons with BPD. Questions for the interview were developed from data collected in the first round of a Delphi study[1] conducted as part of a larger research study designed by Dawkins Productions, Inc. and funded by the National Institute of Mental Health (NIMH). The first round of the Delphi study consisted of five questions, posed to 12 leading BPD researchers/clinicians and 13 BPD family advocates, in order to assist in identifying appropriate editorial content to include in a video series for family members of persons with BPD; this video series was being developed as part of the NIMH funded study. One question in the Delphi study asked both the BPD researchers/clinicians and BPD family advocates what interview questions they thought would be most relevant to ask family members in order to learn about their personal experiences with the disorder. Themes were identified based on responses to this question, and these themes formed the basis for the questions that were asked during these subsequent interviews with family members. The goal of these interviews was to learn directly from family members what their experiences have been in four key areas: (1) knowledge about BPD, (2) BPD treatments, (3) coping with BPD, and (4) reasons for hope.

Sample

Participants were recruited from a list of individuals who had recently made inquiries via phone or Internet to the National Education Alliance for Borderline Personality Disorder (NEA-BPD) Family Connections program. The NEA-BPD Family Connections administrator e-mailed a letter explaining the research project to 14 potential candidates on this list and asked whether they might be interested in participating.[2] All family members who were contacted agreed to participate. Interviewers then contacted each family member by phone and explained the project in greater detail. Consent and HIPPA forms were provided to and signed by all participants. Interviewers set up one-hour interview appointments with each participant. As the target sample size was 12 family members, interviewers ceased interviewing after the first 12 were complete. These family members included 2 males and 10 females: 10 parents (including one legal guardian), 1 spouse and 1 sibling.[3]

Interviews

As the interviewees were widely distributed geographically, all interviews were conducted via telephone. All interviews were audiotaped and transcribed with the permission of the participants. Each participant was assigned a code number and assured that their responses would not be identified with their name or the name of their ill relative. Demographic information was collected by interviewers on a separate sheet and only the gender of participant and relationship to the person with BPD were connected with the transcripts for data analysis. Two researchers, both certified in the protection of human subjects, conducted the interviews.

At the start of each phone call, the interviewers administered the McLean Screening Instrument for Borderline Personality Disorder (MSI-BPD) (Zanarini, 2003), a measure designed as a brief diagnostic screen to identify persons with BPD. For the purpose of this study, items were posed in the third person to reflect the family member's perceptions of the ill relative's behaviors. Examples of items include: "Have any of your relative's closest relationships been troubled by a lot of arguments or repeated breakups?" "Has your relative deliberately hurt him/herself physically (e.g., punched, cut, or burned him/herself)?" "Has your relative had at least two other problems with impulsivity (e.g., eating binges and spending sprees, drinking too much or verbal outbursts)?" Those family members who endorsed at least 7 of 10 items about their ill relative were to be accepted for inclusion in the study. All interviewees endorsed the requisite number of items.

Each family member participant was asked the same series of questions, including, "Once the diagnosis of BPD was made how difficult was it to find skilled professional help? (e.g., in medication management, psychotherapy and family support/education)"; "What were your experiences with the healthcare system?"; "How well would you say you have been able to cope with this situation?"; and "How hopeful are you about the future for your family member?"

RESULTS AND DISCUSSION

Difficulty Accessing Information About BPD

The moment that family members first need BPD information is immediately following the diagnosis. When asked if the people who diagnosed her ill relative provided her with any information, one family member said: *"No. In fact they were in such a hurry to get to another appointment that we kind of stood in the door, and I had my mouth open saying . . . This is it? . . . Why couldn't there be somebody who could have given me the sense that there was anything that could be done? . . . That's all we [family members] want–a sense that there's hope."* Family members recounted similar experiences of receiving little assistance from mental health professionals when trying to obtain information and educational resources about BPD. Feelings of hopelessness seemed to pervade their information-seeking experiences.

Left to seek information on their own, family members often located out-of-date resources, mainly through the Internet and in books, that simply described BPD without any guidance on how to locate treatment or updated statistics on remission, further contributing to their sense of hopelessness: *"We initially found this information. And it pretty much said, well, that there's really no hope for people with borderline, that they don't live long. Because they get into their 30s and 40s and commit suicide by that time."* Another family member said: *"I had never heard of it [BPD]. And when I got on the Internet and tried to read about it, I became very depressed myself because it sounds so hopeless for any chance of a better life–let alone recovery."*

Other family members explained: *". . . In flipping through information I've been given, there's a lot of descriptives in there but, as far as what I've come across, there is not much information about what to do to help . . . It seems so hopeless because there isn't a lot written about treatment.*" While describing this search for information, one family member commented about her confusion in trying to read about BPD on her own, "*Well, you know all the books seem like I could pick something out of them, but in a lot of the things that I read, I wonder who's right and who's wrong–you know all these theories.*"

Navigating the Mental Health System

Both before the diagnosis of BPD, when family members recalled numerous misdiagnoses that both they and their ill relative felt were incorrect, as well as after a diagnosis of BPD was made, family members expressed their frustration with attempts to navigate the mental health system. Family members told of ill relatives who had been in and out of the mental health system for years, with little success in finding effective treatment.

One parent was able to tell a positive story of being put in touch with a mental health professional who referred her ill relative to a DBT program, which proved, and continues to prove effective. But the majority of family members told stories of being shut out of the treatment process and being given the run-around: "*It's sort of like running into a brick wall. You get a name and they call them. And they say, well, why don't you call this place? And we call them, and they say call this other place.*" One parent recalled contacting over 200 therapists listed in her insurance company's book, to little avail because as soon as she mentioned that her ill relative was "cutting," she was told that the therapist on the other end of the line was not accepting new patients.

Family members told of miscommunication, both with them and between treating facilities in the system: "*I think the care is fragmented when someone is inpatient . . . She's been hospitalized several times. And everyone has their own way of doing things and their own thoughts about what's going on. There's no consistency. And they don't share [information]. I think that's the biggest thing. One hospital can't send information to another hospital without our signing over our lives–which is not a problem. But then at the next hospital has to happen all over again . . . I mean, even if the first hospital shared [the information] with a second hospital, the second hospital can't share it with the third hospital.*"

Locating Treatment

Striking similarities arose in family member stories of attempting to learn about treatments and subsequently locating a trained therapist or program. As one family member said, *"It seems to me that since we've found out about [BPD], and her therapist has actually said that she definitely has it, that there are so many professionals who don't really know a lot about it. There are a few who know a little bit, but they really are not well versed in it at all. We know more than they do. We're telling them what we've learned through books. And it changes as the information gets updated and people do more studies, [but] they're just not up to date on things."*

Other family members expressed similar sentiments concerning difficulties in finding professionals knowledgeable about treatments: *"And I said, well what can you tell me about any of the places? Which would you say would be the best help for this person? [The social worker] didn't know anything about any of them. I said, so why are you recommending them? . . . So I started calling the places and I started going online trying to read about them myself. And because [my ill relative] was too sick to go, she ended up going back out to [treatment location] and I don't think that she's in a place that's really going to help her."* Another family member recalled, *"All this time, all these therapists that [my ill relative] has seen over the years –some of the best and some that are somewhat mediocre–there has never been anyone who has helped us to understand what [my ill relative] is dealing with."*

Family members reported that instead of receiving assistance from mental health professionals, they often were left to seek out their own resources, research treatment options, evaluate what might work best, and then locate appropriate facilities where those treatments are offered. Excited at first about the possibility that DBT holds, some families experienced further hopelessness when searches for trained professionals and programs for DBT in their area were unsuccessful. *"We're still searching. We have called New York City. We have called a lot of . . . we went online. We've talked to a lot of people. And there's no one in our area. And there's not a lot of help trying to find something that is doable for us. So it's very difficult."*

Coping

Hopelessness: During the interviews, most family members said that they have already resigned themselves to the possibility of having to care for their ill relative with BPD alone and for years to come. When asked how well they are coping, family members responded by saying, *"Well, there's that saying–that which doesn't kill you makes you stronger. And I do think I'm a pretty strong person, because I've had to be. But I'm so weary; I don't want to cope any more. I just want to live my life and be joyful and not be so hurting with all these problems."* Similarly, another family member said: *"Even though I want to do something, I don't know what to do. I don't know where to go to get her help or deal with the financial issues. Just because I can put a name on it . . . it would be like saying you've got AIDS. There's nothing you can do, really. You know when [AIDS] first came out, it was just a death sentence, and that's what this feels like."*

Family members have struggled for months and years without support and assistance from the very professionals who are trained to provide such services: *"Why couldn't there be somebody who could have given me the sense that there was anything that could be done . . . That's all they [families] want–a sense that there's hope."* This sense of hopelessness pervaded the majority of interviews conducted. After multiple failed attempts at treatments, dwindling support systems, and emotional and financial exhaustion, family members expressed desperation for a sense that their lives and the lives of their ill relatives would ever improve. As one family member commented, *"I just feel like I'm drowning, and there's not a ship or a life preserver or anything in sight."*

When asked about the moments when they have felt the most hope, some family members mentioned learning of possible treatments: *"When we found out that there's some kind of behavior-related therapy that has experienced some success."* Others spoke of having located family support programs: *"Meeting other people dealing with the same issues that we are [and who] might have insight into other avenues to get some help. Even if none of that comes to fruition, just having the support is such a weight lifted off when you know you're not dealing with it completely alone–which is how we feel right now."*

Social Networks: Through the many years during which BPD can go undiagnosed or misdiagnosed, those with an ill relative find it difficult to maintain social relationships with friends and extended families. Most family members reported that their friends and extended families had expressed frustration from hearing about their problems so frequently. Even within immediate families, spouses sometimes disagreed about whether or not their child with BPD truly needed professional help or was simply lazy or acting spoiled. Family members told multiple stories of being criticized by family and friends for "mishandling" the difficulties arising from their ill relative's BPD symptoms.

Very few family members told of having consistent or wide support networks. Quite the opposite: many of the interviewees felt quite alone in this struggle. When asked to whom she turned when she has an emotional crisis, one family member replied, *"Absolutely no one,"* and then began to describe how excited she was to be able to join a family support and education group (Family Connections) that included other family members in similar circumstances.

Adding considerably to their difficulties in coping is the insinuation that parents are to blame for their child having BPD. This stigma compounds the guilt that many family members already experience for not having understood what was wrong with their ill relative: *"When initially, during the first hospitalization, [the therapist] wanted to know whether I felt that I ever bonded with [my child] as an infant, I made a comment: . . . So this is the mother's failing–again. And he [said]: I didn't mean it that way. And I said: Yes, you did mean it that way. I know people tell you that I've never loved [my ill relative], never understood [my relative]. I know what [my relative] will say to you, but I don't think that's true."* Another family member with a similar experience recalls: *"The first thing they said to me was that they viewed it as, you know, because of non-maternal bonding."*

Another family member who recognized this blame as a myth commented, *"I actually just recently read something that said it was earlier believed that the lack of mother's nurturing as a young child [was to blame–and all these fallacies. Also, that anyone who has it had to have had some sort of trauma . . . some sort of abuse, either physical or sexual abuse when they were younger. And I think people just automatically assume that that's the given. A lot of the professionals in the beginning would start trying to find out what exactly happened to [my relative] . . . I think that the whole thing with borderline is, if the right treatment is given, it can work. But getting to get to that point is so frustrating because people don't recognize this as really a disorder, and that's the frustrating thing."*

Financial Burdens

Interviews with family members were characterized by worries about financial burdens, including problems with insurance companies: *"If you're poor and have Medicaid, you can get all the help in the world. If you're rich you can pay for it out of pocket. It's the in between people that really get the short end of the stick."* Family members hit road blocks when insurance companies were unwilling to cover their ill relative's needed resources: *"I wish I knew where to find help. Her health insurance does not cover mental health issues. I don't even know what insurance does cover mental health. But you know to try to get her some help I mean, you'd probably have to sell your house and live on the street to be able to afford the kind of help that she probably needs."*

Beyond insurance issues, some family members reported being financially able to cover the costs incurred by treatment, medications, hospital stays and their loved one not being able to work; other family members faced severe financial burdens: *"You know, I would have had to get a loan or sell my house. But in the end, I will do that. I mean, if that's where my back ends up, you know all I want for this child is for her to have a normal life."* Another family member expressed a similar sentiment about last resorts: *"We don't want to lose our house. But taking care of her is a priority."* Beyond direct medical costs, some family members reported financial stressors caused by covering costs incurred by their loved one with BPD: *"You know, she gets herself involved with bills that she can't pay. And I pay them. I'm seriously, seriously in debt because of a lot of her behavior."*

CONCLUSION

Although the experience with BPD in these families spanned from a few months to almost 10 years, remarkable similarities emerged from their experiences, including searching for a correct diagnosis and accurate information about the diagnosis, attempting to learn about and locate treatment, struggling to find reasons for hope, struggling to cope in their own daily lives, and dealing with BPD-related financial burdens.

Sadly, what makes these families' stories so striking is the contrast of their experiences with the growing body of information over the past decade describing effective therapies for persons with BPD and support programs for family members such as NEA-BPD's Family Connections (Hoffman, Fruzzetti, Buteau et al. 2005; Hoffman, Fruzzetti, & Buteau, 2007) and NAMI's Family to Family (Dixon et al., 2004). These experiences signal the need for members of the mental health community to become more knowledgeable about BPD and its treatments, the availability of support groups for family members, and ways to communicate this information to those who need it. With social work, now the profession most involved in the direct service of BPD, it is imperative that those in the discipline become professional advocates for this community of families and patients, and provide them with the hope that is needed and so clearly evident.

NOTES

1. A Delphi study is an iterative research method for soliciting information about a specific topic to be examined and subsequently understanding where agreement does and does not exist among individuals who are experts on that particular topic.

2. The administrator only contacted family members on this list who did not have a familial affiliation with professionals in the BPD community or prior involvement with existing BPD family support programs. All family members contacted by the administrator agreed to be interviewed for this study.

3. These 12 family members represent 12 different families; no more than 1 person was interviewed from any family.

REFERENCES

Bateman, A. & Fonagy, P. (1999). Effectiveness of partial hospitalization in the treatment of borderline personality disorder: A randomized controlled trial. *American Journal of Psychiatry*, 156 (10), 1563-1569.

Dixon, L., Lucksted, A., Stewart, B., Burland, J., Brown, C.H., Postrado, L., McGuire, C., & Hoffman, M. (2004). Outcomes of the peer-taught 12-week family-to-family education program for severe mental illness. *Acta Psychiatrica Scandinavica*, 109, 207-15.

Fall, K.A., Levitov, J.E., Jennings, M., & Eberts, S. (2000). The public perception of mental health professions: An empirical examination. *Journal of Mental Health Counseling*, 22 (2), 122-134.

Frances, A. J., Widiger, T. A., & Pincus, H. A. (1989). The development of DSM-IV. *Archives of General Psychiatry*, 46(4), 373-5.

Friedel, R. O. (2006). Early sea changes in borderline personality disorder. *Current Psychiatry Reports*, 8, 1-4.

Gunderson J.G., Daversa, M.T., Grilo, C.M., McGlashan, T.H., Zanarini, M.C., Shea, M.T., Skodol, A.E., Yen, S., Sanislow, C.A., Bender, D.S., Dyck, I.R., Morey, L.C., & Stout, R.L. (2006). Predictors of 2-year outcome for patients with borderline personality disorder. *American Journal of Psychiatry*, 163 (5), 822-6.

Gunderson, J. G., Shea, M. T., Skodol, A. E., McGlashan, T. H., Morey, L. C., Stout, R. L., Zanarini, M. C., Grilo, C. M., Oldham, J. M., & Keller, M. B. (2000). The collaborative longitudinal personality disorders study: Development, aims, design, and sample characteristics. *Journal of Personality Disorders*, 14(4), 300-15.

Hoffman, P. D., Buteau, E., Hooley, J. M., Fruzzetti, A. E., & Bruce, M. L. (2003). Family members' knowledge about borderline personality disorder: Correspondence with their levels of depression, burden, distress, and expressed emotion. *Family Process*, 42, 469-78.

Hoffman, P. D., Fruzzetti, A. E., & Buteau, E. (2007). Understanding and engaging families: An education, skills and support program for relatives impacted by borderline personality disorder. *Journal of Mental Health*, 16 (1), 69-82.

Hoffman, P. D., Fruzzetti, A. E., Buteau, E., Neiditch, E. R., Penney, D., & Bruce, M. L. (2005). Family connections: A program for relatives of persons with borderline personality disorder. *Family Process*, 44 (2), 217-25.

Hooley, J. M. & Hoffman, P. D. (1999). Expressed emotion and clinical outcome in borderline personality disorder. *American Journal of Psychiatry*, 156 (10), 1157-1562.

Linehan, M. M. (1993). *Cognitive-behavioral treatment of borderline personality disorder*. New York: Guilford Press.

Widiger, T.A. & Frances, A. (1985). Axis II personality disorders: Diagnostic and treatment issues. *Hospital and Community Psychiatry*, 36, 619-627.

Yeomans, F. E., Clarkin, J. F., & Kernberg, O.F. (2002). *A primer for transference-focused psychotherapy for borderline personality disorder*. Northvale, NJ: Jason Aronson.

Zanarini, M.C., Frankenburg, F.R., Hennen, J., Reich, D.B., & Silk, K.R. (2005). The McLean Study of Adult Development (MSAD): Overview and implications of the first six years of prospective follow-up. *Journal of Personality Disorders*, 19 (5), 505-23.

Zanarini, M.C., Frankenburg, F.R., Hennen J., & Silk, K.R. (2003). The longitudinal course of borderline psychopathology: 6-year prospective follow-up of the phenomenology of borderline personality disorder. *The American Journal of Psychiatry*, 160, 274-283.

Zanarini, M.C. (2002). Family perspectives conference. From research to community. Columbia University College of Physicians and Surgeons. New York.

doi:10.1300/J200v06n01_16

Fostering Validating Responses in Families

Alan E. Fruzzetti
Chad Shenk

SUMMARY. Families and family interactions can play a role in the development (vs. prevention), maintenance (or remediation), and treatment of borderline personality disorder (BPD); and, having a family member with BPD can have a significant impact on family functioning. This paper reviews a transactional model for the development and maintenance of BPD, with implications for treatment, particularly from the perspective of dialectical behavior therapy (DBT). The paper also describes a subset of DBT interventions specifically developed for work with couples and families to turn the destructive "inaccurate expression/invalidation cycle" into the constructive "accurate expression/validation cycle," which is illustrated by a case example. doi:10.1300/J200v06n01_17 *[Article copies available for a fee from The Haworth Document Delivery Service: 1-800-HAWORTH. E-mail address: <docdelivery@haworthpress.com> Website: <http://www.HaworthPress.com> © 2008 by The Haworth Press. All rights reserved.]*

KEYWORDS. Families, borderline personality disorder, validation, accurate expression, dialectical behavior therapy

INTRODUCTION

Although the etiology of borderline personality disorder (BPD) continues to be much debated, there is a virtual consensus that families and

[Haworth co-indexing entry note]: "Fostering Validating Responses in Families." Fruzzetti, Alan E., and Chad Shenk. Co-published simultaneously in *Social Work in Mental Health* (The Haworth Press) Vol. 6, No. 1/2, 2008, pp. 215-227; and: *Borderline Personality Disorder: Meeting the Challenges to Successful Treatment* (ed: Perry D. Hoffman, and Penny Steiner-Grossman) The Haworth Press, 2008, pp. 215-227. Single or multiple copies of this article are available for a fee from The Haworth Document Delivery Service [1-800-HAWORTH, 9:00 a.m. - 5:00 p.m. (EST). E-mail address: docdelivery@haworthpress.com].

family interactions can play a role in the development (vs. prevention), maintenance (or remediation), and treatment of this disorder (Fruzzetti, Shenk, & Hoffman, 2005). Unfortunately, a good deal of clinical lore has blamed parents, in particular, for the development of BPD in their children, even in the absence of longitudinal data to support such a position. In reality, having a parent, partner, child, or other loved one with BPD can be extremely difficult: people with BPD suffer a great deal, have high rates of suicidal, self-harming, and other impulsive behaviors, along with concurrent disorders such as depression, substance use, post-traumatic stress disorder, eating disorders, anxiety disorders, and other problems. High levels of anger and aggression, and/or shame and withdrawal, along with relationship problems in general, are commonly part of the picture with BPD. Thus, it is no surprise that family members of people with BPD also report high levels of distress, depression, grief, and burden (Hoffman et al., 2005) and that their family interactions are also distressed (Shenk & Fruzzetti, 2006).

Yet only recently have programs been developed to address the needs of both patients and their families (Fruzzetti & Boulanger, 2005). Clinicians, theorists and researchers have had to extrapolate from case studies or more sophisticated family research associated with other disorders, such as depression, bipolar disorder, or even schizophrenia. However, some evidence suggests that families with BPD may be different in important ways from families with these other problems (Hooley & Hoffman, 1999), and that the quality of family relationships can have a significant impact on the overall functioning of people with BPD over time (Gunderson et al., 2006).

Family interventions utilizing the principles of Dialectical Behavior Therapy (DBT) have become increasingly popular (Fruzzetti, 2006; Fruzzetti, Hoffman, & Santisteban, (in press); Hoffman, Fruzzetti & Swenson, 1999), and these interventions have begun to accumulate empirical support (Fruzzetti & Mosco, 2006; Hoffman et al., 2005; Hoffman, Fruzzetti, & Buteau, 2007; Santisteban et al., 2003). This paper will first describe the transactional model that provides the foundation for family interventions utilizing DBT. We then highlight a core subset of DBT interventions with couples and families used to turn the "inaccurate expression/invalidation cycle" into the "accurate expression/validation cycle," and provide a case example to illustrate how to use these interventions with families.

TRANSACTIONAL MODEL FOR BPD

Marsha Linehan and colleagues have described a *transactional* model for the development and maintenance of BPD (Fruzzetti et al., 2005; Linehan, 1993a). The idea of a transactional model is that the factors in the model are not static. Rather, they are reciprocal, influencing each other over time comparable to other systems, including family systems models. In the case of BPD, it is hypothesized that an individual has certain vulnerabilities to negative emotion and emotion dysregulation that may be more biologically determined or temperament-based or a result of early learning, or any combination of the two. These dispositions transact with an "invalidating environment." In such an environment, normative and accurate expression of private experience (thoughts, emotions, wants, etc.) is pervasively not validated and/or invalidated, and concurrent problematic or inaccurate expressions are intermittently validated and reinforced. The nature of the transaction suggests that, over time, increased vulnerability leads to increased invalidation, while increased invalidation leads to increased vulnerability, and so on.

Individual Vulnerability to Negative Emotion

The idea behind vulnerability is that it makes a person more likely, all other things being equal, to have negative emotional reactions and emotion dysregulation across a variety of situations. In this model, emotion dysregulation is postulated to be the core problem of BPD. This painful, negative emotional arousal is high enough to disrupt effective emotion management and general self-management, to lead the person to focus increasingly on arousal reduction via any available means (including dysfunctional escape behaviors such as self-injury, substance use, angry outbursts, etc.), and to have a negative impact on many others. Three factors are suggested to contribute to high vulnerability: sensitivity, reactivity, and a slow return to emotional baseline (Linehan, 1993a; Fruzzetti et al., 2005; Fruzzetti, 2006).

Sensitivity refers to the person's low threshold for discriminating or noticing emotionally relevant stimuli in the world, especially interpersonally. A person may be highly sensitive or highly insensitive, or anywhere in between, but being acutely sensitive leaves a person vulnerable, in part because he or she is therefore constantly bombarded with stimuli that have a high emotional quality. A less sensitive person simply does not notice those same stimuli, just as a less sensitive person does not notice as many different tones or sounds in the world. Similarly, a more sensitive person may also experience greater pain from big emotional events than a less sensitive person. *Reactivity* simply describes how much a person reacts *after* noticing something with an emotional quality. A person can react in a big way or a small way; neither is inherently healthy or pathological. Finally, having a *slow return to emotional baseline* means that it takes the person longer to return to equilibrium, or baseline, after becoming emotionally activated.

It is important to note that it is the combination of all three factors, not just one or two of them, that leaves a person highly vulnerable to emotion dysregulation. Then, when negative events occur, including negative interpersonal events such as being misunderstood, criticized, blamed (i.e., invalidated), high negative reactions and dysregulation are more likely to occur.

Invalidating Responses

Invalidating responses are those that communicate high negative emotion (e.g., disgust, contempt, condescension, or other emotions associated with disrespect), high levels of negative judgment (e.g., the person's feelings, desires, actions, or thoughts are just "wrong"), or that the person's valid experiences are otherwise not legitimate (Fruzzetti & Iverson, 2004; 2006; Linehan, 1993a). It may also be invalidating to respond to dysfunctional behaviors with support or acceptance (i.e., to validate invalid behaviors).

Invalidation is common in communication, and no one enjoys this type of response. However, the combination of being emotionally vulnerable and being invalidated is most likely to result in escalating, dysregulated emotion and the kinds of impulsive behaviors associated with BPD.

Destructive Transactions

When we are invalidated, our arousal escalates (Shenk & Fruzzetti, 2006; Swann, 1997). Conversely, being validated typically soothes us and helps ameliorate painful negative emotional arousal. Of course, when we are highly emotionally aroused we demonstrate less and less cognitive capacity, notably broad self-awareness and the ability to solve problems. Thus, our expression becomes less accurate, and it becomes more difficult for people to understand; validation becomes less likely. Instead, invalidation becomes more likely, which only further increases emotional arousal and further decreases accurate expression (Figure 1).

The cycle continues, typically until the point at which one person becomes highly aversive and the other withdraws, or until both become highly aversive and destructive conflict ensues. In either case, one or both parties to the transaction may engage in dysfunctional behaviors to escape their high negative emotional arousal. These may include aggressive behaviors to push the other person away, or destructive and impulsive behaviors to facilitate escape from the emotional arousal, such as self-harm, substance use, binging or purging, etc.

FAMILY INTERVENTIONS

It is this cycle of inaccurate expression, followed by invalidation (and vice versa) that DBT with couples and families seeks to remedy. Although there are many other intervention targets and strategies, helping the person with BPD express him- or herself more accurately and helping family members respond in a more validating way are the foci of the next section. (See Fruzzetti, 2006; Fruzzetti & Fruzzetti, 2003; Fruzzetti & Iverson 2004; 2006 for other, related interventions, and additional details.)

Accurate Expression

Many factors affect a person's ability to express or disclose accurately and effectively. This section will highlight both the skills that are necessary in advance that make it possible to verbalize accurately, as well as factors that can detour effective and accurate expression.

Regulating Your Emotion Before You Speak: It is very helpful to be mindful of one's emotions and goals before beginning any expression. Patients and family members alike often get stuck in high levels of reactive or *secondary* emotions (Greenberg & Johnson, 1990) that interfere with accurate expression. Therefore it is important to find the *primary* or normative (and healthy) emotion in a given situation, one that is not a product of judgmental thinking (Fruzzetti, 2006). If emotional arousal is moderate (or lower), it is much easier to communicate effectively, both as the person expressing and the person listening and responding. That is, when arousal is reduced, other factors like facial musculature, body posture, and muscle tension more readily communicate openness and willingness to communicate.

Choosing the Context: Picking an effective time to speak is an important component of effective disclosure. When people are reactive, they

FIGURE 1

The Inaccurate Expression ←→ Invalidation Cycle

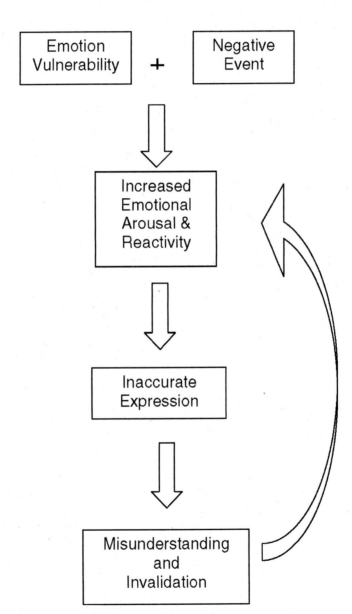

often forget to pay attention to whether the other person is too tired or hungry to be effective, about to go to work, or engaged in something important to him or her. It is important to help families be award of timing. In addition, there are many things people can do actively to minimize distractions. For example, an individual can turn off the television or the cell phone, find a quiet and comfortable place, and do something soothing before starting a conversation.

Matching Your Strategy to Your Goals: Finally, at different times a person may have a very practical or concrete goal (such as getting a ride somewhere), while at other times she or he may have a more relational goal (e.g., getting or giving support, wanting more closeness, wanting to be understood). If the person's goal is clear, it is much easier to match the strategy to achieve that goal. When a person wants support, it may be much more effective to state that clearly than to list a variety of problems. With a list of problems, a family member might start to attempt problem solving, which the person would not experience as supportive. Similarly, if a person wants instrumental help, he or she should ask for it clearly. For example, if someone wants help doing the dishes and cleaning the kitchen, it is less effective to say, "I am so tired!" than to ask, "Could you please help me clean up here? I'm really tired and would appreciate the help."

Regardless of the goal, an important part of any response to accurate expression and any self-disclosure is the communication of understanding, the legitimacy of the person's experience, and acceptance. We call this kind of response *validation*.

Validating Responses

There are many ways to validate what another is thinking, feeling, wanting, or sensing, just as there are many ways to invalidate a person's experiences or desires. Of course, what is validating depends on the context: a simple "uh-huh" may be very validating in one situation and absolutely useless or even counter-productive in another. The following types of validation are informed by Linehan's work on the ways that therapists can validate clients (Linehan, 1997), and by research evaluating validating responses specifically in couples and families (Fruzzetti & Jacobson, 1990; Fruzzetti & Iverson, 2004, 2006; Fruzzetti et al., 2006). See Fruzzetti (2006) for more description and details.

Just Pay Attention: Although often referred to as "active listening," this approach emphasizes using mindfulness to reduce reactivity and make active, unbiased listening possible, and to listen to and understand what the family member is saying and experiencing descriptively. The listener minimizes interpretations and judgments about what is being expressed or disclosed, or about the person expressing it. Thus, "relationship mindfulness" is also a basic way to validate because it conveys this willingness just to listen openly, accepting the other person's descriptions as valid in one or more ways. Of course, in order for mindful listening to be conveyed, the listener must make effective eye contact, cease other activities that might interfere, and otherwise communicate that she or he is listening mindfully and paying attention willingly.

Acknowledge or Reflect: This type of validation includes statements such as "I can see that you are ___ (e.g., tired, sad, excited)," or "I know you are ___ (e.g., frustrated, unhappy, angry, relieved, thinking X, wanting to Y)." The essence of validation here is that the listener is not invalidating or reacting negatively to what is being expressed, but instead is understanding accurately and accepting the reality of what the family member is thinking, feeling, or wanting.

Clarify, Be Curious: In many situations the listener is genuinely trying to understand the other's experience, but that understanding may be incomplete. At these times, asking gentle questions to facilitate understanding is an important part of being validating. Thus, rather than asking questions Socratically, or as a means of showing the other person how he or she should not feel or think in a certain way, these questions communicate curiosity and interest, a willingness to accept and understand, and constitute a genuine invitation to accurate expression.

Put "Mistakes" and Problematic Reactions in Perspective: Sometimes loved ones with BPD (and others, of course) do things that are dysfunctional or problematic, or have reactions that only make sense given their unique pattern of behavior resulting from either biological dysfunction and/or negative learning experiences. When a person reacts in such a non-normative way or engages in some problematic behavior, it is common for family members to be critical, judgmental, and invalidating. Alternatively, they can try to understand the larger context of the person's reactions or mistakes: their loved one is more than just this reaction, more than just this problematic behavior. Recontextualizing the behavior this way does two important things that otherwise would be quite invalidating: (1) it does not pretend that the problem is not a problem and therefore validate something invalid; and (2) it acknowledges that problem descriptively, without judgment, keeping the behavior in context and perspective and allowing problem-solving to follow, if needed. Part of this kind of validation includes understanding the impact of previous experiences and how they contribute to current problematic reactions and behaviors. For example, a person who has experienced a series of relationship losses might become highly sensitized to, and fearful of, more such losses, and might do problematic things (e.g., threaten suicide) to keep a parent or partner from taking a vacation. Although such behavior is clearly dysfunctional (and likely, paradoxically, to create the very problem–abandonment–that he or she desperately wants to avoid), it does make sense if we understand the person's history. Thus, validation here requires the family member to acknowledge that history and to be mindful of the many loving and relationally effective things the person has done at other times, while at the same time to recognize that the behavior is problematic.

Normalize: Often, even a family member with BPD has reactions (thoughts, feelings, desires) that are completely normal and just like those anyone would have. But, because people with BPD also commonly have more sensitivity and reactivity than is normal, it is easy for family members to misattribute normative reactions to the disorder or to dysfunction, which is extremely invalidating. Here, the validating thing to do is to normalize normative reactions. Saying things like, "Of course you feel that way," or "Anyone would react that way," or "I would (think, feel, want) that, too in your situation," communicates the utter normality of the person's reactions, rather than making them seem pathological.

Be Vulnerable, too: Sometimes a loved one makes him or herself quite vulnerable to a parent or partner via an accurate disclosure (e.g., "I feel so badly that we haven't been getting along," or "I know I have not been a great parent/partner/child lately."). When the vulnerable person expresses these sentiments, to be truly validating the family member also must be willing to be vulnerable (e.g., "I have been feeling bad about our conflict, too," or "Yes, I've been feeling distant and frustrated with you, but I have not always reacted at my best, either"–or, simply, "Me, too").

Be Responsive with Deeds, not Just Words. Provide Soothing: Sometimes it is important to react to a loved one's situation with action, not just talk. For example, if the person is hungry, we can get her or him some food; if tired, we can help reduce demands; if unhappy, we can provide soothing. This type of validation actually demonstrates that we understand the person's experience by helping to alleviate suffering. Although such validating actions can be accompanied by validating words, these often are not necessary.

CASE ILLUSTRATION

The following case illustration highlights the usefulness and importance of accurate expression in the elicitation of validation as well, as the subsequent effects of validation on emotion regulation and family satisfaction. In this example, 13 year-old has just received a second failing exam grade in math class. Historically, he has done well in math and has enjoyed the subject, that is, until this most recent school year. When the adolescent arrives home from school, the parent is in the kitchen getting a snack for a younger sibling. He enters the house, slams the front door, and walks noisily up the stairs to the bedroom. The parent, sensing something is wrong, soon follows him upstairs to the bedroom.

Parent: Honey, what's wrong?

Child: Nothing. Leave me alone.

Parent: Clearly something is wrong. I can see that you are upset. Did something happen at school?

Child: Come on, I said leave me alone. I don't want to talk about it right now.

Parent: OK. Can we talk about it after dinner if not now?

Child: Fine (exasperated). But there is nothing to talk about.

(After dinner the parent approaches the child to discuss the event at school)

Parent: So is it OK if we talk about what happened at school today?

Child: (taking a deep breath . . .) Fine. There's not much to talk about though. I hate math and Mr. Lynn is the worst teacher in the world.

Parent: It seemed like you were pretty upset when you came home. I take it something happened in math class?

Child: Yeah, something happened. I failed another test because Mr. Lynn can't teach. Either that or I am totally stupid.

Parent: Honey, you sound frustrated but I'm wondering if maybe you are feeling really disappointed about something, or even afraid?

Child: What do you mean?

Parent: Well, you do seem to be struggling this year in math, but you are doing well in all your other classes and have done well in math before. Now, I also struggled in math in school, and when I did I felt pretty disappointed in myself. I was also afraid that I would not be able to do better on the next exam and that people might think I was dumb. Is that something like how you are feeling, too?

Child: Yeah, like, I know I can do better, but I'm afraid that I just won't. I don't get it. I was doing well in math and now I am not.

Parent: That is a really hard thing, but you know, I can't imagine anyone else in your shoes feeling any differently.

Child: So what do I do?

Parent: Well, what do you think? I know this is tough. But, I am willing to try to help you through it any way you want. For example, I could help you with your homework if you want, or I can help you get a tutor.

Child: Mr. Lynn is probably not as dumb of a teacher as I said before. Maybe I could ask him what I should be doing differently. Or, I could talk with Ms. Rosemont, my teacher last year. I think she liked me, and I did OK in her class. There has to be something I can do; I was pretty good in math before. Then, I can decide whether to get a tutor or have you help me.

Parent: That sounds like a great idea. Keep me posted on what Mr. Lynn or Ms. Rosemont suggests.

Child: I will. I feel a little better about it now.

This example illustrates many of the important components of accurate expression and validation. The parent was willing to pick the right time to talk about the child's feelings about the math exam, which allowed the child to modulate his heightened emotional arousal and be more likely to disclose his feelings about the situation. Then, the parent was able to reflect the child's expressed feelings while being curious about other, more accurate emotions the child may have been feeling. This allowed for a more validating exchange of the primary emotions that the child felt about failing this second math exam. Once that occurred, a decision about further validation or problem solving could be made in order to further assist the child in accomplishing his or her goal to do better in math.

This example was about disappointment about school performance, but of course the child (or partner, parent, or sibling) could have reactions to a variety of situations. Social and relationship situations are "triggers" for significant emotional reactions in all people, and in particular for those with BPD. Regardless of the situation, validation helps soothe frayed emotions and helps the other person to express what she or he is genuinely experiencing more accurately. This, in turn, makes validating easier and problem management possible, and builds the relationship in important ways.

REFERENCES

Fruzzetti, A. E. (2002). Dialectical behavior therapy for borderline personality and related disorders. In T. Patterson (Volume 2 Ed.), *Comprehensive handbook of psychotherapy, Volume 2: Cognitive-behavioral approaches* (pp. 215-240). New York: Wiley.

Fruzzetti, A. E. (2006). *The high conflict couple: A dialectical behavior therapy guide to finding peace, intimacy, and validation.* Oakland, CA: New Harbinger Press.

Fruzzetti, A. E., & Boulanger, J. L. (2005). Family involvement in treatment for borderline personality disorder. In J. G. Gunderson & P.D. Hoffman (Eds.), *Understanding and treating borderline personality disorder: A guide for professionals and families* (pp. 151-164). Washington, DC: American Psychiatric Publishing, Inc.

Fruzzetti, A. E., & Fruzzetti, A. R. (2003). Borderline personality disorder. In D. Snyder & M. A. Whisman (Eds.), *Treating difficult couples: Helping clients with coexisting mental and relationship disorders* (pp. 235-260). New York: Guilford Press.

Fruzzetti, A.E., Santisteban, D.A., & Hoffman, P.D. (2007). Dialectical behavior therapy with families. In L.A. Dimeff & K. Koerner (Eds.), *Dialectical behavior therapy in clinical practice: Applications across disorders and settings* (pp. 222-244). New York: Guilford Press.

Fruzzetti, A. E. & Iverson, K. M. (2004). Mindfulness, acceptance, validation and "individual" psychopathology in couples. In S. C. Hayes, V. M. Follette, & M. M. Linehan (Eds.), *Mindfulness and acceptance: Expanding the cognitive-behavioral tradition* (pp. 168-191). New York: Guilford Press.

Fruzzetti, A. E., & Iverson, K. M. (2006). Intervening with couples and families to treat emotion dysregulation and psychopathology. In D.K. Snyder, J. Simpson, & J. Hughes (Eds.), *Emotion regulation in couples and families: Pathways to dysfunction and health* (pp. 249-267). Washington, DC: American Psychological Association.

Fruzzetti, A. E., Shenk, C., & Hoffman, P. D. (2005). Family interaction and the development of borderline personality disorder: A transactional model. *Development and Psychopathology*, 17, 1007-1030.

Greenberg, L. S. & Johnson, S. M. (1990). Emotional change processes in couples therapy. In E. Blechman (Ed.), *Emotions and the family: For better or for worse* (pp. 137-153). Hillsdale, NJ: Lawrence Erlbaum Associates.

Gunderson, J.G., Daversa, M. T., Grilo, C. M., et al. (2006). Predictors of 2-year outcome for patients with borderline personality disorder. *American Journal of Psychiatry*, 163, 822-826.

Hoffman, P. D., Buteau, E., Hooley, J. M., Fruzzetti, A. E., & Bruce, M. L. (2003). Family members' knowledge about borderline personality disorder: Correspondence with their levels of depression, burden, distress, and expressed emotion. *Family Process*, 42, 469-478.

Hoffman, P. D., Fruzzetti, A. E., & Buteau, E. (2007). Understanding and engaging families: An education, skills and support program for relatives impacted by borderline personality disorder. *Journal of Mental Health*, 16, 69-82.

Hoffman, P. D., Fruzzetti, A. E., Buteau, E., Penney, D., Neiditch, E., Penney, D., Bruce, M., Hellman, F., & Struening, E. (2005). Family connections: Effectiveness of a program for relatives of persons with borderline personality disorder. *Family Process*, 44, 217-225.

Hoffman, P. D., Fruzzetti, A. E., & Swenson, C. R. (1999). Dialectical behavior therapy: Family skills training. *Family Process*, 38, 399-414.

Hooley, J. M., & Hoffman, P.D. (1999). Expressed emotion and clinical outcome in borderline personality disorder. *American Journal of Psychiatry*, 156, 1557-1562.

Linehan, M. (1993a). *Cognitive behavioral treatment of borderline personality disorder*. New York: Guilford Press.

Linehan, M. (1993b). *Skills training manual for treating borderline personality disorder*. New York: Guilford Press.

Santisteban, D. A., Coatsworth, D., Perez-Vidal, A., Kurtines, W. M., Schwartz, S. J., LaPerriere, A, & Szapocznik, J. (2003). The efficacy of brief strategic/structural family therapy in modifying behavior problems and an exploration of the mediating role that family functioning plays in behavior change. *Journal of Family Psychology*, 17, 121-133.

Shenk, C., & Fruzzetti, A. E. (2007). The impact of parental validating and invalidating behaviors on adolescent emotion regulation. (Manuscript under review).

Shenk, C. & Fruzzetti, A. E. (2005). Mindfulness based interventions with parents and their distressed adolescent children: A pilot study. Symposium paper presented at the Fifth International Congress of Cognitive Psychotherapy, Göteborg, Sweden.

Swann, W. B. (1997). The trouble with change: self-verification and allegiance to the self. *Psychological Science*, 8 (3) 177-180.

doi:10.1300/J200v06n01_17

Family Connections:
An Education and Skills Training Program
for Family Member Well Being:
A Leader's Perspective

Dixianne Penney

SUMMARY. This chapter describes the Family Connections (FC) program, a 12-week, two-hour, interactive, manualized, education/skills training course for relatives of persons with borderline personality disorder (BPD) that is co-led by trained family members. It explicates the training of co-leaders, the registration process for participants, a detailed description of the curriculum's six modules, and consideration of the on-going challenges faced by participants after the program ends. The introduction describes historical development of the program. Subsequent sections are organized into two parts: each opens with a segment that presents key ideas, which is followed by *"Leader Observations"*—the reflections of a seasoned leader. doi:10.1300/J200v06n01_18 *[Article copies available for a fee from The Haworth Document Delivery Service: 1-800-HAWORTH. E-mail address: <docdelivery@haworthpress.com> Website: <http://www.HaworthPress.com> © 2008 by The Haworth Press. All rights reserved.]*

KEYWORDS. Psychoeducation, coping skills, well being

[Haworth co-indexing entry note]: "Family Connections: An Education and Skills Training Program for Family Member Well Being: A Leader's Perspective." Penney, Dixianne. Co-published simultaneously in *Social Work in Mental Health* (The Haworth Press) Vol. 6, No. 1/2, 2008, pp. 229-241; and: *Borderline Personality Disorder: Meeting the Challenges to Successful Treatment* (ed: Perry D. Hoffman, and Penny Steiner-Grossman) The Haworth Press, 2008, pp. 229-241. Single or multiple copies of this article are available for a fee from The Haworth Document Delivery Service [1-800-HAWORTH, 9:00 a.m. - 5:00 p.m. (EST). E-mail address: docdelivery@haworthpress.com].

Available online at http://swmh.haworthpress.com
© 2008 by The Haworth Press. All rights reserved.
doi:10.1300/J200v06n01_18

INTRODUCTION

This chapter describes Family Connections (FC), to date the only program for families in the journal literature that targets the well-being of family members who have a relative with borderline personality disorder and related symptoms researched (Hoffman et al., 2005). The 12-week program, under the auspices of the National Education Alliance for Borderline Personality Disorder (NEA-BPD), has shown that family members can be helped to manage the despair they feel and the family chaos that accompanies BPD.

The Family Connections curriculum is based on the strategies and skills of Dialectical Behavior Therapy (DBT) (Linehan, 1993). It provides for participant knowledge about the disorder and training in coping skills in a supportive and validating environment. FC is an adaptation and synthesis of two family programs that have served hundreds of families for over a decade (Hoffman, Fruzzetti & Swenson, 1998). The program was further revised and re-designed by Drs. Hoffman and Fruzzetti, several family members, and a consumer, so that the course could be brought into community settings and taught by family leaders (Fruzzetti & Hoffman, 2004). Pilot research has documented significant reductions in grief and burden and a significant increase in mastery from pre- to post-group assessment for participants in this program, with changes that were maintained at six months post-baseline (Hoffman et al., 2005).

This 12-week, two-hour, interactive, manualized course is taught by trained family members. Each group is typically capped at 12 family members, so that participants have the opportunity to be fully involved in discussions and the practice of skills. In order to be accepted into the leader-training program, the leaders must have a relative with BPD. Much care is taken in the selection of leaders in order to ensure their ability to teach the curriculum and conduct a family education series. The importance of their suitability for group leadership is at the core of the success of the FC program and cannot be overemphasized. Prior to participation in the training, prospective leaders either must be known previously to the FC trainers or to another FC leader, or must have an in-person (or phone) interview.

All potential leaders undergo two days of criterion-based training in a retreat setting. As their teaching resource, Drs. Fruzzetti and Hoffman utilize the manual the leaders will use subsequently to lead their own groups. The training simulates the FC group experience, while at the same time instructing the new generation of leaders in group dynamics and family education techniques. In addition to the two-day training, future leaders are encouraged to take Dr. Fruzzetti's course on validation when it is offered in their area. Acceptance into the two-day training does not guaranty automatic approval as a leader. A final decision concerning the appropriateness of an individual to become a FC leader is made by the trainers in discussion with the potential leader at the completion of the training course.

THE PROGRAM

The Registration Process

Potential participants learn about FC through a variety of sources: therapists; word-of-mouth from previous attendees; regional NAMI offices; facilities treating persons with BPD; NEA-BPD's Web site; flyers distributed at NEA-BPD-sponsored national and regional conferences; and under the section "Resources for Families" in several educational books on BPD (Friedel, 2003; Gunderson & Hoffman, 2005). Family members then contact the NEA-BPD administrative office to seek further information.

> Leader Observations: *With increasing frequency, FC groups include parents whose child is under age 18. A recent paper by Kessler et al. (2005) reported that, "About half of Americans will meet the criteria for a DSM-IV diagnosis at sometime in their life, with first onset usually in childhood or adolescence. Interventions aimed at prevention or early treatment need to focus on youth" (p. 593). This finding would not come as a surprise to the parents who attend the FC course. Thus it makes sense that if there is a program to assist parents of adolescents to learn the kinds of skills that are taught in the FC curriculum, they should not be asked to wait until their child reaches the arbitrary age of 18 when the DSMIV declares a person is now ready to be diagnosed with BPD.*

The Curriculum

The FC curriculum (Fruzzetti & Hoffman, 2004) is divided into six modules: Introduction, Family Education, Relationship Mindfulness Skills, Family Environment Skills, Validation Skills, and Problem Management Skills, Each module serves as a foundation of competency for the modules to come. Each module will be described separately followed by discussion with examples under "Leader Observations."

Module 1: Introduction (Week 1): The Introduction sets the mission, tone and goals for the entire course. Topics include: the meaning of CONNECTIONS (an acronym); the specific goals of the program; the weekly format; the rights of relatives; the nine criteria for diagnosing BPD; the five areas of dysregulation (Linehan, 1993); and exercises for participants to take home to be reviewed the coming week. Attendees are asked to sign an informal agreement committing them to attend meetings to the best of their ability, and to the need to keep confidential any information shared within the group. The weekly format is also described: (1) The "go-around" (a brief up-date of how things have gone in the previous week; (2) Practice exercises (in all successive weeks assigned from the didactic material of the current week's lecture, explained in class and completed during the week at home, then reviewed the following week together in class); and (3) Questions and discussion.

Leader Observations: *In addition to the introduction of didactic material, most of the first evening is spent getting acquainted and answering questions about the goals of the program. Occasionally, family members arrive believing they have come to FC to learn skills to change their ill relative's behaviors. Leaders explain that while participants will develop a better understanding about their loved one, most importantly, they will learn skills for themselves and their own well being.*

Most participants arrive with trepidations, many of them participating for the first time in a multi-family setting. Each person may believe initially that his/her family is unique in its isolation and dysfunction. This first night is important in dispelling that notion. To introduce the initial "go around," my husband offers to begin by telling our story. We have found it important for the men in the group to know from the start that it is acceptable for a man to speak about grief and despair, to admit to being afraid of the future, and not to know all the answers or how to fix what's wrong. I then add a few thoughts about how our daughter's illness brought on the estrangement from most of our extended family, how we stopped sending Christmas cards after her first hospitalization, and that she is well now. I also speak about how much hope there is for so many people who have this diagnosis. Next, we turn to the group and ask if anyone else has had similar experiences. Then the shyness drops away, the floodgates open, the grieving starts, and the healing begins.

Module 2: Family Education (Weeks 2-3): This module covers both general information and some of the research that propelled the creators of FC (Fruzzetti & Hoffman, 2002) to develop the program. For example, in a seminal paper, Hooley and Hoffman (1999) found that emotional "over-involvement" of family members predicted a *better* clinical outcome in patients who had BPD, underlining the importance of family relationships. Finding a way to help make relationships healthy is a primary goal of FC. The module continues with a discussion of "Important Considerations," for example, that medication effects are usually only modest and partial (i.e., that there is no "magic bullet" that can stop BPD in its tracks), followed by a list of other psychiatric disorders that can occur with BPD–one reason this disorder is so difficult to diagnose and treat. There is also discussion of the high percentage (75%) of persons with BPD who self-injure and of the estimated at 10% of persons with this disorder who commit suicide. Nevertheless, an on-going message of this section is that many persons with BPD do get better.

This module also includes discussion of the biosocial theory on the origin of BPD, namely, that persons with BPD are thought to be born with an emotional vulnerability that is the basis for their rapid emotional dysregulation coupled with factors in their environment that interact with and intensify their emotional vulnerability. We also offer a primer on emotional sensitivity (quick and intense reactions to emotional stimuli) and emotional reactivity (extreme reactions that affect thinking), which can lead to the emotional dysregulation and slow return to normalcy or "baseline" see in individuals with BPD.

Leader Observations: *One of the most difficult concepts in this curriculum requiring extensive discussion is the biosocial theory, particularly the impact that factors in the environment may have on triggering BPD. This is exemplified by the phrase "invalidating environment" (Linehan, 1993). Participants report that this seemingly unforgiving phrase, coupled with accusations of abuse and neglect that may have been leveled at them by some professionals, only adds to the guilt they already carry. As clarification, leaders explain that while it is true that some persons with BPD may have been severely abused emotionally and physically, many others have no abuse history at all. Rather than characterizing home life as an "invalidating environment" (although that may have been the case for some), the situation might more accurately be described as a "poor fit" between the child and the parent. Leaders point to other environments where to our loved ones may have been exposed to damaging invalidation, such as in school settings (peers and teachers), religious institutions, and camps.*

Module 3: Relationship Mindfulness Skills (Weeks 4-5): This module covers individual and relationship skills that promote participant emotional well-being. These include: emotion self-management; mindfulness (being aware of another person and your interaction with them, paying attention but not passing judgment); decreasing vulnerability to negative emotions; and skills to decrease participant emotional reactivity. There is an introductory segment on validation that lists seven components of a validating family environment; a later module covers validation more extensively. Attention is paid to aversive control (nonvalidating) and how contagious that tactic can be. For example, it can be difficult not to overreact when you come home to a kitchen strewn with dirty dishes, but yelling is not likely to get the job done. On the other hand, it can be a potent technique if it is almost never used: e.g., in the woods at the top of your lungs: "Don't move! There's a rattle snake 10 feet ahead in the path!" A major section focuses on how to remain nonjudgmental and presents specific skills to help participants reduce judgments. Attendees are taught that judgments about others are toxic not only to relationships within the family environment but also to their own wellbeing. This module also introduces the concept of three states of mind or being: (a) emotion mind (where we find ourselves in a mental place in which emotions dominate our thoughts and often determine our behaviors); (b) rational mind, the opposite of emotion mind, where logic dominates (think of Mr. Spock in TV's Star Trek); and (c) wise mind, which is a synthesis of emotion and rational mind, a state of centeredness, which is what we aim for and how we want to think and function in our daily lives.

Leader Observations: *This initial segment on validation (particularly dropping aversive control– the opposite of validation) and letting go of judgments frequently comes as a surprise to many participants. Many say they did not realize how often their actions were spiked with aversive control method, and their conversation laced with judgments, such as, for example, "You're acting like a two-year old!" One week later, participants return reporting that practicing validation and suspending judgment have already made big changes. Beginning to implement these skills gives them the awareness that they have the capacity to make change themselves, and hence the ability to modulate previously unsatisfactory or explosive interactions.*

Module 4: Family Environment Skills (Weeks 6-7): This module covers family and relationship skills to improve the quality of family interactions. These include letting go of blame and anger and increasing acceptance skills in relationships. The sub-sections include a discussion of what happens within the family that makes it so difficult to function when a member has BPD. Participants are introduced to Linehan's (1993) four basic assumptions: (1) People need to interpret things in the most benign way possible; (2) There is no one or any absolute truth; (3) Everyone is doing the best he or she can in this moment; and (4) Everyone needs to try harder.

Following a discussion of the four basic assumptions, the curriculum covers the most difficult acceptance skill for participants, namely, radical acceptance: total and complete acceptance of things that are hard to accept, a "letting go" of fighting a reality that you cannot change at this moment.

Leader Observations: *To explain Assumption 1, we use as an example the phone ringing in the middle of the night. My husband just mumbles, "Wrong number," and goes back to sleep. I bolt out of bed, grab the phone, and croak, "Who's been in an accident?" Of course, it's a wrong number.*

Some participants confuse Assumption 2 with religious belief; rather, it pertains to explanations of the opinions or actions others. It is very easy to think that one's own opinions are facts; however, no one has a corner on the whole picture, and when two people disagree, there is a kernel of truth in each person's point of view. For example, let's say your child stays up very late at night and sleeps very late in the morning. Parents may perceive this schedule as "not getting anything done." The late sleeper perceives that if he/she doesn't get enough sleep, it is certain that nothing will get done. Who is right? They all are. Who is wrong? No one.

Assumption 3 is hard to swallow if your ill relative is engaged in self-harm. What this assumption allows us to do is manage a diffi-

cult situation. A leader might offer as illustration a loved one who is cutting, because for the moment, an act that is beyond our understanding has brought her relief from unbearable anxiety, allowed her to feel reality for a few minutes, or given a brief respite from never ending depression. The cutting was the best that individual could do at that moment in the face of unremitting psychic pain.

Assumption 4 is comforting to participants when we assure them that they can expect their loved one to try harder. The fact that the attendees have chosen to participate in the FC program is an example that they already are trying harder to make changes in themselves and their relationship. To explain the concept of radical acceptance, Fruzzetti (2005) offers a comparison with the Serenity Prayer–*"God grant me the serenity to accept the things I cannot change, the courage to change the things I can, and the wisdom to know the difference"–but cautions that radical acceptance deals more with events that are occurring in this moment. For example, parents may be deeply concerned about an unsuitable boyfriend or girlfriend. It is so tempting to jump into the fray and try and save a child from what seems like a life-ruining decision. Rather than saving them, our actions may instead be helping them to dig their hole even deeper. Fruzzetti offers that Radical Acceptance is when you move toward disappointment and away from anger or judgment. Radical Acceptance is not hopelessness; it is moving from, "I have to fix it" to, "I can manage it" in a way that allows a participant to say, "I can also take care of myself."*

Module 5: Validation Skills (Weeks 8-10): This module comprises the definition and skills of validation, including: accurate and effective self-expression and how to do it; why validation is important; targets for validation; different levels of validation the many ways to invalidate the valid; validation tips; a section on self-invalidation and its consequences; and a list of self-validation skills.

There is also a section on "observing your limits," explaining why it is helpful to one's well being to learn to recognize one's own limits, then teaching the skills to accomplish it. Leaders then introduce three major priorities in DBT (Linehan, 1993): (1) Objective effectiveness (obtaining one's goals); (2) Relationship effectiveness (getting or keeping a good relationship); and (3) Self-respect effectiveness (preserving or improving one's sense of self-respect). They subsequently teach participants one of the major DBT self-expression skills with the acronym of DEAR MAN (Describe, Express, Ask, Reinforce, Mindful, Appear confident, Negotiate), fundamental to success in observing limits.

Leader Observations: *Earlier reference was made to the work of Hooley and Hoffman (1999) in which they found that emotional "over-involvement" predicted a better clinical outcome in patients who had BPD, and that a major goal of FC is to teach how to be effectively emotionally involved. Since validation is the ability to acknowledge another person and be able to communicate with them with empathy, it is one of the most important tools leaders can model and teach participants. It is important to underscore that validating is not placating, nor is it problem solving; rather it is a tool to communicate your understanding of the legitimacy of another person's point of view, opinions, or feelings. It is also essential that participants validate themselves, because so many of us, as parents, have considered ourselves abject failures. An example of accurate expression of validation of both yourself (self-disclosure) and another person (self-doubts) that sets up the possibility for change is, "I'm scared too, but we're going to get through this."*

When the section on "Observing Your Limits" is taught, participants often report that they have attended "Tough Love" classes but have not found those harsh techniques helpful. Attendees are invited to share situations in which having a relative with BPD has pushed them at times to do or accept things that they would not allow or tolerate in others, or allow others to treat them in ways that were disrespectful or hurtful. While each family and each situation is different and depends on specific circumstance, there are themes that will repeat over and over if we do not recognize or learn how to observe our limits. We may give until we have nothing left to give (both literally and figuratively); we may find ourselves resenting the relationship rather than preserving it; or we may hold back in the relationship for self-preservation, increasing our existing sadness or guilt because we are not giving as much as we would wish. The recounting of these stories provides the perfect transition into the teaching and practicing of the DEAR MAN skill, because in each situation where a line has been crossed, either by the participant or the person with BPD, there is the potential solu-

tion for change through DEAR MAN. This skill shows the partici-
pant how to ask for something that he/she wants, how to request it
respectfully in a way that is positive for the overall good of the re-
lationship, thus preserving the participant's sense of self-respect.

Module 6: Problem Management Skills (Weeks 11-12): This final
module on problem management covers defining problems effectively,
solving problems collaboratively, and knowing when to focus on acceptance and when to focus on change. It is divided into sub-topics that include accurate self-expression and the importance of timing; sorting out
the difference between goals and strategies; and setting up strategies.
Some examples of strategies include: always beginning with something
positive; being specific; expressing your feelings; identifying your role
in the problem; dealing with only one problem at a time; summarizing
what the other person is saying; avoiding making inferences about the
problem behavior; and being sure you want to solve the problem. There
is also a section on techniques for non-collaborative problem solving,
including what techniques to use if those skills are not successful.

Leader Observations: *One of the indicators of success with these*
groups is that the participants have bonded with one another and
have developed a network of social support that most did not have
prior to starting the course. Inevitably this also has meant a grow-
ing sense of connection and attachment to the leaders. Thus, in ad-
dition to teaching the new material and corresponding skills, it is
important during the final two weeks for leaders to recognize that
this is a transition period for the group, to allow time for discus-
sion, and to help participants prepare for life after Family Con-
nections.

In addition to teaching practical skills in managing problems, the
curriculum offers some practical advice, which provides excellent
subject matter for discussion and summing up. The specifics of the
change strategy skills are particularly crucial at this time. The
first of these is "Timing." This means that even before launching
into a DEAR MAN, for example, it is important to stop and think
about when you are doing the asking. This is comparable to the
strategy of "managing up" with a difficult boss. Participants will
need to take the time to think out our timing with their ill relative in
the same way. Then there is the question of prioritizing subject

matter. To practice your skill in change strategies, leaders suggest that participants start with a subject they believe may be the least volatile, gradually working up to those subjects that are likely to be more difficult. For example, checking in by phone every few days might be on the low end of volatile subjects and could make its way through a DEAR MAN very successfully without having the kettle boil over. On the other hand, it could take many months before it would be safe to have a conversation about money management. Whatever the situation for which you may be seeking change, there are three crucial caveats: (1) Deal with only one problem at a time. Once we have captured the attention of our relative, it is so easy to blurt out a litany of complaints; this is also the surest way to ensure a delay before we'll be given a hearing; (2) Own up to your role in contributing to the problem; and (3) Avoid being judgmental, because it could cost you the entire effort.

When there is clearly no desire to engage in collaborative problem solving, other techniques are called for. Let us return to the subject of money management. It is possible to try the "Foot-in-the-door" technique, an example being, "Would you like to talk about it later?"

The module closes with "Taking a Step Back." This section deals with situations where family members may need to observe their limits in order to remain healthy themselves or make a decision about what is healthy for their ill relative. The kinds of "Steps Back" that are available can be as simple as going into another room while saying, "When you are screaming, I can no longer focus on our conversation. I am going into the next room for a few minutes. When you can lower your voice, I'll be glad to listen to what you have to say."

In some cases, it may become necessary for family members to take some time away (more than a few hours) or put some distance (as determined by the situation) between themselves and their ill relative. There was only one time in all the years that our daughter was ill that this became necessary for us. It was when she was so ill with an eating disorder that her life was hanging in the balance. We felt that unless she were geographically so far away from us that we couldn't physically get to her short of boarding a plane for a six-hour trip, and she couldn't easily come home, we all might not survive this. And so she went for treatment 3,000 miles away for two years. It was the hardest decision the three of us ever made and the precursor to her eventual recovery.

LIFE AFTER FAMILY CONNECTIONS

Borderline personality disorder is not cured in 12 weeks, nor have the challenges faced by FC participants vanished after the 12-week program. It would be ideal if NEA-BPD were to offer a formally researched graduate FC program for as long as family members felt they needed to attend. Until that time, some FC groups have bonded so closely during the 12-week period that they have decided to continue meeting monthly, frequently holding these meetings in one another's homes. At other sites, the leaders offer a more formalized meeting on a monthly basis. NEA-BPD also keeps in touch with participants, ensuring that they know about its regional conferences presented in their areas. More recently, a number of the FC attendees have participated in research for two educational videos about BPD, one under the aegis of the Borderline Personality Disorder Resource Center, and the other, funded by NIMH Grant # 1 R43 MH069050-01A1.

Leader Observations: *A very important principle of Family Connections emphasized throughout the 12 weeks is that the curriculum was created for the wellbeing of the family members them- selves, and that its primary purpose is not to make their sick relative better. Anecdotally, participants report that as they are making changes in their understanding of BPD and the way they deal with situations that arise, they perceive that their ill relative is changing too. We remind our family members that knowing the right words and the right time to say them, and how to ask for a change in their loved one will help the participant to feel stronger, more centered, more empowered, and more secure. The ill relative may very likely start to notice these changes, and sense that their family members are observing limits and learning how to stick to them. Over time, such behavior on the part of family members can help their relatives with BPD to find a more centered place within themselves.*

ACKNOWLEDGMENTS

The author wishes to thank Kiera Van Gelder, director of Middle Path, and Thomas Penney, co-leader of the Westchester, New York Family Connections group, for their thoughtful reading of this manuscript.

REFERENCES

Fruzzetti, A. E. (2005). Family Connections Leaders Training, Reno, Nevada, March 4-6.

Fruzzetti, A. E. & Hoffman, P. D. (2004). *Family Connections Manual: Teaching Notes.* Rye, NY: National Education Alliance for Borderline Personality Disorder, Inc.

Fruzzetti, A. E. & Hoffman, P. D. (2004). *Family Connections Workbook and Training Manual.* Rye, NY: National Education Alliance for Borderline Personality Disorder, Inc.

Gunderson, J. G. & Hoffman, P. G. (Eds.) (2005). *Understanding and Treating Borderline Personality Disorder: A Guide for Professionals and Families.* Washington, DC. American Psychiatric Publishing.

Hoffman, P. D., Fruzzetti, A. E., Buteau, E., Neiditch, E., Penney, D., Bruce, M. L, Hellman, F., & Struening, E. (2005). Family connections: A program for relatives of persons with borderline personality disorder. *Family Process,* 44 (2), 217-225.

Hooley, J. M., Hoffman, P. D. (1999). Expressed emotion and outcome in borderline personality disorder. *American Journal of Psychiatry,* 156 (10) 1157-1562.

Kessler, R. C., Berglund P., Demler, O., Jim, R., Merikangas, K. R., & Walter, E. E. (2005). Lifetime prevalence and age-of-onset distributions of *DSM-IV* disorders in the National Comorbidity Survey Replication. *Archives of General Psychiatry,* 62, 593-602.

Linehan, M. M. (1993). *Skills training manual for treating borderline personality disorder.* New York: Guilford Press.

doi:10.1300/J200v06n01_18

Inhabited by a Cry:
Living with Borderline Personality Disorder

INHABITED BY A CRY

Shortly after I received the diagnosis of borderline personality disorder at age 31, I came across a poem by Sylvia Plath (1965), a poet famous for her sensitivity, her intensity and her self-destruction–a poet many people with BPD consider to be one of their own. The poem is called "Elm" and in it, Plath writes:

I am inhabited by a cry.
Nightly it flaps out
Looking, with its hooks, for something to love.

There are many ways to describe the experience of living with BPD, but no other words have captured my condition so precisely. "Inhabited by a cry" is not simply sadness, where the cry comes and goes. It is not depression, where heaviness sets in and the life force ebbs out. "Inhabited by a cry" means living with something inside myself that is so bloated with grief and longing and rage and fear that it can't find words or solutions. It is being possessed by a type of pain that is so desperate for comfort and relief that "nightly it flaps out looking, with its hooks, for something to love."

[Haworth co-indexing entry note]: "Inhabited by a Cry: Living with Borderline Personality Disorder." Van Gelder, Kiera. Co-published simultaneously in *Social Work in Mental Health* (The Haworth Press) Vol. 6, No. 1/2, 2008, pp. 243-253; and: *Borderline Personality Disorder: Meeting the Challenges to Successful Treatment* (ed: Perry D. Hoffman, and Penny Steiner-Grossman) The Haworth Press, 2008, pp. 243-253. Single or multiple copies of this article are available for a fee from The Haworth Document Delivery Service [1-800-HAWORTH, 9:00 a.m. - 5:00 p.m. (EST). E-mail address: docdelivery@haworthpress.com].

doi:10.1300/J200v06n01_19

In this chapter, I want to give you a sense of what it's like to live with borderline personality disorder, but I have to admit that I'm nervous. By identifying myself as a person with BPD, I run the risk of losing my credibility. Who, I have to wonder, would hire a person admitting to being a borderline? And more importantly, who would willingly enter into a relationship with him or her? Like many people with BPD, I am excruciatingly sensitive to other people's perceptions of me. At times, a negative word or look can drastically redefine how I feel about myself. It even has a physical effect, like being hit with a soccer ball in the solar plexus. With this kind of vulnerability, it seems almost masochistic to publicly identify oneself with a disorder that has such negative associations. But here's the catch: enduring human connection and mastery comes only after facing oneself and sharing that self with others.

It has taken a long time arrive at an understanding and acceptance of this disorder, to be properly diagnosed, to receive the treatment and support that directly addresses my suffering. I began seeing professionals when I was 12 years old, when the cry was already so loud that I'd tried silencing it with a bottle of pills, and then, when that didn't work, with a steady supply of alcohol and drugs. By age 15 I was cutting and burning myself every day, fantasizing about suicide, writing letters in blood and sending them to schoolmates who, understandably, had withdrawn their friendships in the face of my neediness and self-destruction.

My family, baffled and fearful, sent me to a psychiatrist and what began with a doctor suggesting I had adolescent depression grew, over the years, into a hydra of diagnoses, each one seeming to have a life of its own: PTSD, drug and alcohol addiction, panic and generalized anxiety disorder, social anxiety disorder and bi-polar disorder of an unspecified numeral. All told, I wandered the maze of psychiatric diagnosis, medications and treatments for almost two decades. Twice I went on disability. I had numerous hospitalizations. I went to 12-step meetings and got sober. I took medication and worked on my issues. I tried to build myself up after every breakdown, but a horrific truth was revealing itself the older I got. No matter what I did, I always ended up back where I'd started: suicidal, self-hating, unable to keep a job or a relationship, a failure at everything, an exposed nerve.

SNAPSHOTS OF YOUTH

I duck into the bathroom in between classes. In the stall, I pull a thumbtack from my pocket and drag the rough point across my forearm, over and over. I watch with a detached fascination as the skin reddens and tears. Then, as the blood appears, it happens: a wave of calm rinses my chest; the intense pressure in my head temporarily diffuses. Relieved, I go back into the hallway, into the churn of eyes and feet and slippery facts. I am 14 years old and I don't know it yet, but I already have all the symptoms of borderline personality disorder.

* * *

My head is shaved. I wear all black. The people around me seem wooden. Sometimes I can't feel myself. Sometimes, I feel so much pain and self-loathing I sit on my bed and bang my head against the wall. Bad girl. Ugly, evil girl. I carve patterns into my arm with razor blades. One night I down a bottle of aspirin with orange juice and wake up in the morning with my ears ringing. I throw up seven times, the taste of the aspirin making me gag and shudder. I am 15 and I am diagnosed with depression.

* * *

My hair is long. I wear Indian print skirts. I have run away from home to follow a band called the Grateful Dead. I take LSD and practice my particular version of free love. When I return home, my family brings me to a psychiatric hospital. I am one month shy of my 18th birthday and am diagnosed with borderline personality disorder, but no one tells me this. I am discharged to my own care.

* * *

I often wonder what my life would be like if someone had intervened sooner. What if a knowledgeable teacher or counselor had noticed my symptoms and brought my family together, describing to us the nature of my disorder, the importance of our working together, the necessity of treatment and support and patience. What if we'd gotten a good referral? I want to turn the years back and reel in my family, dysfunctional and fragmented and each person caught in a private web of confusion and ask each of them to look at me, to pause, to be present, to observe me without judgment, and let my pain exist as it was: raw, overwhelming, something beyond my control at times. I want to say to my younger self "You are not a bad person, you are in constant pain. You are not irresponsible, you just don't have the skills to handle life as other people do. You are not alone. This all makes sense, and you will get better."

But I slipped away at age 18, unmoored, my hooks catching whatever would hold me for the moment. I had sex with men simply to be touched and to imagine what love must feel like. I put any chemical in my body that promised a temporary respite. Even in recovery and on medication throughout my 20s, I lived as a hostage to my inner turmoil. The world was unsafe; I was contaminated and unlovable. People couldn't be relied on; I was unable to take care of myself.

* * *

Twenty years after my first suicide attempt, I formally received the borderline diagnosis. At that point, I was living on social security and disability insurance. My previous three teaching jobs had resulted in breakdowns, and I had just ended another tumultuous relationship. Ten years sober, I found nothing in the 12 steps to soothe the cry inside of me. Bile rose in my throat every time I was advised in meetings to "work the steps" harder, or to have more faith in God. If anything, my years of sobriety had given rise to more emotional turmoil. I didn't understand how I could be doing everything "right" and still not function and live the way other people did. At the advice of my frightened ex-boyfriend, I made an appointment with a clinician randomly assigned by an outpatient receptionist at the local psychiatric hospital. And, like every other intake, I sobbed my way through the laundry list of difficulties, abuses, hospitalizations and diagnoses. Dr. P. nodded and scratched notes onto the clipboard. Symptoms of emotional distress, flights of escape, medication, more medication. At the end of my story, the doctor put his clipboard aside, spread his fingers over the pressed blue fabric of his knees and said, "I know your problem."

I strained in my chair, ready to catch his words. He was like a palm reader, eyes interpreting my hands. He only had to skim over the lifeline, no need to trace the smaller creases of my hand. "Borderline personality disorder," he declared, then waited a beat. "It's a condition of extreme mood instability, a fear of abandonment, an uncertain sense of self." He leaned forward in his chair. "Does that make any sense to you?" I nodded. "A pervading sense of emptiness," he continued, now ticking off his fingers. "Recurrent suicidal behavior, self-mutilation." He listed the nine criteria, and when he had finished, I'd mentally checked off all nine. "Of course, saying you have BPD is just a convenient way of explaining your behavior. A personality disorder," he continued, "can't simply be cured with a pill." He took a white business card from the pile stacked at his elbow and wrote down the contact number for the local Dialectical Behavior Therapy program, explaining that it was a therapy designed particularly for my kind of problems. Our 20 minutes, I realized, were up.

"You will learn equanimity," Dr. P promised, tamping his hands down in a gesture of settledness. Then he extended his hand in farewell. "You are a woman of great passion. What you'll learn to do is channel that energy, to control it, rather than the other way around. And when you do," he smiled, "there will be no need for a diagnosis."

Relief flooded my body as I left the doctor's office. Until then, nothing had been able to describe the pain I'd experienced since I was a young girl. Things I'd never been able to manage–the impulsive and self-destructive behaviors, the desperate clinging to relationships, the over-sensitivity to rejection and judgment, the obsession with suicide, my shifting identities and drastic changes in perception–suddenly made sense. A voracious need for more information followed quickly. I have heard other people with BPD describe a similar experience: when the diagnosis is revealed, there is an "ah-hah" moment, and for the first time, a sense of control enters the picture. It's not so much that one suddenly gains control of the symptoms, but that the awareness, itself, becomes empowering. I remembered from 12-step meetings, people would say, "You can't rearrange furniture in a dark room. First you have to turn on the light." Those nine criteria were a spotlight into a warehouse full of rampaging armoires.

SCORCHED TO THE ROOT

In 2001, when the country grieved the tragedy of 9/11, I sat in a hospital day room with three over-medicated women and felt oddly comforted by the fact that the rest of the country was also in a state of distress. The orderlies, the nurses, the news anchorman on television, all seemed to finally share what I'd been feeling all along, as though the entire nation and my interior world had something to finally agree on. Plath writes about this state of mind:

> I have suffered the atrocity of sunsets.
> Scorched to the root
> My red filaments burn and stand, a hand of wires.

Now I break up in pieces that fly about like clubs.
A wind of such violence
Will tolerate no bystanding: I must shriek.

It is as she describes: Some days it feels as through I am nothing but a hand of wires, exposed filaments, scorched by something as simple as a sunset. How well she connects that sensitivity to the breakdown of self, the breaking up in pieces that fly about like clubs. Intolerable, the cry becomes a shriek. Reactivity. Impulsivity. Hostility. Self-destruction. There is no safety when the slightest breath of life affects you like a violent wind.

Try as I might to subdue it or escape it, this sensitivity and impulsivity are a part of me, hard-wired, and like all things biological, they exist whether I approve of them or not. When I understood this, a form of mastery began to take root. In DBT terms, this is the beginning of mindfulness practice: the ability to observe my own suffering without reacting to it. In gaining a bit of space between my feelings and my reactions, I begin to notice how antagonistic I am, with myself, with the world around me. There is no calm abiding. Even in mindfulness, I am aware of this struggle. It is exhausting, being at war with myself, wrestling with the feelings, negotiating the thoughts and reactions. Even more exhausting is the need to appear normal and not lose control. Some days I must sleep for 16 hours simply to reset my self back to operational mode. "Apparent Competence" is Marsha Linehan's term for living with the constant threat of losing your composure, at any moment, for the slightest reason, while other people cannot understand why.

SHADOWS

I remember being four years old and waiting in agony for my goodnight kiss. It was a very important kiss, promised to arrive as soon as I pulled on my footy pajamas and climbed into bed. Downstairs there was a dinner party with adult laugher, the tinkling of silverware, jazz music on the record player. My little brother was already sleeping, but I waited, tense with anticipation. The minutes passed painfully, each of them like a stone stacked along a wall confirming my separation, my insignificance. By the time a shadow fell across the doorway and my mother entered the room, I was hot with rage and remorse. She bent down and a brown curtain of hair fell over me.

"I'm sorry I'm late honey," she whispered, and put her mouth on my forehead for an instant. Tears of relief and anger spilled over my eyelashes, and I felt a rage beyond the scope of kisses and apologies. It is the same rage I would feel when my boyfriend smiled at another woman on the street. In that smile, I'd watch his love for me dry up and blow like a cloud of dust towards the woman walking past. In a moment, our years of togetherness dissolved and I could barely keep from howling. I'd lash out verbally, accuse him of betraying me. "But I didn't do anything," he'd argue, which somehow proved to me, all the more, how much he didn't know. My weeping would take on a life of its own, and I'd only start to calm down when he'd hold me, like a child, like a baby, waiting for another kiss. Plath writes:

> Love is a shadow
> How you lie and cry after it
> Listen: these are its hooves: it has gone off, like a horse.

There is this overwhelming desire to be saved, as though I were an orphan perpetually standing in a line-up waiting to be taken home. Pick me! Pick me! But who is out there, who can give me the thing I lack? It is not love I am crying after. I have love. I just can't recognize or absorb it as others do, can't incorporate it into my core and know, "I am lovable and this cannot be taken away." Because it feels as though it is always leaving me.

LIFE WITH DBT

I am sitting in my studio, waiting for the phone to ring. My boyfriend isn't calling and I'm crawling out of my skin. I eat a bag of cookies and leave a message on his voicemail, nicely, but there's no reply. I go out for ice cream and then call him again. This time I am weepy. "You always do this to me," I cry. In the third message I am shouting, "I'm sick of this! I don't exist to you!" Exhausted, I climb into bed and feel as though the world's bottom has dropped out. I am swirling in rage and despair–my life hangs in the balance of a boy's cell phone call–and I cry myself to sleep, imagining he's with his ex-girlfriend. Then at midnight I get a call. "What the hell happened to you?" He asks. He reminds me that he was out with his best friend at a movie.

"I was having a borderline moment," I mumble, flooded with shame now that I am safe again with his voice in my ear.

"Don't you have skills for that?" he asks. I think back to the cookies and ice cream, hitting the redial button. I know I'll need to do a chain analysis the next morning in therapy with Saul. I am 32 years old, six months into DBT, three weeks into a new relationship.

* * *

I am sitting on the couch with my boyfriend when he answers the phone. I think it's his ex-girlfriend, judging from the faint girlish voice coming from the receiver. He talks to her thoughtfully, but doesn't say much, mainly listens. I want to run from the room in tears but I'm also rooted to the couch. Out of a perverse wish to be proved right, I construct in my mind the conversation we'll have when he hangs up, how I'll get him to admit he's still interested in her, and how I'll demand his allegiance, then make an ultimatum. The more I think of this, the more upset I become until finally the tears begin rolling down my cheeks. I am ready to go the freezer and put ice cubes on my palms to quell the longing for physical pain, but at that moment, my boyfriend says goodnight. "Goodnight MOM." He turns back to me and sees my face already puffy from the tears. I want to control these reactions. I want to be strong and self-confident and not fall apart at the sound of a woman's voice on the phone. We practice distraction by watching a movie, and in an hour, I've forgotten why I was so upset.

* * *

He is talking to his ex-girlfriend. This time it's real. "Hi Amber," he says when he picks up the phone. We have just sat down to watch a movie. I feel my whole body tense up, my breathing get shallow, I start to get up but my boyfriend holds my hand. With his eyes, he implores: sit with it. He talks to Amber, who I imagine is tall and shapely, with honey colored hair and big green eyes. They dated for a couple months but that was years ago. I repeat to myself, "years ago" and while my boyfriend rubs my back, I sit and fiddle with the remote, practicing the tortuous "opposite action" of staying with what feels intolerable. He says goodbye to Amber, whose voice I imagine to be like velvet and honey and then he turns to me. "That wasn't so bad, was it?" I am soaked with sweat and exhausted, as though I've run a great distance. But I notice, after that, I don't worry about Amber's calls.

WHAT I KNOW

There are things I know about myself now, such as the fact that I may see rejection where others perceive indifference, and that I will interpret neutral faces as hostile. That sounds can set me on edge and when I'm under stress and feeling trapped, I will start to believe people are against me. I know that being with groups of people exhausts me and that if I spend too much time with one person, I'm liable to lose touch with my own feelings and sense of self. If I feel wronged by someone, unjustly judged, disregarded when I deserve to be noticed, the world will lurch and I have to work hard to regain my balance. But there are other things that I do not know. Plath writes:

> I am terrified by this dark thing
> That sleeps in me;
> All day I feel its soft, feathery turnings, its malignity.

If you take away cutting and burning, the suicide attempts, the impulsive sex with strangers, the drugs, drink and geographical cures, the rages and dissociations, there still remains this person, this me. Who is this person inside borderline personality disorder?

I used to think there was something terribly wrong with me, something more than a problem or a condition or even a disease. I thought if you smelled my breath, or came too close, you'd be contaminated by the stench of my rotten core. Now when I look in the mirror, I'm no longer filled with disgust, but neither am I comfortable with myself. Who and what I am continue to fluctuate drastically from day to day. This sense of being unmoored is disorienting. It is hard to have self-confidence if you never know how you're going to be from day to day. Often it's a game of let's pretend and a puzzle that needs constant solving. Are you my mommy? Where do I belong? The pieces never stay in place. Last week I was a writer, reading my work on stage; this morning I am a worm burrowing through the carcass of a once-promising life. In an hour, I will enjoy a cup of coffee and laugh. It's as though I'm traveling at a different speed, the way fast moving light can bend time; these seismic shifts in feeling throw the world into a hall of mirrors. What I see depends on where I am and who I am with, or if I am alone.

I wonder, though, if this need to be certain of oneself and to be stable and concrete is an expectation we impose on each other and ourselves. To some, the ability to shape-shift and merge into different environments is a talent and an asset, and some have made careers in performance and art because of this very nature. In cultures where empathy and connection are valued over individualism and competition, the borderline sensitivity may not be such an isolated experience; it may well be a shared consciousness. Why do we hold the expectation that we should be able to thrive in a word that is shifting so quickly that not even the dictionaries and cartographers can keep up?

When the overt symptoms of BPD are taken away, you are still left with a person who needs a community and a way of life that will not recreate the same conditions in which the disorder developed. The people closest to me know what I struggle with and are sensitive to my vulnerabilities. There has been no greater gift than the validation I get from people who are willing to understand and accept me in all my troubling and curious ways. And over the past few years, this widening circle of understanding and support has transformed my life. Rather than seeing myself as different from other people, I now understand my experience as an aspect of being human, for everyone has strong emotions, fears loss, fantasizes about escaping and despairs on occasion. There are still times when the cry within me shrieks and I find myself with hooked talons, poised for flight. But I am no longer alone, possessed like a marionette, decomposing at the core.

To be alone with this condition is almost unendurable, and that is the real tragedy of borderline personality disorder. Our symptoms–the cry, the desperate clawing for a savior or a fix, the consequences and remorse of being unable to manage our reactions–only shame and isolate us more. In showing my face as a person with BPD, I run the risk of more shame and isolation. This compounded impact of the illness perpetuates the deep sense of ugliness so many of us feel. How do people with BPD live with the disorder when we are still unable to share it with the world?

How do we have faith that we can get better if those who survive this ordeal disappear and the success of their recovery is measured in the distance between themselves and the borderline label?

When I read Plath's words again, her terror of "this dark thing that sleeps in me," I write my own reply:

I am transformed
by this dark thing
that shrieks in me.
Its desperate talons,
its violent love,
all part of me.

I must tender these cries,
each one held in the palm
and wept, until the wings
fold back and in.
I know intimately
the resonance and depth
of my cry, but I am
just discovering what
it means to be a wild
and feathery thing.

REFERENCES

Plath, S. (1965). *Ariel: Poems by Sylvia Plath.* New York: Harper & Row.

doi:10.1300/J200v06n01_19

Index